FRANÇOIS FÉNELON

FRANÇOIS FÉNELON

A BIOGRAPHY ✦ THE APOSTLE OF PURE LOVE

PETER J. GORDAY

PARACLETE PRESS
BREWSTER, MASSACHUSETTS

François Fénelon: A Biography—The Apostle of Pure Love

2012 First Printing

Copyright © 2012 by Peter Gorday

ISBN 978-1-55725-801-4

Library of Congress Cataloging-in-Publication Data

Gorday, Peter J.
  François Fénelon : a biography—the apostle of pure love / Peter J. Gorday.
    pages cm
  Includes bibliographical references and index.
  ISBN 978-1-55725-801-4 (pbk.)
  1. Fénelon, François de Salignac de La Mothe-, 1651-1715. 2. Authors, French—
17th century—Biography. 3. Theologians—France—Biography. I. Title.
  PQ1796.G55 2012
  282.092—dc23
  [B]   2011052032

10 9 8 7 6 5 4 3 2 1

Published by Paraclete Press
Brewster, Massachusetts
www.paracletepress.com

Printed in the United States of America

CONTENTS

"So it is to ensure that the operation of grace may remain a mystery of faith that God permits it to be slow and painful. . . .We would much rather be consumed at once by the flames of pure love, but so speedy a process would cost us nothing. It is utter selfishness that we desire to attain perfection so cheaply and so quickly."

—INSTRUCTIONS AND ADVICE, 36 (TR. EDMONSON)

"As for myself, I am in a dry peace. . . . But the world seems to be like a bad comedy, which is going to disappear in a few hours. I distrust myself more than the world. I classify everything as a 'makeshift,' and it is in the depth of this 'makeshift' status of everything here below that I find peace."

—LETTER TO THE COMTESSE DE MONTBERON
NOVEMBER 7–8, 1700

Man, Quietist, Mystic

T he winter in northern France along the border with the Low Countries that year was particularly harsh: It was the final strain on the increasingly frail health of the sixty-four-year-old archbishop and duke of Cambrai, François Fénelon. People noticed at Christmas services when he presided in the stately Gothic cathedral that he looked extremely drawn and feeble. He described himself as "a walking and talking skeleton that sleeps and eats a little bit."[1] He had already been asking officially for help with administrative duties that were beyond his strength, although his mind was as sharp as ever. His mood and spirit were resigned, yet tranquil and hopeful. In the first week of January—the year was 1715—he took a sharp turn for the worse with what seems to have been bronchial pneumonia.[2] Medical help was summoned to no avail. Friends, family, local clergy, and supporters gathered in order to be with him as the end approached. There were final devotions and exchanges of affection, administration of the last rites, and the last blessing from the archbishop on all present. He was in considerable pain that night. By early morning on January 7, though, he was more peaceful; he kissed the crucifix for the last time and quietly expired.

Fénelon's will was uncomplicated, because, as his secretary Ramsay said, "after his death he was found to be penniless and debt-free; he died as poor as he lived."[3] He swore his allegiance to Louis XIV in a final statement, asking His Majesty only to assure a pious successor to the archbishopric and the continuing supervision of the seminary by the Society of Saint-Sulpice. He had requested that the funeral observances be kept as simple as possible, so that, he said, "the modesty of bishops' funerals would teach the laity to forgo the vain expenditures" that had become customary. It was decided also to dispense with any eulogies despite his saintly reputation.[4]

He was deeply mourned and fondly remembered as an exemplary priest and pastor. It is extraordinary, therefore, that such a beloved and revered man should have left such a complex legacy. Yet complex it is, at least partly because of the fascinating spiritual currents that will always swirl around his name.

At the center of this whirlpool was the fact that he had spent the last years of his life under the shadow of a papal condemnation that his own monarch, Louis XIV, had aggressively sought. By official pronouncement in March 1699, Pope Innocent XII had censured in the work of Fénelon certain theological propositions about the nature and import of "pure love." The matters were highly technical in nature, and the force of the censure was somewhat unclear. But, nonetheless, Fénelon had immediately and in good faith submitted. Others quickly disseminated his controversial writings, however, and his ideas spread like a devotional flood that could not be suppressed. Louis's disapproval and the pope's judgment failed to hold back the tide.

Thus, the lack of eulogy at his funeral notwithstanding, massive praise of Fénelon (as well as heated criticism) had already begun during his lifetime, only to mushroom after his death in a process that continues to this day.[5] Our retrieval of the man and his message can still bear much good fruit.

The Maxims of the Saints

François Fénelon is either idealized or demonized because he continues to strike deep chords in the life of the spirit. For students of the history of Christianity he is remembered primarily as the author of the notorious work that led to his papal condemnation, the *Maxims of the Saints* (its full title is *Explication of the Maxims of the Saints on the Inner Life*). First published in 1697, then condemned in 1699, its further publication was suppressed until the nineteenth century. Modern readers are always surprised that such a dry composition should be so controversial. The *Maxims* is a strikingly innocuous composition at first glance.

Each of the "maxims" is actually an affirmation, or contention, about some aspect of how it is that the human soul, hungering for the perfection of spiritual life, can draw closer to God in prayer. After being stated in what Fénelon considered a correct and orthodox form, the individual maxim is then coupled with an erroneous and distorted statement of the same central point. The intention is to help the reader separate a "true" from a "false" formulation of what is at issue. The core argument of the whole work, the underlying theme, is that "all interior paths tend toward pure or disinterested love" and that "this 'pure love' is the highest degree of Christian perfection."[6] In other words, if you want to grow in your relationship with God, then you must practice what Fénelon calls "pure"— that is, totally disinterested—love. The terms are slippery, but the claim is bold and is raised by Fénelon to the very highest level of intensity. The implications are radical and unsettling. And yet, says Fénelon, such an idea of "pure love" has always been at the heart of the best spiritual teaching in all times of the church's life. Consequently, the *Maxims* actually stirred up a hornet's nest.

But there was even more to it. By publishing the *Maxims* Fénelon aimed at accomplishing something else on a deeply personal level. He wanted to vindicate the essential insights of his friend Madame Jeanne Guyon. She had been a catalyst in his development. He considered her a saintly, well-intended, but misunderstood and mistreated spiritual teacher. Her book, *A Short and Easy Method for Prayer*, had been well received initially by seriously devout readers in the most aristocratic circles. Then doubts arose. Careful examination by church authorities had turned up some troubling expressions. Her personal history was also controversial, even scandalous. In the prolonged struggle that was set in motion Guyon was apprehended, then interrogated by Jacques-Bénigne Bossuet, bishop of Meaux and senior theologian of the French church, and then invited to produce a defense. Fénelon rose to her side in the *Maxims*, but failing to exonerate her, he brought about his own condemnation as well. As part of the complex fallout Fénelon came under official censure, and his intimate relations with Louis XIV and his consort, Madame de Maintenon, were ruined for good.

The grounds of the condemnation are somewhat obscure to us today. In essence Fénelon was accused (as had been Guyon earlier) of the doctrinal heresy known as "quietism." The label had come to be linked specifically with the notorious heretic Miguel de Molinos, whose writings and life had already been condemned by the pope in November 1687, following which Molinos was thrown into prison. His rejected teaching, now labeled "quietist," made use of the concept of "pure love." So in the minds of many people "pure love" automatically implied "quietism," and "quietism" meant the forbidden teachings of Molinos. Fénelon's name and his ideas about "pure love" thus came to be permanently associated with a formal heresy, and the very concept of "pure love"—despite a respectable legacy in orthodox theological discourse—became tainted. It is *this* version of the quietist Fénelon that is best known to students of church history.

Two Problematic Terms: Quietist And Mystic

So it is that we must come to grips with two terms if we are to begin to understand Fénelon. The first charge is that he was a "quietist." And the second is that his spirituality is "mystical" and that he is a "mystic." Both concepts are closely associated in the tradition and thus must be taken in tandem. What makes definition difficult here is that they had achieved a kind of red-flag status in the later seventeenth century because each of them had become an "ism," that is, a set of doctrines. There was quiet*ism* and there was mystic*ism*. As soon as one of them was used, people judged their orthodoxy or unorthodoxy. Can good Catholics be quietists and mystics? At the very least, both terms suggested to the minds of many people dangerous tendencies in religion.

But there was distortion here. In the Molinist form in which it had been condemned, quietism consisted, to be sure, of a set of (officially objectionable) theological propositions, and this is how it is defined in theological encyclopedias. In its more original and more general usage the term referred, as Ronald Knox argued,[7] not to an articulated doctrinal posture of some sort, but rather to a type of pastoral guidance common in the seventeenth century. Pious souls were encouraged to embrace what was sometimes called the "sleeping devotion" or "the prayer of quiet" or "the prayer of simple regard." In theoretically articulated form it was a devotion that had roots in Spanish and Italian circles and was then popularized in France by Francis de Sales. Traditionally considered a higher and more advanced form of prayer for monastics, it proved to be quite helpful for ordinary layfolk as well. The purpose of this kind of prayer was to help devotees avoid two perennial traps in the disciplined practice of prayer, especially where concern with method was paramount: scrupulosity about intention (am I doing this with the right spirit?) and self-conscious preoccupation with technique (am I doing this in the right way?). What then happens, ironically, is that the "self" of the worshiper becomes the center of attention instead of God. Henri Bremond, the great historian of the history of French spirituality (to whom I shall refer often), described the dilemma in terms of the anxious "disquietude" that easily fills our hearts when we are "self"-focused in prayer.[8] The "prayer of quiet" is then a way to shift the focus onto God, so that the soul of the one who prays might be filled with trusting "quietude." It was a bit like telling someone who is learning to dance to stop thinking about their feet and just swing with the rhythm. The goal is a worthy one.

So, where's the problem? While everyone agreed that the prayer of quiet is a good thing for particularly distressed and fretful souls—which is all of us at times—there are deeply important questions about the nature of this prayer. What exactly happens between the soul and God in such prayer? If we practice such prayer, what are the implications for more ordinary meditative practices and devotional disciplines, for the use of the sacraments, for relations to church authority, and, most of all, for Christian ethics? All of these require methodical attention to duties and "correctness." How is the requirement to love thy neighbor affected? Or loving God? If I quietly *love* God in my prayer, is it acceptable to *hope* for something as well? Or does that let anxiety about whether I am doing it "right" slip in by the back door? Fénelon addressed all of these questions eventually. As we shall see, much of this devolved into a debate about the relation between "self-love" and love of the "other," in this case God, or "a love of God for what he does [for me] and a love of God for what he is [in himself]"[9]—a debate just as alive in our own time as in that of Fénelon.

The core quietistic idea is solid. It is the belief that God is found by the still, resting, empty, and *contemplating* mind, not by the mind as it *actively* manipulates quasi-visual imagery or verbal constructs, that is, not by *discursive* mental labor or *meditation*. When God "comes" to the patiently waiting and expectant soul, it is because we *listen* and cease talking; it is because we sit in stillness and wait for God and (seemingly!) cease to *do*

anything. We do not find God, but God finds us: it is one way of emphasizing the priority of grace and gift, of receptivity, in the spiritual life.
Quietist writers often make this point by saying that we must get the
"self" out of the way in making ourselves available to God. This "self" may
be understood morally as our prideful, arrogant, conceited, self-important
self, but also more cognitively as our consciously thinking, analyzing,
self-reflexive (thinking about ourselves and self-aware) self. Notice also,
though, that this contrast may be formulated as "the self doing something"
in the presence of God, that is, in "action," versus "the self at rest" in the
presence of God, that is, in a "state" of repose. It is one small step, then, to
say that this "self" must be "annihilated" if we wish to give ourselves over
to, or "abandon" ourselves to, God's presence and then to divine providential care. The intention is clear, but the language is risky.

The point at which "mysticism" enters the picture is with the contention
that this abandoning of ourselves or giving ourselves over to God must
proceed by means of a rediscovered, intensely felt, and profoundly
inward sense of the immediate presence of God.[10] The consequent
yielding of the self to this experience of God must happen at a hidden
location deep within the individual's inner "space," often called the
"center" or "fine point" of the soul. "Mysticism" then denotes this sense of
being "filled" with divine presence deep within. We should notice as well
that the sense of being "filled" may be expressed positively or negatively.
That is, God may be present, for example, as a burning fire (positive) or,
paradoxically, as a desolating emptiness (negative). Likewise the presence
may be depicted with vivid imagery (positive) or, contrariwise, by means
of an abstract language of negation (negative). The experience may be
one of joy (positive) or agony (negative). And so on. There was also the
issue, often heard in Fénelon's time, of whether mystical experience was
reserved only for adepts or something to be desired for all Christians.

Now in the early stages, this inward experiencing of the mystic is
marked by a retreat from the mundane, from the outward, superficial,
and distracting world of daily concerns and activities, in order to pursue a
re-centered, "purified" sense of the self (a "losing of the self to find the self"
experience). But then in its more advanced stages the soul, no longer or
not entirely invested in a retreat from the outward, may move back to the
mundane with "eyes that have been opened," with, we might say, "the eyes

of God." Bremond's more technical definition is that "mysticism" denotes "that natural disposition which leads certain souls by a sort of sudden compulsion to seize with direct and daring love on the spiritual beneath the veil of sense, the one in the many, the order amid the confusion, the eternal in the transitory, the divine in the created."[11] The mystical consciousness *generalizes*; having started in prayer, it becomes a way of perceiving everything. For Fénelon, as we shall see, it is not so much that the world looks different because of mystical experience, but that he understands it differently (as being providentially ordered by grace, rather than meaningless), and he can now ethically relate to it differently (with the will of God, rather than with his own).

It is useful, then, to combine the terms. If we say that this quietist prayer of repose combined with the deep inwardness of the mystical experience is something genuine, even something beautiful and highly to be desired, it may also have a dangerous and subversive quality about it. Sometimes the mystic, immersed in a deep and inward quiet with God, overlooks and even bypasses the ordinary practices and disciplines of community life. Trouble then begins and conflict ensues with authoritative traditions and offices in the church. The stage is set for charges of heresy, or immorality, or "special revelations" vouchsafed to mystical "prophets." Precisely because of their unregulated nature, quietistic-mystical spiritualities tend to be manifestations of individual religious genius. They may be freewheeling, undisciplined, ineffably private, vulnerable to the one-sidedness of idiosyncrasy, bizarre and extreme language, and grandiose claims for personal authority. Religious fanaticism, pathology, and delusion, as well as outright charlatanism, may enter the picture. All of the rules are broken, or at least stretched. The mystic does not have to live by the ordinary requirements because he or she operates on a higher level of consciousness and "knows" better.

Fénelon was exceedingly careful here. We will see how hard he labored to restrain what appeared excessive with Guyon. Quietistic-mystical spirituality *does* tend toward overstatement, he admitted. But abuse does not do away with correct use. We will also see that he was equally intent on preservation of a rich essence as well. This spirituality is fecund with spiritual renewal for all of us, but it must be *rightly understood*. It was the function of the titanic struggle with his archrival Bossuet about these matters that allowed him to craft the all-important distinctions and clarifications. His purpose was to "detoxify" quietist-mysticism, to show that it contains a *way* of relating to God and a *way* of living that are authentically Christian. That *way* is "pure love." And in this he was eminently successful, despite the official condemnation of his masterwork.

Fénelon the Man and the Spiritual Teacher

For most modern readers of spiritual texts, the old ecclesiastical disputes with their sometimes arcane and off-putting technical language may seem, perhaps, like dinosaurs. We are more likely to know Fénelon as the benignly smiling figure (in the famous Vivien portrait) who graces the book jackets of anthologies. These are usually abbreviated selections drawn from compilations put together after his death or excerpted from his vast correspondence. In such collections we do not meet Fénelon the embedded controversialist and polemicist on matters of seventeenth-century church dogma. Instead, we encounter a more user-friendly Fénelon, who seems more contemporary because he is dealing with perpetual matters. *This* Fénelon is an expert on prayer, a passionate lover of all that is beautiful and exalted, and a therapist for the sin-sick soul, all at once! One danger in such a way of experiencing Fénelon, though, is that his ideas about "pure love" can have a certain vapid quality, as if the very notion is a harmless vagary of "sweet" Fénelon! One of the purposes of this biography is to honor our modern interest in Fénelon the man, but also to re-immerse the concept of "pure love" in Fénelon's own context, so that it might shine more clearly, as it were, with its own peculiar light.

Typically in the volumes of selections we hear Fénelon at work as a spiritual director. Serious Catholics at the court of Louis XIV, the group known as the *dévots*, sought out certain clergy or laypersons with a reputation for mature spiritual wisdom to function in the role of spiritual directors. Either in direct meeting or through letters, the director kept the directee hard at work in the development of mature interiority. Growth in the practice of prayer, sensible regulation of the passions and appetites, the practice of devotional habits (such as the cultivation of silence), appropriate preparation for sacraments, thoughtful and balanced self-examination, and practical charity might all be included. Much stress was laid on faithfulness to role, duty, and vocation, as director and directee discerned and understood these. Practically from the beginning of his priestly ministry, Fénelon was sought out as a director, and thus passages of direction are often cited in modern collections.[12]

His directees were male and female, young and old, laity living very active lives in the world (including soldiers), and especially members of religious orders. It is in this capacity that he eventually became known as "the Swan of Cambrai," renowned for his charming presence, graceful literary style, and disarming gentleness of manner (the source of his "sweetness"). We should be clear, however, that just as he was a rigorous thinker, a determined and sharp opponent in debate, and a biting adversary when he wished to be, his spiritual direction was nothing if not forceful. The contrast with Bossuet as "the eagle of Meaux," with razor-sharp talons ready for the defense of churchly orthodoxy and royal absolutism, is often overstated, with the implication that Fénelon was "soft." In fact, he operated, as we shall see, with a velvet-gloved fist—all smooth and soothing on the outside, but hard and potentially crushing on the inside. To some people he seemed cunning and arrogant, but the truth is that he operated with the kind of street smarts that the aristocratic milieu of Versailles required. People experienced him (mostly) as a good friend or (on occasion) as a rugged adversary, although he could be both at different times with the same individual. Call it versatility.

Part of what makes him so enjoyable to read is that he had the ability to use words in that polished lapidary fashion that is a mark of the high literature of the French seventeenth century. His way of stating ideas often has a gem-like, proverbial quality. This style of smooth, pellucid writing (called the "Fénelonian style") made him, in French literary tradition down through the nineteenth century, an acknowledged master of classical literary elegance and an exemplar to be imitated. We know from the popularity of his slightly earlier contemporary La Rochefoucauld (1613–80) that epigrammatic writing was vastly popular at this time, and surely Fénelon exemplified the trend in a powerfully evocative way. (One of my favorites, packed with Fénelon's theology, which we will unfold in the course of this biography, is: "Privations are the bread of the strong.")[13]

Spiritual truth simply stated and with maximum economy of words has a timeless quality.

His personality comes through as well in these letters, and there are famous descriptions of Fénelon's graceful, almost mesmerizing self-presentation from his Versailles contemporaries. Many of them were captivated by, but some were maliciously envious of, his suavely aristocratic demeanor (his *politesse*), and others were just put on edge by him. The descriptions often come from courtiers and royal officials, that is, people who appreciated subtlety and nuance in the arts of self-presentation. As descriptions they may, of course, say more about the describer than the one being described. The most sophisticated characterization comes from the royal chancellor Henri d'Aguesseau and deserves full quotation: "Never has one man better united in himself qualities so contrary and incompatible with one another. Uncomplicated but fine-grained, transparent but profound, modest but ambitious, feeling but indifferent, able to desire and yet have disdain for everything, always agitated but always tranquil, aloof from everything but entering into everything, Sulpician and missionary and yet a courtier, ready to play the most brilliant roles and yet to live in obscurity, finding his sufficiency in everything and yet self-sufficient, a versatile genius who could assume any character without losing his own, whose depth was an imagination fecund, gracious, and dominant without causing one to feel that domination."[14]

But the most famous description—archly ambiguous and deliciously cutting—is drawn from the reminiscences of the frustrated and envious aristocrat, the Duc de Saint-Simon, a man "of misanthropic character and satirical spirit, more given to censure than praise."[15] To him Fénelon was marked by "a charming wit and pleasing manners," mixed with much "ambition," and "a piety which made him all things to all men," so that his "constant craving for admiration" allowed him to please everybody.[16] Indeed, Saint-Simon's favorite words for Fénelon would be "ambitious" and "charming." Thus, Saint-Simon is the source for the common perception that Fénelon's "softness" was a mask for cunning. Literary personality portraiture was almost a cult in the time of Louis XIV, and we should be careful here of some overembroidering. Sabine Melchior-Bonnet, Fénelon's most recent biographer, goes so far as to make the bewitchment that people experienced with Fénelon's person (*Fénelon l'enchanteur*) the central mystery of the man.[17]

I suggest, by contrast, in this biography that our present *intellectual* perceptions of Fénelon are much the more important ones, the ones that can make him spiritually significant and edifying *for us*. In fact, he was a first-rate mind capable of articulating a tough and continually compelling spiritual vision. Appreciation of Fénelon as a thinker, therefore, is critical. A short recalling of the history of the interpretation of Fénelon's thought can frame our narrative and position us to hear him afresh.

The Archbishop's Legacy: The First Two Hundred Years

So, as low-profile, quiet, and austere as his earthly end was, in the relative obscurity of pastoral responsibility in a frontier diocese for his last twenty years, Fénelon died as a hero and martyr for his many contemporary admirers. He had been officially "disgraced" because of the condemnation of the *Maxims* and the friendship with Guyon. But he also had aimed impolitic criticism at Louis as well as sharp reproof to his consort, Madame de Maintenon. The result was banishment (being dismissed from Versailles was tantamount to exile) to Cambrai. But well before his death his work was being anthologized for posterity, and in due course he passed into the French national heritage as an icon of various spiritual, political-moral, and cultural values. But in different ways for different generations, since "each age has 'its Fénelon' in accordance with the sensibilities of the time and the records that historians have managed to unearth."[18] In broad terms the history of his veneration, or as it may be, his vilification, has passed through three phases.

The initial phase, that of the eighteenth century with traces persisting to the present, was inaugurated by means of the first, profoundly hagiographical biography (1723) of Fénelon, that written by his devoted disciple, the chevalier André-Michel Ramsay (actually a Scot, Andrew Michael Ramsay).[19] He was the first to argue that the idea of a pure love for God in which the lover eschews all self-interest is the heart of Fénelon. By going on to suggest that this "pure love" can be seen as the universal master key to the truth of all religions, Ramsay created the image of Fénelon that endeared him to the Enlightenment. Unselfish loving is the ideal for human goodness everywhere. This way of viewing what Fénelon meant by "pure love" made him the ultimate liberal and model of Christlike goodness. The paradox here was that a devout Catholic archbishop became the mostly secularized arch-representative of tolerance, reason, and humanity.

Enlightenment readers loved certain of his compositions. As the author of a treatise advocating liberal education for young women, the *Treatise on the Education of Daughters*, he was seen as a forebear of the progressive ideas of the great Jean-Jacques Rousseau. As the author of an apologetic work, the *Demonstration of the Existence of God*, in which some arguments, traditional (part 1) and contemporary (part 2), for the reality of God are set forth with grace and clarity, he was seen as an orthodox but also intelligent and urbane philosopher of religion. As the author of animal fables in the style of the ancient Aesop and the modern La Fontaine and moral dialogues in the style of the ancient Lucian of Samosata and the modern Fontenelle, he was seen as an educational writer and moralist of particular elegance and charm. But most of all, as the writer of *The Adventures of Telemachus*, a spin-off from Homer's Odyssey and a long lesson on the virtues of the enlightened ruler, he was seen as a great defender of a humane political order of universal justice far in advance of its time. Study of the *Telemachus* eventually became a mainstay of French culture and maintained that position until the First World War. *Telemachus* made Fénelon a champion of freedom and earned him an honored place, despite the changed and lowered status of the Catholic Church, in the roster of heroes of the French Revolution.[20]

But with the reestablishment of the church's authoritative position under Bonaparte, and then the return of the monarchy at Napoléon's downfall, the time was ripe for the retrieval of Fénelon as a widely respected writer, *but also* a good Catholic. A Fénelon dusted off and taken back from the secularists for churchly use, despite the charges of error and the old condemnation, was much to be desired. In order to effect this reappropriation it was important to recognize all of his enlightened values and writing, but also to downplay the stains left by the quietist controversy. It became customary on the part of Catholic defenders now to minimize, or qualify, the official condemnation by arguing that the pope had frowned only on certain tendencies, certain dangers, in Fénelon's expressions, but that his essence and his person, solid and good, remained orthodox and untarnished. Protestants, as they had from the beginning, continued to see the old condemnation as simply unjust, another example of unevangelical ecclesial repression and papal tyranny.

For both sets of interpreters, much depended on an assessment of Madame Guyon. Was she an asset or a liability? How valuable and sound was her teaching on the spiritual life? What was the degree and nature of her influence, for better or worse, on Fénelon? There were some few Catholics who defended her. On the one hand, the marquis Gabriel-Jacques de Salignac-Fénelon, grand-nephew of Fénelon and the first comprehensive collector of his personal papers (published 1734), acknowledged and valued her influence.[21] On the other hand, a spiritual writer such as the Jesuit Jean-Pierre de Caussade, already eager to respect the views of both Bossuet and Fénelon on mystical prayer by synthesizing them, completely ignored Guyon's existence.[22] It was entirely different with Protestant writers, who, beginning with Pierre Poiret's early edition of her collected works in nineteen (!) volumes between 1713 and 1732, greatly valued her quietist spirituality. Moreover, distinguished American Protestant readers of Fénelon in the nineteenth century, such as Horace Bushnell and William Ellery Channing, tended to see Guyon and Fénelon as inextricably linked in a favorable mutual influence.[23] All of these efforts at reclaiming Fénelon's writing had the effect of vindicating either his essential orthodoxy (for Protestants), or his essential Catholicism (for Roman Catholics), or his spiritual usefulness (for both readerships and others as well), while the status of Guyon remained controversial.

But then there was the matter of his relationship with Bossuet. Protestants saw the bishop of Meaux primarily as a fawning ecclesiastical tyrant of the ancien régime, while for Catholics, especially in France, he always remained an esteemed figure. Considerable effort was invested in showing that at heart there had been no real disagreement between the great Fénelon, whatever his errors in the *Maxims*, and the great Bossuet on substantive matters. It had all been just a morass of personal animosities, hurt feelings, rivalries, and misunderstandings, with a bedrock of real love and affection underneath. Interpreters of Fénelon's work, while greatly valuing his perspectives, were able to appreciate important elements of truth in Bossuet's side of the debate as well. A consensus view emerged in which it was argued that Fénelon was wrong with regard to those dangerous quietist leanings on which the church, led by Bossuet, condemned him, but right on a range of disputable questions, where Bossuet was obtuse. They tended, as we say, to talk past one another. The battle between them was a draw.

Such was the posture, for instance, of Cardinal Pierre de Bausset, author of the first multivolume critical biography of Fénelon (first published in 1808, third edition in 1817), and of Jean Gosselin, general editor of the two major nineteenth-century editions of Fénelon's collected works. Furthermore, after a long period of obscurity the letters between Fénelon and Guyon became widely available to scholars only at the beginning of the twentieth century, so that major reassessments were in order. One result was that Guyon's influence over Fénelon appeared to have been less comprehensive than had been thought, and the struggle with Bossuet began to look more political and psychological than theological. Thus Henri Bremond, eager to revive the pure-love spirituality of Fénelon by reinstating him with all good Catholics, produced his famous 1910 *Apologie pour Fénelon.* The book is a defense of *both* Bossuet and Fénelon, who as wise spiritual teachers, Bremond thought, aimed at the same truths, loved the church dearly, and were ultimately upholders of true Catholic orthodoxy. Ronald Knox in *Enthusiasm* (1950) articulated a similar, mediating position, but with this difference: Bremond admired Fénelon's depth, beauty, and boldness, while Knox admired Bossuet's balance and caution.

And, of course, rarely is the whole truth in complex debates on one side, and the tendency is for opponents to caricature one another through overstatement. The critics and historians agreed that Fénelon had indeed tapped into a powerful and important stream of spirituality, but that Bossuet, better informed than often realized (or than Fénelon could admit), had been right to raise warning flags, especially in light of the sometimes bizarre nature of Madame Guyon's contribution.

Context is all-important here, because profound-sounding statements can be tweaked in so many directions. When, for instance, Fénelon tells us that privations are the bread of the strong, he is articulating a classic quietist tenet—that by divine intent suffering is gracious and loss is gain, so long as they lead us into the death of self and a closer relationship with God. Is such a statement a mere truism, dangerously one-sided, or profoundly wise? Certainly it is more than a banality ("no pain, no gain"). Nor is it mere popular Stoicism ("through bitter things to the stars"). Nor with the insight of our post-Freudian and feminist age can it be seen as an invitation to a kind of spiritual masochism with a perverse delight in, or rationalization of, passive acquiescence in suffering ("living is hurting"). Bossuet came close to understanding Fénelon that way. Bossuet was only being sensible, so the argument goes, whatever the lack of subtlety in his own thought, to be deeply suspicious of the incautiousness, the exaggeration, the fondness for extreme statement, and the subjective enmeshment with fantasy and fanaticism attending some quietist thinking. The only problem was that he had misunderstood Fénelon, who was, I suggest, voicing a deep insight into the nature of love—an insight that tends to escape merely "reasonable" people.

Fénelon and Jansenism

Before we can fully appreciate Fénelon in the twentieth century and for our own time, we must address one more major factor in how he is viewed by historians. In addition to "quietism" and "mysticism," another seventeenth-century "ism" dogs his steps, not because he is labeled with this "ism" but precisely because he is not. This is the phenomenon known as "Jansenism," which has played an immense role in French religious and cultural history.

Eventually condemned by the pope for certain of its doctrinal tenets, Jansenism is often compared with the teachings of figures collectively labeled as the "French School" of spirituality. The followers of the French School, which would include Fénelon (although technically he is not classed with them, because he came later), supported mystical prayer, whereas the followers of Jansenism did not. Writers of the French School *inclined* toward quietist practice, and the Jansenists hated it. We will deal with the French School in chapter two, but let us glance here at the nature of the Jansenist movement and then consider why it is important for understanding the complexity of pro- and anti-Fénelon positions.

Jansenism has been described by its opponents as a Catholic crypto-heresy and by its defenders as a form of Catholic orthodoxy hostile to the powerful Jesuit order.[24] Essentially it was a movement of church reform. But it ended up having profound political and cultural ramifications for all of French society up to the time of the Revolution. It began with a Dutch theologian at Louvain, Cornelius Jansen (1585–1638), and his book *Augustinus* (posthumously published in 1640). Jansen set out for his academic readers his own interpretation of controverted matters in the theology of Saint Augustine. Issues of the nature of human sinfulness, grace, free will, and predestination—central concerns of the Protestant Reformation and the Catholic Counter-Reformation—were the focus. Jansen took a hard position. We are *utterly* depraved by sin, he said, and reduced to total helplessness, and salvation must be *entirely* by means of a special dispensation of God's grace given *only* to that portion of human-kind destined for salvation. Prickly questions abounded. How does grace work? What about human free will in salvation? Does the depth of our sinfulness disable the power of human reason? And so on. Jansen's reading of Augustine was within orthodox boundaries, but the devil was in the details and the implications that others drew.

Indeed, others *did* pick up Jansen's ideas, because a hard reading of Augustine lent itself to a "get tough" policy in church discipline. And in a time of heightened secularism the atmosphere was ripe for it. Jean Duvergier de Hauranne, known as the Abbé de Saint-Cyran (1581–1643), and the famous Sorbonne theologian Antoine Arnauld (1612–94) translated Jansen's teaching into a "rigorist" set of prescriptions for devotional practice. One of the most controversial was that, given our radical sinfulness, we should come to Holy Communion infrequently. We must receive the Eucharist not just in a state of *attrition*, or simple recognition of the wrongfulness of our sin coupled with a salutary fear of divine judgment—as the Jesuits taught—but rather in a state of deep *contrition*, that is, love for God's holiness and deep sorrow for the insult to God caused by our sin.

This is harsh talk, but it caught on like wildfire. Catholic monastic orders and schools were deeply affected, and some became predominantly Jansenist in practice. The culmination was in the spiritual and cultural life generated by the two massively influential religious communities named Port-Royal in the Paris area. Under the influence of scholar-teachers in these communities, a whole generation of distinguished thinkers, artists, and writers provided some of France's best minds. The most famous are the dramatist Racine, the philosopher-theologians Pierre Nicole and Antoine Arnauld, and the mathematician–spiritual savant Blaise Pascal. Many clergy and laity were indirectly affected. Jansenist influence suffused everywhere.

Initially supportive of all aspects of culture and learning, Jansenist thinkers gradually became, as their doctrine hardened under persecution, more puritanical, more austere, and more hostile to any practice that seemed to weaken Christian witness by compromising with a secular spirit. With regard to ecclesiastical politics, they tended to operate with a sectarian mindset, resisting the control of local bishops, even when backed with royal authority, where this conflicted with their basic theology or practice. When the backlash came, the church hierarchy was aroused and eventually charges of heresy were raised; the upshot was a papal pronouncement in May 1653. Jansenist doctrine was condemned as Calvinist error in the famous five propositions supposedly extracted from Cornelius Jansen's work. A subscription oath was placed on clergy and university teachers. Public conformity coupled with private resistance on various levels followed. Complicated and convoluted debates continued until finally Pope Clement IX terminated the furor with an imposed silence. We will address some of the subtleties of Jansenism later and will see Fénelon's part in all of this during his Cambrai years.

Where the modern understanding and assessment of Fénelon enter the picture, though, is with the viewpoint often articulated since the nineteenth century: that the Jansenist movement was the real spiritual center of authentic Christian spirituality in Fénelon's time. The usual reasons for this view have to do with admiration for Pascal and the power of his emotional, passionate witness for Christ—and this admiration is then generalized to all of Jansenism—and admiration for the resistance that many Jansenists made to an absolutist monarchy and an authoritarian church when constraints were imposed. The Jansenists are seen as advocates for freedom against tyranny. But *if* the Jansenists are the spiritual heroes of the age, then their opponents, including Fénelon, are the villains. This contrast has been worked up in many ways.

Two noted examples illustrate the point. The most distinguished pro-Jansenist, and thus anti-Fénelonian, writer of the nineteenth century was the literary critic Charles-Augustin Sainte-Beuve. He has been closely followed by the twentieth-century expert on French ecclesiastical history, John McManners. In his famous study of Jansenism, the five-volume *Port-Royal*, finished in 1859, Sainte-Beuve presented the Jansenists of Port-Royal as truly Christian, as having "spiritual magic."[25] He admired the sturdy, vigorous quality of their belief and practice. In the excellence of their writing he saw them as the true forerunners of all that would be progressive, free-spirited, and aesthetically superior in the artistic productions of later times. Their resistance to churchly authority made them harbingers of the Republic. Even their negativity to aspects of their contemporary culture manifested the ability to be "critical" in an age of fawning panegyric. Referring to the hermit-scholars of Port-Royal, for whom he had the highest regard, Sainte-Beuve praised them for their "exceptional moral adventure" and for representing "the magnificent example of a society of beings, pure and courageous."[26]

Fénelon, by contrast, Sainte-Beuve described[27] as an admirably spiritual man, a man of beautiful thoughts, whose intentions were good (he taught the Duc de Bourgogne that "a king is made for the people"[28]) and his writing elegant, but whose actions manifested weakness and vacillation (a man of an "excellent mind," but also an "irritating gentleness"), who is always counseling "submission" to authority.[29] In a similar way, as well, he saw a certain manliness and robustness in the great Bossuet, despite the wrongheadedness of that court-prelate's royal absolutism, since his vigorous statements of Catholic truth always contrasted with a certain "feeble side"[30] in Fénelon, even if the latter had truth on his side. "His piety had wings," said Sainte-Beuve of Fénelon,[31] but he was a "patriotic dreamer" in the end, and a "deviser of pastoral utopias," says McManners.[32] Furthermore, by comparison with Pascal, that great martyr of human moral struggle and the stormy, agonized search for God, Fénelon's piety, contended Sainte-Beuve,[33] had a smooth, unruffled, overly intellectualized quality about it (a "feline deftness," says McManners).[34] And so on, in a comparison of virile "strength" and feminized "weakness"—in which making the Jansenists look good entails making Fénelon look bad!

Again as an arch-example, the counterbalance to Sainte-Beuve is Bremond, who popularized the idea that the Jansenists were basically

Catholics in the tradition of the French School, but who, under Calvinist influence, gradually slipped more and more into a dark and anti-mystical reading of St. Augustine.[35] Catholicism rightly understood, argued Bremond, is a "devout humanism," that is, a combination of the central Catholic dogma of the Incarnation and the affirmation of all that is best in human culture. The seventeenth century, begun by Francis de Sales and then blossoming in the French School, represents this authentic Catholic balance. The point is that Fénelon and "pure love" captured and completed the work begun by Francis de Sales, whereas the Jansenists in all of their puritanical rigor, all of their sense of the dark tragedy of sin and the mystery of God's separation of the saved and the damned, were the antithesis.

Bremond was a Catholic Modernist. He was one of those scholar-historians who, around the turn of the twentieth century, were beating the drum for the more disciplined use of historical scholarship in Catholic self-understanding. By publishing his 1910 work on Fénelon, and then in composing his massive eleven-volume *Histoire littéraire du sentiment religieux en France* between 1916 and 1933, he was attempting to make a case for what he considered the more humanistic, less dogmatic side of Catholicism, namely, the tradition of the great mystical writers. In this perspective where spiritual inwardness is placed at the center and strict doctrinal orthodoxy is subordinated to the dynamics of religious experience, Fénelon was once again tending to be read with respect. What historians call a "pietist" tradition of spirituality now began to link up with nineteenth-century romanticism and the renewed interest in emotional and aesthetic experience as a reaction to the rationalism of the Enlightenment. Mysticism moved center stage, because it involved *feelings;* it is *soulful,* not denatured by the (seemingly) cold intellectuality of dogmatic theology, or the formal creeds of an institution, or the logical constructs of the rational mind. Heart-religion is coming to seem more authentic than intellect-religion. We will see in due course, though, how valid this contrast is in understanding Fénelon.

Quietism and Mysticism in Fresh Perspective

With the new availability of critical editions of his work in the nineteenth century, especially his letters, and with the church's own increasingly historical-critical understanding of its own past, Fénelon was rediscovered. People began to encounter him in the way that most of his contemporaries knew him, that is, as a sage and guide for the inner life, a sophisticated psychologist for the spiritually hungry soul. Such subjects as the nature of prayer, the pursuit of holiness, and the desire for "perfection," gifts of the Spirit, and the discernment of vocation, the interest in meditation and the cultivation of contemplative practices, and so on, began to make Fénelon a favorite for pious readers. What then happened is that this kind of reading tended to bring back into focus the whole story of the quietist controversy once again, along with all of the debates with Bossuet about the "states" of prayer, the nature of passivity in the devout soul, the meaning of "indifference" in Christian living, the hope for salvation, and the elimination of the "self" in the quest for God. The whole relationship with Madame Guyon and her "short way" to God comes back into focus again as well.

The difference is that the quietism and mysticism of Fénelon and Guyon could now begin to be viewed as *modes* of religious experiencing and as *ways* of spiritual practice. They could be viewed as *spiritual phenomena*. What I termed above the "ism" quality of quietism and mysticism—their status as a set of technically formulated doctrines—was coming to seem less important than the record of divine-human interaction that they might contain. If we can understand that record, empathize with it, grasp its essence, then it may become accessible to us as well. Even more, quietism and mysticism may in their own way contain elements that are vital components of all living religion and thus have something to say about the universal human condition.

The question that the nineteenth century addressed to Fénelon was not about the orthodoxy of his teaching, but about its *meaning*. It is this meaning that makes it relevant for us as well, and potentially of very great interest. The way we say this today is that we are looking for "wisdom," wisdom that is convertible and usable, in Fénelon's experience and teaching. We seek insight into spiritual truth. But these insights will take the form not so much of theological statements as of reports of what it is like to be close to God and how we can get there too.

The answer that Fénelon gives here is that the way to God is open. In order to walk that way we must become serious about what he calls "pure love." We can enjoy the deep satisfaction—what he terms "dry peace"— of the quietist practice of inward prayer, as well as the mystical sense of immediate encounter with God, once we recognize that "pure love" is the indispensable key. But then we must spend some time pondering what this "pure love" really is, because its nature is not self-evident. Some deep reflection is in order, since misunderstanding is perilously easy. It is impossible to obtain a firm grip on what Fénelon meant by "pure love," I would suggest, without retracing the steps and the history by which he worked out his mature thought.

"Pure love" has its critics, even in our modern age. For many there is a suspect air about the concept because there is the sense that it contains something overstated, angelic, unrealistic, ultimately inhuman. This is Bossuet's old criticism, implied as well in Pope Innocent XII's condemnation of the *Maxims*, and more recently echoed by Thomas Merton in the 1960s.[36] One is also reminded of Reinhold Niebuhr's criticisms of utopianism in the name of "realism." "Pure love" as something highly desirable is not necessarily obvious or legitimate. The case has to be made.

The problem always is to get clear about what Fénelon meant by the phrase, because he insisted that, however deserved the papal condemnation, he was only trying to say in a perhaps inadequate and misleading way what great teachers had always said. Augustine himself, after all, had asserted in a famous passage from the *Confessions* "that we are to love God and then do as we wish," and all will be well. Everybody, including Madame Guyon, quoted that tag from the *Confessions*, but the question for Fénelon was: how seriously, really, do we take that statement? So it is that we will have to revisit Fénelon's use of classical sources, including Augustine, to appreciate his thinking about "pure love." Everything depends, says Fénelon, on what this "love" is, and what it means for it to be "pure," if we are really to approach God and really to be transformed. A great deal is at stake indeed.

So, in what follows, we are going to be looking for points of entry into what Fénelon meant by "pure love." We will discover that a galaxy of themes, gradually emerging in the course of his biography, crystallize and cohere around this concept. By way of introduction, let us hear from Fénelon himself as his earthly end approached, when, in an offhand manner, he offered a concise summary.

In the last of his extant letters of spiritual advice, posted from Cambrai on December 30, 1714, one week before he died, Fénelon hit the essential notes of his life's work. The letter is a very occasional piece, and written to someone whom he did not know, a woman member of a religious order, but all the more significant and touching because of that. He had been urged to write to her, and possibly visit, because informants had indicated that both he and she would profit from a spiritual conference face-to-face. He indicates that he cannot make this visit, although he urges her to open her heart "in all simplicity" to him. From his side he would like nothing more, he says, than to be instructed by God's spirit working through her, since his personal desire always is to be "the least and smallest of God's children," however much he has been invested with high pastoral authority. To receive her advice, and even correction, would be a joy to him. For, after all, his sole goal has been always "to be without a will of his own" in submitting to the maternal embrace of the church. He then adds, tellingly, that this desire to give up his own will arises from a more fundamental urge to place himself in submission to every human being (1 Peter 2:13), "so as to die to self-love and his own pride." He apologizes for his intimate directness in this letter, since he does not know her personally, but his sense is that she genuinely seeks God, and thus, as he finishes this short letter, he indicates his wish to engage in that search with her.

There we have it. Simplicity, spiritual childhood,[37] the release of the selfish self, the transformation of the will—these are major points of entry into what Fénelon means by "pure love." They were themes that reso- nated with the sweeping spiritual currents of his time and culture. They were themes that he evoked with a kind of transparent freshness to the very end. His critics accused him of hypocrisy—of exalting himself by means of the language of self-abnegation, where all talk of the rejection of self-love is nothing but a cover for the most egregious forms of the thing itself—but we shall have to assess that for ourselves as we revisit his biography, allow ourselves to be enlightened as to the nature of love of God, and attempt to reclaim Fénelon's legacy.

"Beware of your own intellectual gifts and those of others. Judge no one according to them. God, the only wise Judge, takes a very different tack: he gives preference to children and the childlike mind."
—LETTER TO SR. CHARLOTTE DE SAINT-CYPRIEN, NOVEMBER 27, 1695 (TR. EDMONSON)

"However, religion ought to be in practice what it is in speculation. That is, it has to actually go as far as knocking our intellect off its feet and surrendering us up to the foolishness of the crucified Savior. How easy it is to be a Christian on the condition that we are wise, masters of ourselves, full of courage, great, punctual in fulfilling our duties, and marvelous in every way!"
—MANUAL OF PIETY, "GOOD FRIDAY" (TR. EDMONSON)

ONE

Classical Education and Priestly Formation

1651–1677

Ll of Fénelon's biographers bemoan the lack of information about his early years. The fact is that we know virtually nothing. His extant correspondence begins only when he is eighteen or nineteen years old and already a student in Paris. And we begin to have a real abundance of material in the form of letters only during the time of his first encounter with Madame Guyon (1688–89). Indeed, by that time he is a well-known and popular figure, beginning to move easily within the circle of the aristocratic dévots at court. Before this time, though, we have the barest outline of dates and names and places in Fénelon's life, combined with some scanty reminiscences from his later years of the flavor of his childhood in an idyllic place.

Most of what can be reasonably surmised with regard to Fénelon's formative years has to do with the quality and depth of his educational and priestly formation. So, after a brief look at his place of origin and family circumstances, that is the place to start.

Born François de Salignac de la Mothe-Fénelon either on August 6, 1651 (the traditional date), or in the early weeks of 1651,[38] he was the second son of Pons de Salignac de la Mothe-Fénelon and his second wife, Louise de la Cropte, sister of the Marquis de Saint-Abre. The family is described as "impecunious old nobility," as marked by "genteel poverty," but also as living in a state of complex fiscal *"ruine,"* although "no less distinguished for its antiquity than for its celebrity."[39] Fénelon appears always to have had a strong sense, throughout his career, of "illustrious origins" and aristocratic standing.[40] The paternal estate and chateau, still there today, where young François spent his childhood, and which he always remembered fondly, are in the picturesque

Périgord region of France, east of Bordeaux in the Dordogne river valley.[41] Surrounded by siblings from his father's first and second marriages,[42] he enjoyed a robust family life in what apparently were moderately comfortable and privileged material circumstances. He is described as having been of "a weak and delicate constitution" but "amiable dispositions."[43] The family was devoutly Catholic, a number of close relatives having been active with groups strongly committed to the renewal of pious Catholic practice, but also appreciative of humanistic learning. Fénelon seems to have been one of those younger sons who were often marked out for the priesthood early on. The standard procedure thus was to give him a solid foundation in the classical languages and texts along with the cultivation of habits of personal religious devotion. This blend is his earliest formative matrix, and its influence would stay with him forever.

Because of the social standing of his family, and given the generally mediocre quality of schools at the time, his education was conducted at home under the supervision of a "governor" or lay tutor, as well as a priest-tutor and chaplain to the family, from the local parish of Sainte-Mondane. One scholar describes his home environment this way: "he lived in an atmosphere both Christian and cultivated, where learning was not oriented to novelties but to steady development of good character, and where nothing is forced or hasty, but always given time to ripen in a setting of 'ambitions pursued in a peaceful spirit.'"[44] Another has written that Fénelon had "a solitary and privileged education" with nothing "schoolish" about it.[45] We should recall also that at this time there is nothing like a French national literature, but instead only a mass of medieval lore and material layered on top of the heritage of Greece and Rome. The whole spirit of the European renaissance in the centuries before Fénelon had been one of recovery of, and deep veneration for, this ancient heritage, slow and deep immersion in which was the absolute prerequisite for cultural sophistication. In due course Fénelon would encounter the artistic experimentation and creativity of the newer Parisian salon culture, but such innovation was not typical of the provinces, which were conservative in spirit. What he received in his childhood was aristocratic education in the elegant and polished style of France's grand siècle in the environment of a country chateau.[46]

There are various indications that Fénelon was a brilliant student from the first, and in due course he did some study at the Jesuit college in Cahors, from which he eventually received a degree. The religious orders of the Oratorians and the Jesuits largely controlled higher education. We know enough about the curriculum in these provincial Jesuit academies of the time to know that he would have received an excellent grounding in Latin and Greek, in rhetoric and the arts of verbal expression, and in the rudiments of dramatic composition. The Jesuits were also quite open to the new science and may have encouraged an interest in Descartes and contemporary thinkers as well. One description has it that "his education had a Jesuit character about it" in that it was "well balanced and always directed to the formation of the will and the development of a 'spiritual aesthetic' grounded in the good use of language." The Jesuit teachers, known for their cosmopolitan humanism, may have imparted "that particular accent which gives his Catholicism such a generously opened aspect."[47]

His father having died in 1663, he spent some substantial time under the tutelage of an uncle, François de Fénelon, the bishop of nearby Sarlat ("a loving pastor to his flock, and beloved of them," wrote Fénelon in a letter of 1706 to Pope Clement XI).[48] We have no way of knowing when and how his vocation to the priesthood began, but it seems to have been there early on and then to have been taken for granted. By 1674 he had been taken under care by another uncle, Antoine de Salignac, Marquis de Magnac (known as the Marquis de Fénelon), "a man nourished in the purest principles of religion and of honor"[49] and a lieutenant general in the king's army. Under uncle Antoine's watchful eye he could continue his higher education in Paris, which had only in this century and quite recently become the cultural and intellectual center of French life.

Becoming a Priest

The intention was that he would begin priestly studies with two years of pre-seminary study in the humanities at the Collège du Plessis under a Sorbonne professor, Charles Gobinet. That academician seems to have been especially acceptable to the Marquis as preceptor for his

nephew because he was an ultramontane, that is, a Catholic with a strong
preference for papal authority over against the ancient autonomy of the
French church.[50] The Marquis also set up young Fénelon in residence
with the gentlemen-priests of the parish of Saint-Sulpice in Paris, where
he would become subject to their spirituality and discipline. As Gobinet
further drilled him in classical learning, the Sulpicians introduced him
to the teachings of the French school. The principal figures here would
be St. Francis de Sales (just canonized, in 1665!) as precursor, then
Cardinal Pierre de Bérulle as principal and founder of the Oratorians,
followed by the Sulpician founder, Jean-Jacques Olier.

The Sulpician order of clergy, initially an offshoot of the Oratorians,
had as its mission the upgrading of seminary education and the setting of high standards for well-educated pastoral work by parish priests.
Henri Bremond has described the Sulpician tradition as an important
part of that "devout humanism" that marked the best in Catholic revival,
where sincere faith is coupled with a sophisticated understanding of
the psychology of human development.[51] These years spent with the
Sulpicians provided for Fénelon an important means for integrating
more deeply the humanistic values of classical learning and the dogmas
of the church. After his death the priests of Saint-Sulpice would become
the keepers of his letters and personal documents and would produce
some of the first critical editions of his oeuvre. In their spirit he himself
would be both a pastor and priest-pedagogue.

A Classical Education

French culture of the seventeenth century is so saturated with the
literature of ancient Greece and Rome that this period is called "the age
of French neoclassicism." In a manner that would be hard to overstate,
the ingestion of aesthetic standards as well as substantive content
from classical models was the very engine of artistic inspiration. The
literature of ancient Greece and Rome provided models for imitation
and standards to be emulated in all artistic production, on the one hand,
but also a repository of texts to be mined for plots, characters, and ideas
that would serve as instruments for new and contemporary expression,

on the other. Whether the goal was the reproduction of classical forms and sentiments or the use of those same forms as a springboard for novel expression, the ancient sources provided the artistic point of departure. The fundamental attitude of this classicism was most famously stated by Jean de La Bruyère in his massively popular, steadily reprinted and expanded *Les Caractères*: "Everything has been said already, and one comes too late after 7,000 years in which men have lived and reflected on their existence. On the subject of human behavior the best and the better have been harvested, and one can only glean behind the ancients and the most talented of our contemporaries."[52] The best mind does not say anything essentially new; it only says it *differently*.

The sources of this seventeenth-century French fascination with classical art forms lie ultimately in the dynamics of political and social stabilization in France after the end of the Wars of Religion at the end of the last century. Under Louis XIII, and then even more under Louis XIV, France was organized, ordered, structured, and bureaucratized in every conceivable way, not least of all in the arts. The great heritage of classical Greek and Roman culture with its criteria of beauty and excellence lay at hand as a treasury of riches to be exploited endlessly—and mined, excavated, and plundered it was. Royal support was generous, and the organization of the French Academy created an elite body of practitioners. The practical upshot for us in understanding Fénelon is that the so-called school of 1660, consisting of the dramatists Racine, Boileau, Molière, and the writer La Fontaine, along with the composer of maxims La Rochefoucauld, forms the immediate backdrop to his own literary endeavors. These authors are, in the genres of tragedy, comedy, popular fable, and proverbial philosophy, the literary psychologists of the time. Human personality and its complex dynamics and possibilities are endlessly fascinating for them, not least of all the intricacies of love!

We must then take some time to imagine what it was that Fénelon absorbed from the classics that was to feed into his mature and elaborated thought about the nature of "pure love." Here we can get a sense of what he studied and its impact on him from the scholarly circles in which he moved as a young priest, from his later use of the classics as a preceptor and tutor to others, as well as from his own literary output. The overwhelming impression we get is that Fénelon metabolized early on, and integrated profoundly, the Greek or Hellenic side of the classical tradition, so that there have been many studies by scholars of the implications of his Hellenism.

Of the two great philosophical traditions inherited from the classical world—Aristotelianism, transmitted mostly through the Scholastic theology of the church, and Platonism, transmitted largely through the humanist traditions of the Renaissance—Plato is by far the dominant force for Fénelon. The massive influence of Plato came partly through his own lifelong study, much of this mediated through the study of Augustine and the Augustinian use of Plato, and partly through the Roman Cicero, who was not only a great classical orator but also an encyclopedic compiler of the views of the ancient, that is, Greek, philosophical schools. We also have good reason to think that as Fénelon became immersed in his higher education in Paris, he moved into friendship and discussion with philosophically sophisticated friends, foremost of whom during the 1680s would have been Claude Fleury, like Fénelon a priest-pedagogue, but also a known interpreter of Plato, and eventually his assistant in the educational supervision of the young Duc de Bourgogne.

What philosophical perspective would Fénelon have learned from Plato and the Platonic tradition that would be fundamental for his whole way of thinking and acting? The central idea was this: the goal of human living is the full discernment of what is good, beautiful, and true in a world where all objects partake of these qualities only to some limited degree. All human growth and maturation is a process of moving from less adequate to more adequate discernments of such truth/beauty/ goodness, as the mind discards inferior manifestations for superior ones. The purpose of education is the progressive refinement of the mind's capacity to make these discernments through dialectical reasoning, so that the mind is enlightened and the will is thereby formed for choosing and practicing good ends in one's life.

In Fénelon's time the question of just *how* the mind grasps what is true through this process of discernment involved complex debate about the nature of "ideas" and the means by which they inform thinking and engage the "will." The underlying assumption, though, was that as its discernment improves, the mind's adherence to goodness, beauty, and truth in objects becomes a desire for, a "love" of, an attraction to these objects. So here we have what would have been a first crucible of formation for Fénelon, namely, the Platonic conception of love, *eros*, as the mind's act of discernment, leading to passion, followed by a total yielding to the lovable object.

Furthermore, the mind's ability to make these discernments, to engage in true love, will be steadily improved as the individual herself grows in goodness, beauty, and truth, that is, in character and virtue, since "like perceives like." This is to say that the mind's act of adherence to what is lovable is not just intellectualizing or curiosity, but a movement of the soul or heart of the whole person. The tendency of the physical body and of the material world in general is to cloud this process of discernment by enmeshing the mind in passions that are the propagators of fantasy and illusion. If erotic desiring and possession are to be valid, to be grounded in what is real, they must find a way to bypass, or overcome, this false eros and its precipitation of misjudgment about what is truly lovable in objects. The whole debate about "pure love" in Fénelon's teaching will focus on the effort to distinguish more adequate from less adequate forms of loving what is good.

Thus far, broadly speaking, does Plato take us. What the tradition called neoplatonism (represented preeminently by the third-century thinker Plotinus) then added was a great elaboration in thinking about the nature of the mind's "ascent" to truth. Plotinus makes the mind's rise to higher and higher levels of discernment a kind of mystical journey, quasi-religious in nature, and profoundly inward—increasingly contemplative, wordless, and tranquil—as the mind progresses upward toward the One, who is the transcendent source of all beauty and goodness, and away from external objects. The mind, that is, the seat of the soul, finally obtains that for which by nature it yearns and arrives at a state of perfect unity with this One.

This tradition from Plato, mediated by Plotinus, is what Augustine inherited in the fourth and fifth centuries and passed on to later generations in the Christian form of the restless soul ("our hearts are restless till they rest in thee") enslaved by mortality and sin, yet yearning for redeeming truth and moral goodness. Augustine's contention was that whatever the mind supremely discerns as good, beautiful, and true

is ultimately the work of the God—who is the "One" whom Plotinus
sought—of Christian Scripture. But because the human will is in
bondage to sin through its concupiscent or disordered desiring, said
Augustine, the mind is darkened and cannot perceive truth, beauty, and
goodness accurately. The gift of God's saving grace is to free the will
and enlighten the mind. The redeemed sinner is thereby empowered to
experience the "victorious delectation" of once again taking full delight
in what is good, beautiful, and true. This is to say that the redeemed
sinner can begin to love *rightly* by obeying God's holy law. And that law
prescribes that we shall love God above all things.

Later we will see how Fénelon's views of Augustine put him in direct
opposition to antihumanistic Jansenists like Pascal, who wished to erect
a high wall between the "God of the philosophers" and the God of
Abraham, Isaac, and Jacob. As strongly as anyone, Fénelon will criticize
an overreliance on reason—that is, rationalism—but will always insist
that Christian revelation can be clarified and more deeply embraced
with the help of philosophical tools.[53] More forcefully than anyone else
perhaps, it has been Henri Bremond who has reminded us that all of
the best spirituality of the French seventeenth century is saturated with
Plato, so that "it is not so difficult to pass from the Academy of Plato to
that of the Crib and Calvary"[54]—a short step indeed!

But there is something else as well. It is a combination of classical
factors, compounded of the ancient Greek tragedies, the philosophy of
Stoicism, and the moralizing literature of late Hellenistic antiquity. This
mixture of traditions captures the view that life is not just a spiritual *quest*,
as with Plato, but also a spiritual *struggle*. This struggle is a dark process
of suffering, frequent defeats, and the emergence of enduring wounds.
On the one hand, our spiritual lives are an upward movement toward
higher ground, but on the other hand, there is the daily encounter with
the insidiousness and intractability of human limitations and all of the
destructive urges—our own and those of other people. We must imagine
Fénelon immersed in his formative years in the sunniness, so to speak, of
a Platonic worldview, but also increasingly aware of the shadowside of
our mortality and dust. The great Roman Stoics, who conveyed Greek
ideas to a wider audience—writers like Marcus Aurelius and Seneca—
but also the ancient playwright Sophocles, or the late moralist Plutarch,

were great favorites. We must take a moment to capture the flavor of their perspectives, especially on suffering, in order to appreciate a critical factor in Fénelon's makeup.

For the Stoics, as the French understood them, human existence is unremitting conflict with the powers of nature. The most that we can hope for is the excellence of our own virtue in the face of every contingency. When challenged by temptation, by hardship, and by the overwhelming forces of circumstance, we have nothing left in the final analysis but the personal integrity of ethical uprightness. Life may often be tragic, but it is potentially meaningful in the courageous integrity of the person who suffers what he or she does not (at least, not entirely!) deserve. The reason, or soul, of such an individual is transcendent over all, even though the dark passions and inveterate perversity of human society, and finally the sheer travail of mortality, are practically insurmountable. Practical wisdom consists of the ability to choose what is truly good and to be willing to pay whatever price is required for its pursuit, even if the result is disaster in worldly terms. The danger always is that we become pretentious. The great French dramatists, such as the tragedians Corneille and Racine and Molière in his comedic way, work these themes incessantly, and thus they provided the stuff of a certain kind of moral reflection for their lettered listeners. Fénelon drank deeply at this well, as did all of his contemporaries, with the result that the Christian concept of sin, with Augustine's help, easily merges with Stoic/tragic views of the kind of moral suffering required by the conditions of human existence. This combination will play out richly throughout all of Fénelon's thought.

Now, a concept that Fénelon would have picked up from his classical studies, especially in the Platonic and Stoic philosophies just described, is the notion of "indifference." The wise person, the good person, the Christian person is in love with what matters, and this means that he or she is "indifferent" to all of the rest, because the rest is inherently inferior. In Jeanne-Lydie Goré's formulation, indifference is "the cessation of desire . . . in order to rise above the immediate, the moment, to attend to an infinite horizon."[55] It is thus both a mental posture and an ethical commitment. "Indifference," for Christian writers, was then an ideal way of describing the spiritual state of the believer open to God's direction and hanging loose (the technical word is *detached*), as it were, from the things of this world as it passes away.[56] Indeed, Christ teaches us to seek only God's righteousness and God's kingdom, to focus only on the "one thing," and to cease concerning ourselves with other things. That is, we are to practice "indifference" by seeking *only* the supreme value. As will become evident, not only did Fénelon appropriate the idea of indifference from his classical and Christian sources, but also he made it central to the correct understanding of "pure love."

A Spirituality Distinctively French

In his formation at Saint-Sulpice Fénelon would have followed the daily routines and disciplines of that community, with its regular round of sacraments and prayer, its instruction and study, and he would also have been under the care of a spiritual director. This last was the popular and beloved director of the seminary, Louis Tronson (1622–1700), for whom Fénelon came to have a deep veneration. Much later in a letter to Pope Clement XI, he said of Tronson, "Never was any man superior to him in love of discipline, in skill, in prudence, piety, and insight into character," and to Tronson himself at one point he gushed, "Remember that you have functioned as my father from my early years." Tronson was to be an advisor and consultant to him on numerous occasions and would serve on the board of commissioners examining Madame Guyon at Issy. He seems to have filled a vital emotional vacuum for Fénelon, who trusted him completely.[57]

What would he have learned from his Sulpician teachers? Three key ideas came to him, one each from the three central writers of the French School tradition. From Francis de Sales he absorbed the view that our love for God, if it is to be genuine, must take the form of a radical "holy indifference" to *absolutely everything else*. From Pierre de Bérulle he came to understand that the practice of this indifference is made possible when we embrace the ideal of self-annihilation. This deep denial of the self occurs when we lovingly identify with the *inner state* of Jesus Christ both as a helpless child and as the crucifed One. From Jean-Jacques Olier he learned that our sinful human ego, profoundly crafty and always intent on self-glorification, is our most formidable enemy in this work of learning to practice holy difference in self-annihilation. Fénelon embraced all three ideas with gusto but wove them into his own distinctive synthesis. What they share in common is the insight that love of God and a true life of prayer centered on God must be something that God does in us, when we get ourselves out of the way. In order to experience loving prayer directed at Ultimate Love, we must become theocentric in focus, always letting God take the lead and not allowing ourselves to become distracted by our own inadequacies or our own agenda.[58]

Francis de Sales

In terms of the pervasive effect of his writings on all classes of society, and by his emphasis on practical charity in discipleship, Francis de Sales was the great champion of the spirit of the Counter-Reformation in early seventeenth-century France.[59] He was "the man of genius" who "achieve[d] completely the necessary adaptation and popularization" that "brought the whole Christian Renaissance within the reach of the lowliest in a little book of devotion." The reference is to de Sales's *Introduction to the Devout Life*, which, along with the later *Treatise on the Love of God*, became the virtual "charter of devout humanism" and of the "higher mysticism" in France.[60] Fénelon would lean on him heavily for ideas and constantly appeal to him in later debate as a foundation, calling him "a man who [possessed] a great penetration, and a perfect sensitivity for judging the depth of things, and for knowing the human heart."[61]

Having first published the *Introduction* in 1608,[62] Francis produced a book centered, in the words of one modern interpreter, on "the universal emphatic call of God to all human beings and in every form of life to that charity which was friendship and salvation."[63] The key idea is that God is to be loved with all of the resources of the human heart, once the impulse to a fear-based relationship has been neutralized. The goal of all Christian living, Francis tells us, is "perfection," which is a state where we do good "carefully, frequently, and promptly," making our charity into a "spiritual fire, which, when it bursts into flame, is called devotion." Arrival at this perfection must be a very gradual process in which setbacks and lapses are to be expected as salutary reminders of our continuing dependence on God. Our human desiring, which is the energy of the soul and center of our personalities, will gradually be so purified, Francis says, that eventually all we will want is God and God's glory. We will have found that it is "sweeter" to love and serve God than anything else.[64] Fénelon agreed completely, with the one reservation that the affectively charged language of a "spiritual fire" was, he thought (and as we shall see), risky.

Although, in conventional fashion, Francis is quite clear that the individual must renounce sinful behaviors through a process of purging, what most concerned him is the redirecting and refocusing of desire, of the "affections." Desiring God, in other words, is more important—because it is more fundamental—than godly behavior as such. His key term, then, for the state of desiring God is "holy indifference." In such a state we are resigned to the circumstances and condition in which we find ourselves at every moment, these being in some way the will of God. Most important are our "inner attractions" to what is holy, so that while we may not be able to embrace holy objects completely, we feel *drawn* to make the effort. In that being drawn, we know that grace is at work within us ("God knocks at the door"), however far from perfection we may actually be.[65] Fénelon agreed completely, and it is here that he found support for his idea that our inner "states" are far more important than our outer actions.

Spiritual directors are people who help us clarify these inner states, especially when all is darkness, temptation, and struggle. Francis picks up the traditional idea that our souls have a "superior part" where we can continue to love God, even if the "inferior part" is consumed with either earthly delight or agony. This is a way of saying that there can be a zone of quiet deep within, no matter what may be the case outwardly. When temptations come, as long as the soul does not inwardly consent, all is well. He also introduces the idea that will become controversial in quietist teaching: that the best way to defeat a temptation in the end is to gently ignore it, until "it" goes away. Francis describes the "two hands of God" as consolations and afflictions, both of which come at God's behest, but our job is to persist "in a constant, resolute, prompt, and active will to do whatever we know is pleasing to God," leaving the rest up to God. "Imitate little children," he says, "who with one hand hold fast to their father while with the other they gather strawberries and blackberries from the hedges. So too if you gather and handle the goods of this world with one hand, you must always hold fast with the other to your heavenly father's hand and turn toward him from time to time."[66]

In 1616 Francis added clarifications and theoretical grounding with the *Treatise on the Love of God*. "In holy Church all is by love, in love, for love, and of love," he said in the preface. He argued the so-called voluntarist view that God is essentially loving and purposeful, that the dominant component in our own souls is the will, and that, therefore, we are saved by the purification of the will. Our approach to God must happen by means of the conforming of *our* wills to that of God, where, in the highest stage, we *lose* our wills in the divine Will.

But now, as it would be for Madame Guyon and for Fénelon, the metaphors become crucial. How shall I conform my will to that of God? Francis contends that as human beings (this is his optimistic "humanism") we have a natural taste for God like that of a child for its creator-parent. "There is an infinite workman who has stamped on me this limitless desire to know and this appetite which cannot be satiated. For this reason I must strive towards him and reach out for him so as to unite and join myself to his goodness. I belong to it and I exist for it." As God's children we can learn to love God as "we love our fathers, not because they belong to us but rather because we belong to them. It is thus that we love and desire God in hope."[67] Later on, as we shall see, Fénelon and Bossuet will struggle mightily with the logic of what Francis is saying. Is he telling us that we place our hope for well-being in our parents because we first love them and trust them, or is he saying that we love and trust our parents because we first hope for the best from them?

A holy relation with God, Francis says, "is a form of friendship and disinterested love, since by charity we love God for his own sake because of his most supremely pleasing goodness." This charity, which is disinterested love, "is present in the will as on its throne, to reside there and to make it cherish and love its God above all things." God's love is like mother's milk, which we eat and drink, and the more we learn to trust this divine nourishment, the more it transforms us into its own substance. Francis has an image of the child not as greedy for mother's milk but simply trusting it to be there at the right time. Mature prayer, he says, is like the rapt attention of the baby to its mother, a state so delicate that it no longer feels like attention. "There is a deep, sweet, sleep-like quality to this repose of the soul. It is better to sleep upon that sacred breast than to be awake elsewhere, no matter where it may be." Just as a baby would cry when its mother puts it down, "it is the same with the soul that is in repose and quiet before God. In an almost insensible way it draws in the delight of his presence, without thinking, without working, without doing anything by means of any faculty except the highest part of the will, which it moves softly and imperceptibly." These are crucial passages in which Francis describes what has come to be known as "mystic quiet," not an induced and contrived stillness, be it noted, but a sense of being "held" securely. In a striking anticipation of the whole debate between Bossuet and Fénelon, Francis says that spiritual tranquility happens when we arrive at "holy quiet," where finally we will know the difference between "concerning ourselves with the contentment that God gives" and "being occupied with God, who gives us this contentment."[68]

Finally, in the controversial last sections of the *Treatise*, Francis takes up the theme of tribulations in relation to "holy indifference." Tribulations, he says, "considered in themselves are dreadful things; [but] looked at in God's will, they are things of delight." A loving heart loves God most "in afflictions, but it loves it most of all in the cross, in pain and labor." It is in suffering, says Francis, that we learn to delight in what is truly delightful, and when we yield to that experience, we enter into "the acquiescence, or resignation, of spirits in tribulation [that] approaches perfect love." "Pure" or perfect love is this "holy indifference," which is "the supreme and most delicate point of the spirit." Such love is "so rigorous that it permits love of paradise only with the intention of more perfect love for the goodness of him who gives it." The soul practicing holy indifference is "like a ball of wax in God's hands," a plaything at the divine disposal, we might say.[69]

But then came the notoriously famous "impossible supposition": if it were God's predestinating will that we be in hell, however saintly we may be, we should prefer the delight of conforming to that will rather than the contrary position of being in paradise without conformity to God's will. The loving soul "would prefer hell with God's will to paradise without God's will." If God wants hell for me, I will out of love for him take delight in that eventuality—which is to say that out of love for God I will give up even the hope of my salvation! What makes the supposition "impossible" (in theory) is the orthodox view that God could never have consigned to hell a soul whose love for God was so perfect. Or differently stated in the orthodox view: if I truly love God, the knowledge that God intends me for paradise will be present as well. But the bare statement of the impossible supposition is a way of reinforcing the idea that love of God must be radical. It must be a love of *God*, not of my own salvation, if it is truly God that I love. Jesus himself in the despair and abandonment of his sufferings continued to love God's good pleasure by means of the "highest part of his soul," even while the lower part was overwhelmed with sorrow and anguish. This, says Francis, is where blessed love reigns supreme even in the midst of a nightmare. So it is that "finally, we see that Mount Calvary is the school of love."[70]

Francis de Sales has sowed the seed that Fénelon will water, but he has also sowed controversy, as we shall see. The idea of the indifferent love of God opens many doors in many directions.

Bérulle and Olier

Pierre de Bérulle (1575–1629), a "religious Copernicus," thought Bremond,[71] and eventually a cardinal, is the founder of the Oratorian order in France, an order of priests living in community and following a community rule, but working and practicing in the secular world primarily as parish clergy and as educators in schools. This order has had a succession of leaders and writers, all expressing themselves within the tradition of thought articulated by Bérulle, a tradition now known through Bremond's popularizing as "the French school."[72]

In his writings, which influenced Fénelon's own, Bérulle[73] emphasizes the importance of turning away from self-love in order to focus one's loving energies on God. Thus, he introduced the idea that self-love is the great impediment and the overcoming of this self-love through "abasement," or self-annihilation, is the remedy. Whereas de Sales's preferred strategy is that of the training of affections and the crystallizing of resolutions by focusing on what is beautiful, Bérulle does something different, something more fundamentally inward. He encourages a process of imaginative, at times intensely emotional, identification between the worshiper and the inner "states" of the Incarnate Lord at every stage of his earthly ministry. The goal is an "adhesion" of the soul of the believer to that of Jesus. Since the Incarnation is the supreme dogmatic fact for Bérulle, every moment in the course of Jesus's earthly existence is a fit object for meditation and thus for inner renewal for the believer. By imaginatively entering into this identification, the believer is "elevated" (an important word for Bérulle) so that the Holy Spirit ignites "flames of love" in the human heart.[74] What Fénelon appropriated here was Bérulle's concern for creating a mystical and immediate match between what happens inside Jesus as he is glorified, and what happens inside the believer as he or she grows in holiness. What he disliked, however, was Bérulle's attempt to harness the imagination in creating this match. It is too dependent on our sensual capacities, and thus too vulnerable to mere fantasy.

Bérulle went on to argue that the Incarnation is the most sacred of all "mysteries," and we know that "this mystery is love and only love. For since in it love has united God to man, then also the greatness of God and the lowliness of man are transformed into love by the power of love accomplishing this mystery and triumphing in this mystery."[75] Notice, though that it is the *lowliness* of human existence that provides the point of entry. By means of abasement, the abandonment of self, and detachment from all earthly sources of security and power we position ourselves to enter into the mystery of the helplessness and weakness that the Incarnate Word embraced in our human existence. Now there is no question that Fénelon strongly affirmed this Bérullian perspective, but, as suggested, he will limit it primarily to the state of "childhood" and the state of the "cross." It will be in combining these two in a distinctive fashion, partly under Guyon's influence, that he will develop his own perspective. His sense, though, that he was basically loyal to the heritage of the French school came in the heat of the Conferences of Issy in February 1695, when he signed a statement of loyalty to the principles of Bérulle as a sufficient statement of his orthodoxy.

It is, then, one small step to Jean-Jacques Olier and the stress on self-effacement in priestly formation at Saint-Sulpice. "Their modesty was carried to the point of dreading glory as the most dangerous snare. . . . Strangers to all the feeling that ambition, interest or pride can stir up among men, they would never get involved in party-conflicts, or factions of opinion; they attached themselves only to the decisions and authority of the Church," says one historian.[76] "Never had the spirit of nobility and disinterestedness been expressed to such a remarkable degree."[77] So it is that Olier tells us in his *Introduction to the Christian Life and Virtues* that the practical response of Christians to God's revealing of true religion in Jesus must be the "annihilation" of self in all manner of sacrifice. Humility is the foundational virtue,[78] and we reach its peak when we love our "own vileness, littleness and nothingness in other people's awareness as well as in our own," for then "only nothingness remains, and this is our core and true reality."[79] "Self-centeredness is a horrible monster and the hideous ocean of all sin, just as abnegation is the summary of perfection and the source of the Christian life and virtues," and he made charts that compared and contrasted the qualities of self-centeredness with the qualities of self-abnegation.[80] The fruit of such humility is practical. "Love fosters union among all things. It becomes a center point where every line ends and comes together. Unlike false charity, which divides people who are united in order to draw them to oneself alone, true charity holds together people with the most diverse inclinations. Through its care the most polarized are maintained in relationship."[81]

Bremond contends that Olier carries self-renunciation to a rarified level that approaches Fénelon's best insights and that echoes Madame Guyon's stress on the "disappropriation" of self in relation to God. There is something truly radical at work here. Olier will not tolerate all of the games played by the human ego, when it seeks to please God and then is pleased with having pleased; he can see through the façade of self-serving virtue and self-glorifying religiosity![82] Olier's thought is a direct precursor of Fénelon's insistence that our greatest spiritual enemy is the

ever-present *moi*, the "me" that tends to run the show in everything that
I do and am. It is the greatest barrier to our desire to love God.

So, there we have it. The combination of a Christian Platonism with
Francis de Sales and French School spirituality set the mold, so to speak,
within which Fénelon would operate. In the eventual debates with
Bossuet, and with input from Madame Guyon as a critical factor, we will
be observing an epic struggle to define the "limit-states" of spirituality,
where loving God involves a radical disconnect from all that is not God,
so that everything about us might be "in God."[83] The more powerful the
individual is in worldly terms, the more excruciating this process must
(not just "will" but *must*) be. Putting the mix to work at the Versailles of
Louis XIV would be a major challenge.

By 1677, Fénelon had completed his education, been ordained,
and had begun to preach in Sulpician parishes. He was also starting
to become known to, and befriended by, some of the leading lights in
the church, foremost among them Bishop Jacques-Bénigne Bossuet of
Meaux, official preacher to the royal court at Versailles. Perhaps uncle
Antoine was again the go-between here. But, however it happened, they
became acquainted, and Fénelon quickly found himself in the hands
of one of those older churchmen who have an eye for up-and-coming
talent. Bossuet liked to surround himself with some of the "best and the
brightest," and Fénelon was included.

But there were also rivalries. According to Bausset,[84] Fénelon, after
meeting Bossuet, who had been impressed with him, "cultivated the older
man, somewhat to the chagrin of François de Harlay de Champvallon,
archbishop of Paris, who was a bit jealous and whose feelings were
hurt." Fénelon avoided him because of his unsavory reputation, and so
the story goes that Harlay said to him one day, "You wish to be obscure,
well you shall be just that!" But it was "with eagerness and delight,"
according to that same historian, that Bossuet, about the same time
that he was appointed official tutor to the dauphin, took up the role of
mentor to Fénelon. Under his patronage the young priest's engagement
with current philosophy, his introduction into court circles, and his
awareness of au courant controversy could pick up steam in earnest.

A relationship that began with great affection and much mutual respect would, in time, do a complete reversal as the two priests became the bitterest of antagonists.

"O infinite Truth, you find all truth within yourself. Created objects, far from conferring knowability on you, receive all of their own knowability from you. And since this knowability comes only from you, it means that we have no knowability in ourselves. It means that you cannot know us in terms of what we are, for we are nothing. You can know us only as we are in you, for you are the reason for our existence."

—DEMONSTRATION OF THE EXISTENCE OF GOD
AND OF THE ATTRIBUTES OF GOD DRAWN
FROM INTELLECTUAL IDEAS, 118

"It is better to be vanquished by truth, than by the shame of having distanced oneself from the truth, as Saint Augustine says; truth bestows the crown of victory only on the 'vanquished' who are sincere and humble enough to follow her."

—THE REFUTATION OF FATHER MALEBRANCHE'S
SYSTEM CONCERNING NATURE AND GRACE, 36

TWO

Rising Intellectual Star

1675–1689

Although the date of Fénelon's priestly ordination is uncertain, it appears to have been sometime in the period 1675–77. We know that while he continued to live at Saint-Sulpice, by September 14, 1677 (Feast of the Exaltation of the Holy Cross), at the latest, he was performing sacerdotal functions and preaching in parishes under the care of the Sulpicians, who, along with some efforts by Bossuet, provided him with pastoral work until his first real appointment should materialize.

There are indications that he gained respect early on in the care of souls and as a preacher. Tributes come from both d'Aguesseau and Saint-Simon: "His eloquence was marked more by his ability to please, than by forcefulness"; "he was endowed with a natural eloquence, sweet, flowery, with a pleasing politeness, but noble and proportioned, with an easy precise, agreeable quality, embellished by the clarity necessary for making the most cumbersome, abstract material understandable."[85] We should imagine this period as a time of quiet maturation, in which he honed his ability at clear and compelling presentation. Some clues to his thinking about pulpit style are provided by an early work, the *Dialogues on Eloquence*.[86]

He contends there that the most important thing about preaching is that it be unaffected, simple, and practical, yet stylistically charming and engaging, much as in the writing of classical authors. This ideal of classical "plainness" is then held up in opposition to the inflated, convoluted, and baroque rhetorical style of his own time. Fénelon tells us that all preachers wish to persuade and to please, but one kind does this in order to make a flattering impression on the congregation and thereby advance his career;

another does it without self-interest in order to inspire righteousness and virtue in his listeners. By contrast, Fénelon wants to capture the "heart" of his listeners with a presentation that "touches," that paints a moving picture of goodness, and that does not just entertain them with elaborately contrived verbal conceits, word juggling, and fashionable allusions. One is reminded here of La Bruyère's famous description of contemporary preaching at Versailles: "Christian oratory has become an entertainment. That evangelical gravity which is its essence is no longer to be seen; the lack of it is made good by the preacher's personal appearance, by the inflexions of his voice, by the studied elegance of his gesture, by the choice of diction and by lengthy enumerations. . . . [Preaching] has become a sort of pastime like countless others."[87] Fénelon will have none of it—he wants transparent sincerity.[88]

Here is an example. One of the most beloved of his extant sermons is the one that he preached to great acclaim[89] on the Feast of the Epiphany, January 6, 1687, at the Church of the Missions-Etrangères, on the occasion of the commissioning of a group of missionaries for work in Siam. His theme was "the vocation of the Gentiles," his text was a traditional one for Epiphany, Isaiah 60:1 ("Arise, Jerusalem, arise clothed in light"), and his focus was the importance of the apostolic call to bring the light of the Gospel to a darkened, and ever more darkening, world. Chad Helms, in his recent translation of and fine commentary on this sermon, analyzes its style and formal properties, holding it up as an eminent example of the pulpit eloquence characteristic of the period.[90] The tone is exuberant, robust: Fénelon is cheerleading for these individuals, brave for the Gospel and about to set forth on work from which they might never return. We can imagine them nervous, apprehensive, and eager for all of the uplift and encouragement that the preacher can provide.

Fénelon takes the logic and structure of his presentation straight from St. Augustine's *City of God*. In that classic work Augustine, in order to defend the truth of the Gospel against its pagan critics, had created a systematic contrast between the city instituted by God and destined to endure and the city made by sinful human hands and destined to pass away. The city of God is New Jerusalem, and the earthly city is that of unbelief and moral corruption. In his exhortation to his listeners Fénelon works the same contrast: just as the Magi came to honor the infant Jesus, we must see that God's light is spreading out to the East and that victorious New Jerusalem is coming. The city of God is almost here. At the same time, though, we must see that "some hidden condemnation hovers over our heads,"[91] some divine judgment for sin in the earthly city. As the old world passes away, the new world is coming.

Fénelon's first point is that even now God is raising up New Jerusalem through the missionary labors of those who go to the far corners of the earth, converting the heathen but also (in reference to the Protestants) showing "again the true church to our erring brothers, as Saint Augustine showed her to the sects of his age."[92] This worldwide spread of the true church, bearing much fruit, demonstrates her divine mission, even as worldly nations, including Christianity's original cradles, crumble. Faith is affirmed.

But then comes the second point. "Perhaps it will be on our ruins that these people will rise up," just as the Jews of old were condemned for their rejection of the Gospel and the kind of life it requires. Precisely because of her sins the church has failed in many places, and judgment has come, and, indeed, is coming. "The day of ruin is near, and the time hastens to arrive."[93] God's grace that empowers and God's righteous condemnation that calls sinners to account work in mysterious tandem. Fénelon's castigation of the sins of his times are as intense as those Augustine aimed at the idolatry of ancient Rome. "Sin abounds; charity grows cold; darkness thickens; the mystery of iniquity takes shape. In these days of blindness and sin, the elect themselves would be seduced if they were capable of it."[94] His exhortation is to the missionaries, about to go forth and pure of heart: "Contemplative souls, ardent souls, hasten to retain the faith on the verge of escaping us. . . . With your innocent hand stop the sword already raised." Go forth, we might say, strong for Christ!

Indeed, this particular sermon also shows us how serious he was about the work of missionaries (a special focus of the Sulpicians in North America, where Fénelon's half-brother was working in Canada) in the early years after his ordination. There are indications that early on he considered the possibility, the "extraordinary project,"[95] of a vocation to missionary work in the East. But cooler heads, people like Tronson who seem to have known that his true career lay closer to home, discouraged him. Those who knew him best knew that his "true apostolate" was to be that of "a man of the study" and a "technician" who brings together philosophy and prayer.[96]

First Assignment

Two opportunities for work now came his way. Both were forms of proselytizing aimed at the French Calvinist Protestants, known as the Huguenots. Both of them belong to the time of the Counter-Reformation, in which Catholic authorities attempted to "reconvert," through the use of more-or-less pressurized tactics, those who had left the fold. Sad as this history is by modern standards of tolerance, for persons of good will, like Fénelon, some good sometimes came of it. Missionary work directed at persons who already have a faith of their own constrained him to wrestle with the distinction between what is "true" in all religious practice and belief and what is not. False religion is false, he would discover, whatever the confessional allegiance of the individual.

The first assignment was in Paris and allowed him increased independence. Early in 1679, about the time he moved out of Saint-Sulpice and went to live with his uncle Antoine at the abbey of Saint-Germain des Prés, he was appointed the director of a church boarding school, the Institution des Nouvelles Catholiques.

The school had been organized in 1634 by the Society for the Propagation of the Faith as a place where young women, daughters of Protestant families deemed to be in the process of returning to the Catholic Church, could be suitably domiciled, educated, and indoctrinated. Church authorities had long recognized that if the children of converting families could be separated from the still quasi-Protestant home environment, they could be more suitably stabilized in an all-Catholic setting. Furthermore, since most of these children came from south-central and southwest France—the most heavily Protestant areas of the country—coming up to cultured Paris for an education was a privilege. Thus, the school was a somewhat posh, upscale place for "new" Catholic girls. There was pressure for conversion, we might say, but *gentle* pressure.

But fresh anti-Protestantism had been brewing for some time in France, and in 1685 things took a darker turn. Louis XIV, at the insistence of elements among the French Catholic majority, and on the advice of his chief lieutenants, revoked the Edict of Nantes. This legal charter had regulated Protestant-Catholic relations in France more or less peacefully since 1572, when it had terminated the Wars of Religion between the two groups, by granting the Protestants certain privileges in their enclaves as well as an official share in governance. After the Revocation, however, this status and these liberties were cancelled and persecution was renewed. A new period of civil and financial penalties, combined with orchestrated efforts at conversion, was forced on the Huguenots. Many resisted, some yielded, and many maneuvered manipulatively with the authorities. One way that Huguenot families, seemingly in the process of conversion, could gain favor was to allow their daughters to be taken off to boarding school. So, at this point, Nouvelles Catholiques became more emblematic of the new "push" against the Huguenots, as the pressure to convert was ramped up. And this is where Fénelon found himself.[97]

Probably the directorship of the school devolved on Fénelon through archbishop Harlay de Champvallon's patronage, and perhaps at the instigation again of uncle Antoine. It was a plum appointment and a distinct honor for such a young priest.[98] Nouvelles Catholiques appears to have been a rather strictly run operation with a considerable staff, high standards, and a demanding regimen for the young students. Fénelon's "duties at the Paris convent [that is, the school] were rather those of a visitor or spiritual adviser. His part was to teach, explain, persuade and guide."[99] He represented church authority at graduations and other ceremonies. Most of the actual day-to-day work was done by an order of residentiary nuns and a chaplain. Thus, the tendency of Catholic historians to interpret this phase in Fénelon's career as evidence of his obedient churchmanship and solid loyalty to the policies of the French state, but also the inclination of Protestant historians to decry the intolerance and coercive zeal of such an institution and to lament Fénelon's participation, are both misplaced. He was, in short, mostly a figurehead.

Nonetheless, he took his work seriously, both as a budding theorist about educational technique and as a missionary. There is at least one example of his having converted the parents of one of the girls at Nouvelles Catholiques,[100] and, as his Epiphany sermon cited above revealed, he was intensely committed to foreign missions. One of the girls educated at the school was Charlotte du Péray, who would become the Carmelite sister Charlotte de Saint-Cyprien, with whom, as we shall see, Fénelon exchanged an important correspondence for years.[101] Late in his life at Cambrai he would induct André-Michel Ramsay, his protégé, into the Catholic faith. In his late letters from Cambrai exchanged with the Protestant Pierre Poiret, who is kindly disposed toward the *Maxims*, he would still argue for the superiority of the Catholic Church, and, more controversially, for the supreme authority of the papacy. Indeed, the whole tenor of his spirituality is one of convicted submission to established authority (one thinks of Simone Weil and her idea that it is always better to stay where God has put you). This quality Sainte-Beuve and others in the free-thinking nineteenth century would see as weak and craven in him, even while they admired his eloquence.

A Second Assignment among the Protestants

So it is that Jean Orcibal begins his section "Fénelon et les Protestants"[102] with the statement, "It is undeniable that, for the ten years following his ordination, Fénelon was 'charged' principally with working for the instruction of heretics."[103] He makes the case that mission work aimed at the conversion of Protestants was considered prime duty for young clerics and that the appointment to the Nouvelles Catholiques was a rung on the ladder of advancement. It was only natural, then, that Fénelon would, in due course, be assigned as well to a missionary "combat zone," in his case the part of the country that was somewhat familiar to him, that is, the far southwest, and particularly the area around the Protestant stronghold of La Rochelle. So, commissioned by Louis himself, who had taken a special interest in the project, with a capable group of priest assistants—several of whom would become lifetime friends—Fénelon departed Paris on his second missionary assignment.

For two years he would be based in the province of Poitou (the area around Poitiers), specifically in the coastal area of Saintonge and in the district of Aunis adjacent to La Rochelle. In this old fortified sanctuary the Huguenot communities were particularly recalcitrant. The work would be hard and prolonged. His task was to assist the local clergy in

the process of exhorting the Protestants to attend Catholic worship and
to come for catechizing, their own meetinghouses having been torn
down. Issues of control with the local clergy could be delicate, and
there were other missionaries as well with different operating styles.
Thus, the situation was often tense and conflicted. Since most of what
we know comes from his letters back to the authorities in Paris, we can
sense how nerve-racking and painful the process often was. The sense
that we get is that Fénelon never objected to the ultimate purpose of
the work—to bring erring brethren back to the true church—but that
he developed definite ideas about how the work should be done, and
thus got into confrontations at times. In fact, he began to gain a reputation as a wise and gentle, but firm and determined, teacher and pastor.
He learned how to make real progress with, but also to be exceedingly
patient with, the complexities of the hearts and minds of the persons
entrusted to him. He did sensible, reasonable, even compassionate kinds
of things in a situation that had typically lent itself to mean-spirited
intimidation and bullying.

Various specific measures that would make things more congenial
for the Protestants—omitting certain offensive prayers from the liturgy,
reading the New Testament in the vernacular, a more biblically based
kind of preaching, vernacular psalms for chanting—are specified in
the correspondence that went back and forth between him and his
governmental superior in Paris, the Marquis de Seignelay. Further,
he had originally accepted the mission only on the condition that
there be no use of troops, or forced quartering of troops, to scare the
Protestants.[104] Thus, in a rough situation, he tried to be gentle and
"accommodating" in a manner that also reflects Bossuet's influence. That
prelate had produced a work in 1671, *An Exposition of the Catholic Faith*,
which advocated a gentle, reasoned approach in missionary methods,
so that true inward conversion, and not mere outer conformity, could
take place. Given this degree of sympathy on the part of Fénelon with
the heretic Huguenots, some people actually suspected him of Jansenist
proclivities. And the friendship with Bossuet at this point may have cost
him the bishopric of La Rochelle and even that of the more prestigious
Poitiers, since Harlay in Paris moved to block the nominations when
their possibility was raised. At the least Fénelon's tenderhearted

approach to the Protestants seems to have resulted in substantial loss in reputation and career advancement.[105]

One outcome, though, was that everyone started to take notice of his assured and masterful touch. Here was a priest who knew how to talk to people, who knew the human heart, and who was learning that spiritual, inner change is a mysterious process indeed, however things may look outwardly.[106] There is no point in pushing people to "go through the motions" when the motive is contaminated. Fénelon also began to realize that when people are pressured to make religious changes, their resistance becomes all the more determined. All biographers of Fénelon cite at this point the advice he gave to the Duc de Bourgogne in the 1711 work *Examination of Conscience on the Duties of Royalty*: "Above all never force your subjects to change their religion. No human power can penetrate the last defenses of the human heart. Men can never be convinced by force; it only creates hypocrites. When kings meddle with religion, instead of protecting it, they enslave it."[107]

The First Writing

Fénelon's first two significant writings both appear about this time, that is, in the period 1685–87. They are the *Treatise on the Education of Daughters*, first printed in 1687, and the *Treatise on the Ministry of Pastors*, first printed in 1688.[108] They are different and pursue quite distinct agendas, but they hold out a common vision of the pastoral care of growing souls.

The first treatise has become a classic, and I will discuss it in the next chapter. The second treatise is now virtually unknown, although it is genuinely important as a window into Fénelon's early development. In the *Treatise on the Ministry of Pastors* he enters the arena of confessional apologetics, that is, the defense of the superiority of one's own ecclesial commitments against attacks, criticisms, and counterpositions. Specifically he formulates a rebuttal to Calvinist Protestant, anti-Catholic arguments regarding the sources of true pastoral authority in the church. It gives us our first look at him as a polemicist and debater.

It is a controversial work typical of the period. Fénelon was responding directly to the Protestants Du Moulin, Claude, and Jurieu (and through them to Calvin), who advance scriptural and historical proofs for the superiority of the Protestant pastorate over the corrupt Roman priesthood as the "true" teaching authority in the church. Fénelon lays out the logic of the Protestant arguments and then offers a point-by-point rebuttal.

While the details of the debate often boiled down to disputes about how to interpret this or that Biblical or patristic text, the core issue is immediately clear. The Protestants contend that the Reformed churches have restored the ancient way of choosing and confirming pastors by insisting that such persons be elected by the congregation, which then commissions them in a simple, scripturally based ceremony. This is in contrast to the Roman argument that the church's pastorate consists of a self-perpetuating priesthood, which is ordained by means of a sacramental ritual administered by bishops in historic succession from Jesus's first apostles.

In order to defend the Catholic position, and then refute the Protestants, Fénelon proceeded to show that their use of the ancient sources was skewed. Not only, he argued, are the Protestants divided amongst themselves on exactly how pastors are to be chosen and validated by congregations, but also they make a gratuitous assumption. This is the notion that the congregation has the "natural right" to choose its pastors and that it is the exercise of this "right" that makes these pastors legitimate. Not so, says Fénelon, since the grace for choosing pastors, and then ordaining them, cannot be a "right" but must be seen instead as a gift, a "charism," divinely bestowed. Further, this gift was conferred by Christ once and for all on the church at its very beginning, so that it could operate in an orderly way. This order is maintained by the college of pastors, who raise up and validate their own successors. The Roman hierarchy, with the pope at the head, is that pastorate.

The most sophisticated part of Fénelon's presentation is in response specifically to Jurieu's claim that the Roman structure of hierarchical priesthood is a degeneration from the primitive practices of the early church. It was possible, to be sure, to show that in some instances clergy were selected on the basis of a popular appeal, but, noted Fénelon, their legitimation came only with sacred anointing by the bishop. But the most famous and controversial text was always that in Matthew, where Jesus gives the "keys" to St. Peter. This conferral of pastoral authority, averred Fénelon, was made by Christ through Peter to the *whole* church, not to *each* individual believer. The gift is then exercised on behalf of the whole by the special grace given to Peter and his successors. The implication is that it is a great mistake to set the authority of a congregation *over* the authority of the pastors, since the pastors, having emerged from the congregation in the first place, are empowered to exercise authority on its behalf. To the pragmatic argument that an authoritative priesthood can become corrupt, Fénelon responds that the congregation may be just as corrupt, if not more so. The best strategy is to trust the promises made by Christ to his church that it will be led into all truth, that is, that through its constituted structure it will be given godly pastors with true teaching authority.

It is unlikely that Jurieu and the Protestants would have been convinced by Fénelon's arguments, or he by theirs, but what impresses the modern reader is the seriousness and thoroughness with which the contending parties engaged one another with broad historical and humanistic learning. One is also struck by the moderate tone: Fénelon is respectful and attempts to speak with calm reason as he addresses his opponents; there is no vituperation, no pejorative dismissal, only carefully stated argumentation and the judicious setting forth of authorities. Melchior-Bonnet calls this early *Treatise* "a work solid and methodic,"[109] and I would add the descriptors "competent and impressive." It is a very capable display of the young Fénelon's erudition and of his ability to tackle a hotly debated issue du jour, as well as one with immediate practical implications for his day-to-day work. He knows how to handle himself in give-and-take with opponents, he is an eloquently articulate thinker, and he is a fiercely loyal churchman. These qualities will register with his superiors in Paris and will mark him out for advancement.

There is also further indication of Bossuet's influence in the background in the working assumptions of Fénelon's position. He tends to pick up Bossuet's claim that just as God has created the Scriptures once and for all, God has created the church as a timeless manifestation of the body of Christ, acting through its hierarchical priesthood. There is no need for the congregation to elect pastors, because there is no need to re-create and reconstitute the church afresh every time a new pastor is needed, because *that* has already been done. Present institutional arrangements are divinely willed. This duly constituted order invites submission from believers, whose task it is to believe and obey, not to engage in elections. What tends to put the Catholics Bossuet and Fénelon and the Protestant Jurieu on different sides of a fundamental divide is Jurieu's willingness to trust the mind of the "people" to be more reliable than an elite and established order of well-educated and upright leaders. It is one form of the old contrast between rule by "the best" and rule by the "people," or, in another form, the tension between local autonomy and central authority. Fénelon did not solve all of the problems here, but he demonstrated his ability to handle his tools well. He was becoming a competent craftsman, and people were starting to notice.

A Young Pastor with Influential Friends

With the end of the Poitou mission he was back in Paris—known, respected, and taken seriously as a first-rate mind. He had sparred pastorally and adroitly with competent and formidable Protestant adversaries. Now, by the summer of 1687, he was ready for bigger game in the form of new works addressed to contemporary and challenging theological concerns. He was ready to take on the "big boys" in "the big city," we might say! The spur came from the man who had become his patron.

The immediate context was Bossuet's stimulating circle and "salon" at his beautiful Marne Valley country estate at Germigny, where the bishop of Meaux had invited Fénelon to join the gatherings. The place was beautiful, Fénelon was entranced and deeply grateful to be included, and the sparkling fellowship must have been not only stimulating but also a great relief for a missionary newly returned from the provinces. Goré, and more recently Melchior-Bonnet, have painted lively sketches of this cultivated intellectual milieu, in which historians, theologians, writers, future bishops, and lay humanists all rubbed shoulders. Having started out as a small group of clergy engaged in Bible study, the circle had become a sophisticated meeting place of cutting-edge minds, with Bossuet as the catalyst.[110] That great man was now at the height of his powers, hailed by all France as the rock of orthodoxy and defender of Catholic truth, finest preacher in the land, and intimate of the royal family. We can imagine him organizing the conversations, being sure that good food and wine was served, that the accommodations were comfortable (not too austere for these polished priests!), and that the right persons were introduced to one another.

Among the multitude at Germigny, we should take note of two individuals in particular. There was the young abbé Claude Fleury, a noted commentator on Plato's works and accomplished historian and writer on pedagogical method. He was to become a major indirect influence on Fénelon's life and thought, worked alongside him in the Saintonge mission, and eventually would be his collaborator in the preceptorship with the Duc de Bourgogne.[111] Another figure in the group, important for Fénelon's long-term development, was the abbé François de Langeron, who like Fleury shared with him in the Saintonge mission, who collaborated with him in their mutual love for lyrical, classical poetry, and for whom Fénelon would become a lifelong mentor and guide. In his will, says Barnard, Fénelon calls Langeron "a precious friend, whom God gave me from our first youth, and who has been one of the great consolations of my life."[112]

Taking on the Greatest Mind of the Age

At some point during this first year back at Paris—we do not know exactly when—Fénelon decided to cut his teeth on the greatest mind of the age and the pacesetter for all philosophical development: René Descartes. He did this in the form of two separate writings.[113] The first is his own direct appropriation and adaptation of Cartesian thought for the purpose of a Christian apologetic. The second is an indirect appropriation, since it takes the form of an attack, in the name of a *better* understanding of Descartes, on the work of another great Cartesian, Nicolas Malebranche. Both works are important, because they provide a first glimpse at the process that would move him intellectually in the direction of "pure love." The first writing has the daunting title *A Demonstration of the Existence of God and of the Divine Attributes Drawn from Intellectual Ideas*.[114] For unknown reasons it lay hidden in Fénelon's papers until its first fairly complete appearance, well after his death, in 1731.[115] The second is the *Refutation of the System of Father Malebranche concerning Nature and Grace*, written sometime in 1687–88 (probably, although some put it in 1683–84) at the behest of Bossuet, who was particularly invested in refuting Malebranchian views. This work circulated privately and was never published. It did not see the light of day for a larger public (aborted effort in 1716), so far as we know, until Gosselin reproduced it in the Versailles edition of the collected works in 1820.[116] The one surviving manuscript still has Bossuet's handwritten annotations in the margin. We are dealing here, therefore, with two relatively unknown and obscure writings by Fénelon and yet ones crucial to his development and status as a thinker.

Let us consider the *Demonstration* first. Written as a critique of the increasingly fashionable Spinozan materialism and atheism, it is a sustained effort to restate Descartes's method of universal doubt as a fresh basis for affirming the existence of God and describing the qualities, or attributes, of God. In more technical language it is a Fénelonian reworking of the Cartesian *Cogito* for the particular theological purpose of establishing the reality of spirit as metaphysically real and distinct from matter in the universe. It is at the same time Fénelon's first working up of the Platonist-Augustinian understanding of the human quest for truth, which is at the core of his worldview, in a way that signals forward movement in the direction of pure love as the adequate human response to the nature of God.

Part of what Fénelon had learned from Plato and the Platonist tradition, as it had come to him through St. Augustine, is that the good, the beautiful, and the true in their ideal or perfect form exist as pure spiritual realities, or ideas, within the mind of God. It is by means of these perfect ideas as they become "present" to the human mind that we can mentally grasp the element of goodness, beauty, or truth in some particular, concrete object. Let us recall that this same God, the source of all ideas, is also the Christian God, who is active Love as the source of all being. Our mystical ascent to this God so that we might become true lovers as well is thus a *mental and profoundly inward* process. What then attracted the thinkers of Fénelon's time to the new ideas of Descartes was that this philosopher, intensely focused on the nature of human cognition and inference, enabled them to break free of the rarified categories of

Aristotelian Scholastic theology in order to "rediscover Augustine in a Cartesianized version."[117] The way in which Descartes took with absolute seriousness the self-reflexive nature of the thinking mind, that is, the mind's ability to reflect on its own nature, was especially compelling for Christian thinkers. In particular, Descartes's claim that the mind's recognition of its own existence as the only thing whose reality it cannot doubt, because as it thinks, it knows that it *is*—called the Cartesian "cogito"—was seen as the critical insight grounding Descartes's fundamental argument that mind is actually substantial in nature. That is, mind is a fundamental reality separate from physical matter in the structure of the universe. And if mind is more or less equal to spirit and soul, then in a heartbeat Descartes suddenly becomes a Christian philosopher!

So it is that for Descartes the fact of the self-aware mind's own existence is the first "clear and distinct idea" that it possesses. This first idea then becomes the basis on which more clear and distinct ideas can begin to be formulated, particularly the ideas of mathematics, which possess truly logical rigor of a high symbolic order, thereby gaining the luster of timeless truth. Descartes will come to the conclusion, in his famous dualism, that all of reality consists of a fundamental bifurcation into mind and matter. Mind is "thinking substance" that works with logic, is unable to be spatially localized, and is immaterial. Matter is "extended substance," spatially bounded, inanimate (not self-moving), and mechanical (operating in a purely lawful way), manifesting itself to the uncertain apprehensions of our sensory awareness. In the elaboration of his thought Descartes then uses this cogito to argue that the mind's perception of reality is certain *but with a certainty that it cannot, as finite, give to itself.* For a finite creature to possess truly certain perception, there must be an infinite reality that is the source of that certainty. God exists, therefore.

Now in this Cartesian-Augustinian-Platonist way of conceiving of the nature of things and working one's way back to God, the operation of the thinking mind is the gateway to all of reality. The critical component of the mind is the "clear and distinct idea" with which it operates. Specifying the nature of these "ideas" is critical. What exactly are these "ideas" with which the mind thinks? Where do they come from? How do they enable the mind's grasp both of its inner reality and of the external world? How does the "idea," which is after all an abstraction, grasp the concreteness of individual objects? If we are theists and believe that God is eternal Mind, or Reason, how does that Infinite Reason relate itself to our finite and limited reasoning capacities? The questions were endless.

In the *Demonstration* Fénelon skillfully lays out his own version of what I have just described. His core idea is that the "clear and distinct ideas" by which the mind works cannot originate from our own minds, because that which is primary and originative—that is, the mind—cannot take its existence from what is secondary and derivative—that is, the body. The way he says this is that "thinking immediately [that is, by the very nature of the fact that it is operating at all] discloses being." A "clear idea" is something that comes overwhelmingly and invincibly to the thinking mind; its power does not come from my mind, but from its inherent nature. But here is the key turn. Since the clear and evident ideas that emerge in my mind come from a transcendent source which is itself certain, I can then see that my own nature as a thinking mind is itself a contingent nothingness, deriving its very existence from something transcendent. My own being as a creature comes from the ideas that inform my mind. At this point it is Augustine who teaches us that these ideas come from the mind of God, that is, they reflect the nature of God as the reason (or Logos) that lies behind the structure of the universe.[118]

This is the Fénelonian twist to Descartes. By virtue of our power to think, nothingness that we are, the reality of God can be discerned. The fact that I can think accurately, that my thinking works by means of a *given and transcendent structure*, shows me that God exists as an all-wise and all-good Creator. French scholars of Fénelon particularly, proud of the Cartesian heritage, have accented the way in which Fénelon has utilized the Sulpician language of our "nothingness" before God and used it to describe the implications of Descartes's metaphysic, namely, that as finite creatures we are privileged to have some knowledge of the Infinite. The amazing thing is that we are "nothings" who can know "something"!

Henri Gouhier has emphasized the striking creativity of Fénelon at this point: as thinking creatures we cannot "think nothingness," since thinking by its nature is an affirmation of "something."[119] When we think, we think "being," however inaccurately, and not "nothing," since "nothing" cannot be known. Gouhier calls this move on Fénelon's part a "critique of the pseudo-idea of nothingness,"[120] meaning thereby that he has used the fact that we are creatures who think to show with one stroke that metaphysically we are "nothing" (that is, contingent and mortal beings) and yet mentally we lay hold of "everything" (that is, real existence). The way Gouhier eventually says this is that "the Fénelonian *cogito* is a strange sort of *ego sum*."[121] The demonstrated reality of human cogitation leads not so much to a demonstration of the *fact* of human existence, and thus to God, as it does to a revelation of the *nature* of that existence. The nature of my being is not-to-be, because only God *is*. This line of thought will eventually supply the rationale for the essentially illusory nature of self-love, since it is in loving God that I turn toward what *is*, and in rejecting self-love, I turn away from what *is not*.

The nature of ideas, the means by which we think, is a difficult subject. "Our ideas," he says, "are a perpetual mixture of the infinite being of God, which is our object, and of the limits which he gives essentially to each of his creatures." What he means is that an idea is by nature a "perfect" conceptualizing of that to which it points. For example, the idea of a dog is more perfect than any particular and actual dog. Logically, he contends, the source of an idea will then possess its perfection absolutely. Thus, the qualities of ideas point to the divine attributes, from which they emanate. One way that Fénelon says this is to argue that "superior to my spirit, these ideas constantly correct my perceptions. Are they God? They are within me as my deepest self, yet outside me as perfect. Truly this is God, the universal Logos [that is, Reason], because it is in this Infinite that I am able to see the finite."[122]

Human error, then, will come from hasty judgment, when our ideas are obscure or partial or confused, that is, when we turn away from God and the divine working. The attributes of God, such as unity and simplicity and immutability, mean that God is the principle whereby multiplicity, composition, and change are possible. "God alone is intimately present to the soul, since all other objects become present in some kind of imaging process, by which knower and known occupy separate spaces, but this is not so with God." Gouhier points to an element of pathos here for Fénelon: my daily walk is a process of always being reminded of my mortality, my fragility, and especially my ignorance; the fleeting and imperfect quality of what I think I know is itself a revelation of how infinitely inferior my mind is to the Source that empowers it.[123] Just when I think I know myself, I realize again that I am not the self that I thought I was. I am humbled by this awareness of my real nature, my nonbeing.

A technical problem now emerges, however, for the Christian thinker regarding the precise relationship between the divine Mind and the eternal ideas. It is a difficulty that will dog Fénelon and that will be the basis of his attempt to refute Malebranche. It is also a difficulty that will preoccupy other great thinkers such as Leibniz and Spinoza. If God is the source of all ideas, does that imply that God has created the best of all possible worlds? That is, has God chosen from all of the "possibles" inside the divine Mind the very best and then actualized these in creating the world we know? Fénelon says yes in his own way and Malebranche will say no in his way. The question may seem incredibly abstruse, but it is in fact very practical. Is the world *as we know it* what God intended, or is it in some fundamental way a distortion of what God intended? And what would it mean to say that the world is the "very best"?

Two more questions are implied. What does it mean to say, as we do, that God is "free" in creating us as we are? Fénelon argues for absolute freedom in God's creative activity, while Malebranche tends to see God as "constrained" in some way. The contention that God is "absolutely" free in creating, say, me or you—and this is what Fénelon claims—means that every creative and willed act of God is necessarily "perfect" by definition. It is not a choice that God makes among "possibles," each of which has its advantages and disadvantages within the range of options, so to speak. The kind of, and degree of, perfection that I possess (or am capable of possessing!) within God's creative purposes is *exactly* what God wants, nothing more or less. It is my task on this earth to discern *what* that perfection is and then to give myself to it.

The second question is even more subtle: If God's creative and loving work in the world is truly "free," that is, proceeds only out of the utterly transcendent wisdom of the divine Mind, in what sense can we finite mortals ever be said to "know" this wisdom? Or is our attempt to know only a journey into darkness? Is God's love "reasonable," bound to be rational in nature and "make sense," or are our efforts to fathom it, "nothings" that we are, some kind of plunge into irrational darkness? What is love, anyway?

So, we see that this Fénelon who is so brilliantly capable and so wants us to walk with God as children has found in the Cartesian metaphysic a powerful tool. Where will it all lead?

Taking on Malebranche

Because we have no contemporary testimony to Fénelon's personal situation at this point—from the end of the Poitou mission until he began life at Versailles—my suggestion is that we think of him as being in a kind of intellectual incubator. Germigny was one principal setting, as was to some degree his work at Nouvelles Catholiques, which went on until 1689. My hunch is that he was consumed by books. Bossuet secured him occasional preaching assignments, he began to write his first letters to his spiritual directees, and in late 1688 he first met Guyon. We know that he sometimes attended gatherings at the country houses of the court dévots, and it is clear that he was beginning to compose substantial works. But the picture is frustratingly blurred and fragmentary at best. Not until 1689 and the beginnings of his correspondence can we trace his exact movements. Scholars often complain that there needs to be much more research into the record of Fénelon's early years, but unless more sources materialize, we are at loose ends here! It would be an overstatement to say that until Madame Guyon becomes part of his life, he himself is blurred, but there is an element of truth in it.

Let us, thus, wrestle with one more fledgling intellectual production. It is in this period of the late 1680s, probably sometime in 1687, that Bossuet, now knowing that in Fénelon he had available a competent theological thinker and controversialist, decided to put him on the track of the intellectual enfant terrible of the moment, Nicolas Malebranche. Bossuet had become disenchanted with this magisterial thinker after a period of initial attraction. When Malebranche's first bold work, *The Search after Truth,* had appeared in 1674–75 to critical acclaim, not least of all from the great Antoine Arnauld at the Sorbonne, many including Bossuet saw in Malebranche a new and master synthesizer of Cartesian philosophy and Christian faith. But critics quickly appeared, claiming that Malebranche had compromised essential elements of Christian belief. He responded with various sets of *Elucidations*, or clarifications, of his thought. Then he followed up with a new work in 1680, the *Treatise on Nature and Grace*. It was a bombshell. Though he had sought a prepublication approval from Bossuet, the bishop of Meaux was shocked.

Bossuet's famous and traditionalist theological judgment on Malebranche's new work was that it was "beautiful, but new, thus false," that it "reversed the true system of predestination," and that it "represented a great battle against the Church in the name of Cartesian philosophy." Malebranche attempted here again to respond with revisions. Elaborate attempts were made at conciliation especially between Bossuet and Malebranche by persons who knew both men, but the efforts were inconclusive. In the midst of this process Bossuet asked Fénelon to prepare a refutation, which he (Bossuet) could review and use as ammunition. Fénelon acceded to the request with a work that reflects Bossuet's personal agenda but that also gives us important clues to the development of Fénelon's thought. This composition, *The Refutation of Father Malebranche's System Concerning Nature and Grace*, was a work "rigorous" in method and marked by "firmness, serenity, and breadth of view," in the opinion of one of the major modern editors of Malebranche's works.[124] So, what was at stake?

Malebranche had thoroughly absorbed Descartes's new scientific understanding of the universe as an impersonal "machine," and he was determined to work out its consequences for theology. His central assertion is that God's sovereign rule over the universe as Creator and Redeemer in Christ is exercised through a "general providence," which operates by means of a rational "order" of impersonal causative processes. These processes are the natural laws revealed to us by science. The reason *why* God operates in this fashion is that such a system is the "simplest way" by which the universe can be ordered, such "simplicity" reflecting the greatest glory back onto God the Creator, who is perfectly "simple" (that is, One). This lawful "simplicity" by which the universe works has at its core Malebranche's famous view that God is the one true cause of all motion in the finite world. All natural causation is "occasional" as the means for divine providence to operate, and, in the realm of spirit our own free-willed decisions are the "occasional causes" by means of which God as the absolute cause works in us. All thinking in our finite minds is a direct operation, called "the vision in God," of the divine Mind. We act with the power of God, and we think with the mind of God.

Malebranche's system is beautiful for this reason. If all *natural* process is tantamount to an expression of God's will, then God does not have to tinker with the universe by means of interventions or "special providences," as if the original work of creation were somehow inadequate and needed improvement (this is what Malebranche means by the "simplicity" of the web of natural laws). While God's *purpose* in operating by general providence is to bring glory to himself, the ultimate *goal*—and this is a special feature of Malebranche's thought—is the Incarnation. All of creation exists only for the sake of the Incarnation and the "spiritual temple" of redeemed humanity who will be the fruit of the Incarnation. God has not created the world for you and me to be happy; he has created it so that we might become part of the work of the Incarnation, so that we love and glorify him by becoming a holy edifice. The means by which we will be enabled to play this role is inclusion in the mind of Jesus, the Incarnate Lord. As Jesus presents us to the Father through his "intercessory consciousness," we, if we are predestined, will become "holy stones" in the spiritual temple.

The argument is radical in its own way and offers a sweeping proposal. Because the Incarnation is the justification for God's entire way of working in the universe, it is the only thing that makes the universe "worthy" of God. On the one hand, the natural "simplicity" of the world is in its inexorable natural laws, but, on the other, its supernatural simplicity is in the fact that all of redeemed humankind is funneled through the humanity of the one man, Jesus Christ.

In the architectonic of Malebranche's edifice the only real miracle is the Incarnation, and everything else that ever happens is perfectly lawful. But there was a particular and devastating irony that was pointed out by critics including Fénelon.[125] The assumption was that a loving God wants to redeem all of humanity. In order, however, to explain how it is that God saves only *some* people, Malebranche argued that God is "limited" by the human awareness of Jesus, which, precisely because it is finite, cannot comprehend and thereby incorporate the whole human race simultaneously. One human mind, including that of the Savior himself, can only include a limited number of persons. And salvation requires this incorporation into the mind of Christ. The irony is that because God is *limited* by the human finitude of the earthly Jesus, he *cannot* save all of humankind. God, therefore, is not truly free.

Fénelon's basic distrust of Malebranche's thinking centered on the whole idea that God follows some sort of regulating "order" in the universe, and that this order is identical with natural law. This is to yield too much to the "machine" side of the Cartesian metaphysic. One result for Malebranche is that everything really spiritual in God's action has to be shuffled off, so to speak, to the Incarnation as the one place that God does something with salvific import. But that cannot be true, thought Fénelon. One way to get at the heart of the matter is to recognize that in Malebranche's view God loves the world *only because of the Son*, only for the purpose of the Incarnation, since without the Incarnation the world is, essentially, worthless. Jesus, however, clearly says in Scripture that God gave the Son *because he loved the world*, that is, God loved the world first and only then did he give the Son.[126] Not only can God's love as a sovereignly and freely operating creative force in the universe not be limited to the Incarnation, but, even more, the Incarnation makes no real sense if there is not a lovable universe for God to redeem. God is ceaselessly creating, and *constantly recreates*, the entire order of the universe. We can see here why the whole mechanistic side of Cartesian thinking, which had mesmerized Malebranche, was unpalatable to Fénelon. The way he will eventually say it is that love is not lawful, but rather *it is its own law*.

Much more could be said here, because Malebranche was a subtle and powerful thinker, and Fénelon's response was subtle as well. Indeed, it is a moot point at this juncture whether Bossuet and Fénelon did him justice. What is important for our purposes in understanding Fénelon is the realization that he was working out his own ideas. Henri Gouhier has argued that Fénelon's critique of Malebranche is his own effort to clarify Augustine's teaching, as well as that of Descartes, for himself (indeed, Malebranche claimed to be basing himself solidly on Augustine).[127] The basic problem, Fénelon thought, was that Malebranche worked with a false analogy. For Malebranche, God's "reasonableness" was like that of a mechanic whose skill is manifested in the finished "purity" of his product, where purity is understood as a quality of maximal efficiency present at the outset, imparted at the very beginning of a machine's operation.

By its smooth, unimpeded running, the "simplicity" of the machine then glorifies its creator. It is much better, implied Fénelon, to think of God as an engineer, who continues to be present in what he has built, because its continued operation is dependent on the perfecting, sustaining presence and fine tuning—"tinkering"—of its perfect maker. This is the difference between a God who operates only, or mostly, by "general providence" and is limited by natural laws and a God who can and does operate with unlimited power through special providences.[128]

If we then asked Fénelon how it is that God's action in the world is "rational," he would answer with the traditional idea that all creatures occupy particular positions in the scale of perfections where God has placed them. God's grace operates in my life, through general and special providences, in such a way as to support and assist me in the fulfillment of that level and type of perfection assigned to me. And the same is just as true for social totalities as it is for individuals. So it is that Fénelon and Bossuet both agreed that in divine working God is the God of universal history, where providence is a "continual governance which directs to a final end things that seem fortuitous." We can agree also with Fénelon that Malebranche's idea of the universe as a "vast construction" in which God works through natural laws makes the world look like "a cold administrative fortress, the ultimate in implacable organization"; Fénelon prefers the view of God as being like an earthly father, whose love is immediate, particular, safeguarding, and consoling, and we are his children.[129]

Consider one more idea. Since Bossuet never published Fénelon's refutation of Malebranche, it is possible that there was a particular and, for Bossuet, annoying matter in which the younger man was already going his own way. Involved here was a point that would come up both with the *Maxims* and then in the struggle with the Jansenists. Just how is it that God's redeeming grace in Christ works in the human will to produce that freedom from sin, followed by the true love of God, that is the sign of salvation? The orthodox view—ostensibly derived from Augustine and shared by Malebranche as well as Bérulle—was that God's saving grace produces a "victorious delectation" in the sinner chosen for salvation, an *intensely and consciously felt* pleasure and delight in turning away from love of self toward love of God (the italicized words are all-important here). Fénelon, though, stayed closer to the Sulpician Olier, with the view that for Augustine the delectation we experience in responding to God's grace and loving God is precisely that of the *consecrated will*, which is *our desiring to desire what God wants, and only because God wants it*.[130] Gouhier's formulation is that "Fénelon denounces the egoism which is immanent in the seeking of my own pleasure."[131] It was too early in Fénelon's intellectual development yet for us to be able to see just how this last train of thought—intended as part of his refutation of Malebranche—would land him in deep trouble with Bossuet as well, but that is indeed what happens. Further, this insistence that God's grace works in us to transform the will, without bringing pleasure in any natural sense, puts Fénelon on a collision course with the Jansenists during his Cambrai period.

At this point in Fénelon's career, where he has struggled with the mysteries of the transformation of the intractable human heart as a preacher and missionary and has begun to metabolize the heritage of Descartes, he was in the process of discovering that the practice of pure love and its "indifference" must be a much more radically *inward, interior* experience, which is to say a hidden *mental* experience, than he had quite realized. Missionary experience made that clear to him, and sustained intellectual reflection confirmed it.

The exterior life of a person, the behaviors and habits, the things said and done—important as they are—are superficial at best, but also ambiguous in their spiritual import. It is the spirit of a person that matters, and this occupies space of its own and obeys laws of its own. Love is its own law—but how far to push this?

Then, in 1689, with Bossuet's strong support, Fénelon's career took a quantum leap. He was appointed tutor to the Duc de Bourgogne, grandson of Louis XIV, and from then on the royal court at Versailles would supply the venue for his activity and continued growth, especially as an educator.

"Show that God wishes to be honored with the heart and not with the lips, that ceremonies serve to express and to stimulate our religion, but that ceremonies are not religion itself, because this is something inward and God seeks worshippers in spirit and in truth; that we must love Him in our hearts and consider ourselves as if in all nature there was but God and ourselves."

—TREATISE ON THE EDUCATION OF DAUGHTERS, 8
(TR. BARNARD)

"Dry, hard bread is not as sweet as milk, but it is more nourishing. Correction from a preceptor does more good than soft treatment from a nurse."

—LETTER TO DOM FRANÇOIS LAMY,
OCTOBER 26, 1701

THREE

Pedagogue to Royalty

1689–1697

During the period of the Poitou mission, from 1685 to 1687, Fénelon became involved with the famous Colbert family. The patriarch of the family, Jean-Baptiste (the "great" Colbert), had been Louis XIV's powerful, enormously successful domestic minister and highly trusted adviser until his death in 1683.[132] In 1685, Colbert's eldest son, also Jean-Baptiste, Marquis de Seignelay, as secretary of state had been entrusted by Louis with the responsibility for oversight in the strengthening of the Catholic mission to the Poitou region. And so it was Colbert who had initially recruited Fénelon for this work and then had received dispatches and progress reports from him, generally endorsing the conciliatory and relatively gentle spirit of Fénelon's efforts. As mentioned, much of what we know about Fénelon's actual activity and experience, the measures he took and the frustrations he endured while trying to convert the Huguenots at Saintonge derives from this correspondence.

A byproduct of this administrative connection, moreover, was a growing familiarity with the Colbert family that went well beyond the circumstances of the Protestant mission. Fénelon became a spiritual director to several of the Colbert sons, first to the young Chevalier Antoine-Martin, who was to meet his death in battle in 1690, and then (perhaps) to another younger son, Jules-Armand, who would likewise die in battle in 1704, and finally to the Marquis himself.

An even more important consequence, in terms of Fénelon's developing career, was the fact that two of Colbert's daughters, Henriette Louise and Jeanne-Marie Thérèse, were married to the two noblemen who were now in the process of becoming the closest of advisors and family intimates with Louis, namely, Paul, Duc de Beauvillier (later the second Duc de Saint-Aignan), and Charles-Honoré d'Albert, Duc de Chevreuse. These two councillors, in addition to being favorites of Louis XIV and serious churchmen, were to become lifelong friends, supporters, and followers of Fénelon, and, in the case of Chevreuse, to come under his spiritual direction as well. The exact process, and timing, of his relationship with these families is not known in detail (uncle Antoine, so critical to Fénelon's introduction to distinguished personages, may have been an intermediary; connections through Tronson at Saint-Sulpice may have played a part).

What we should picture, once again, is that by late 1687 Fénelon had made a report directly to Louis XIV on the completion of his Poitou mission and was back in Paris at Nouvelles Catholiques, meeting with other intellectuals at Germigny, developing intimacy with the Colbert family and their friends, and becoming increasingly well known to religiously serious aristocratic circles. From within the specifically dévot group, which included the Beauvillier and Chevreuse couples as well as the royal consort, Madame de Maintenon herself, individuals began to extend social invitations, and some started to reach out to this brilliant and charming abbé Fénelon for spiritual guidance.

The Education of Daughters

At some point in the mid-1680s the Duchesse de Beauvillier, perhaps knowing of Fénelon's work at Nouvelles Catholiques and concerned about the education of her eight daughters, sought out his pedagogical advice. The proximate result was the famous *Treatise on the Education of Daughters*, which, intended originally only as a private communication, was rushed into print because of its excellence, probably by the proud ducal father who had outlined it for himself. It was rapidly to become the best known of Fénelon's early writings, quickly admired by liberal Dutch Protestants as well as Catholics because of its emphasis on inward conviction rather than outward practice,[133] but also because Fénelon shared in the current critique of aristocratic female idleness and supported the consequent call for improved educational opportunity for women.[134] The *Treatise* was also to become a classic statement of the traditional view that the purpose of education is the formation of character and the moral excellence of the student.

The *Treatise on Education* is a fascinating extension into the realm of pedagogy of the spirituality with which Fénelon had been imbued and that formed his bedrock. It gives us an early look at how his evolving ideas about pure love could play out in a setting where, unlike the constrained, somewhat self-defeating context of his missionary endeavors at Nouvelles Catholiques and in Saintonge, he was completely free to show how *he* would go about the work of Christian formation under ideal circumstances.

The central idea of the *Treatise* is that since the purpose of education is the successful development of virtuous character, the teacher must operate in a way that is respectful of the student's nature—that is, her abilities, needs, and potential. The student is a child, not a miniature adult. The spiritual working assumption, furthermore, is that good character in the child will emerge precisely as she comes to know and love God as human nature's final end, so that she will understand that "the essence of Christianity . . . is contempt of this present life and love of the life hereafter."[135] So far as the method of instruction goes, the teacher's responsibility is to make what must be learned *beautiful* at an appropriate level, thereby engaging the student's natural yearning for the goodness of truth.

Fénelon starts out by arguing that the educational formation of women is to be taken with great seriousness, so that they may be prepared for great responsibilities in home and family, and so that they may become morally mature and productive adults in general, not self-indulgent hothouse flowers and passive dependents. Early childhood is the critical period, where the good teacher must strike a balance between dutiful regard for the child's capacities for learning and the overinvested use of children by adults for parental entertainment and agendas. This "modest" approach to children will stimulate their natural desire to learn (in an "age-appropriate manner," we would say), while building a healthy "humility" in the child (that is, good self-esteem but not self-importance). The child must be exposed to what is admirable in adults, so that a "taste" (an enormously important word for Fénelon) for virtue is imparted. It is very important to engage the child's interest with attractive texts, games, and exercises that reinforce good teaching, to manifest patience and candid honesty with the child's questions, to offer suitable physical training, and to administer discipline gently when rules are broken. Learning must be enjoyable, since *responsiveness* in the child is critical. The child must be patiently led to increasingly subtle discernments of goodness and badness in self and others. The best moral inculcation is done in the form of stories, and the best kind of instructional discourse is Socratic, where the child is led naturally and by her own reasoning to grasp certain truths.

Religious training of the child is to be done by means of the biblical narratives, which, "if properly handled, will pleasantly fill the imagination of young and intelligent children with the history of religion from the creation of the world to our own times and will give them an exalted idea of it which will never fade."[136] The child is to be taught obedience to the church as the interpreter of Scripture rather than relying on private judgment, contrite as well as joyful participation in the sacraments, and a humble and sincerely inward practice of personal prayer. He emphasizes as well the importance for women of cultivating open and honest speech and a simple straightforwardness about feelings and thoughts, rather than affected craftiness and manipulation. He urges women to minimize, or at least play down, the focus on beauty and fashion and the consequent "artificiality." He wants *simplicity* (another crucial term for Fénelon) and modesty in all things. "True grace follows nature, and never spoils it," he says, "but fashion destroys itself."[137]

Distaste and boredom, he says, reflect the weakness of disordered minds, while true refinement and good manners are "according to reason." In the final analysis, though, it would be cruel to foster in a young woman impossible aspirations: "in considering the education of a girl one should take into account her position in society, the places where she is destined to spend her life and the occupation which she is likely to take up. Be careful that she does not cherish hopes which are above her fortune and condition."[138]

Fénelon's prescriptions in the *Treatise* are not revolutionary; he is not looking for upheaval in the social order or in gender roles. What is noteworthy, however, and part of what made his work famous, is its remarkable emphasis on the teacher's calling to organize the educational process around a humanistic ideal of moral maturity. There is also the important insight, progressive for its time, that children do their best and deepest learning when the experience has, we might say, a positive valence in the child's memory. This is different from the claim that learning must be *fun*, since in fact it will still be hard, sometimes very hard, work. Educational standards for Fénelon are rigorous but not demeaning or mindlessly mechanical. After all, precisely as moral training, education is directed to the strengthening of the *will*, of the individual's moral determination to love what is truly lovable. In other words, in the good teacher, we have something like a human analog to God, who trains us to love not by providing inducements that stimulate self-love but by directing our gaze to what is good and making it lovely, so that we want that only for its own sake. Thus, he manifests what Melchior-Bonnet calls a "pedagogical optimism"[139] that will make its way straight to Rousseau's *Émile* and, in a way, into some forms of the modern emphasis on "values" in education.

A last implication of the *Treatise*, one more fully spelled out in an associated document of unknown date, the *Advice of Fénelon to a Woman of Quality on the Education of Her Daughter*,[140] is that education as a formative process is better carried out at home than in the convent schools then favored by the nobility. Disapproving of the harsh rigidity of many convent schools, Fénelon was convinced that they produced rebellion, religious hypocrisy, and worldliness by reaction in healthy youngsters.[141] Perhaps Fénelon's attitude on this was hardened by his experience at Saint-Cyr, as we shall see.

Bourgogne

Not only were the Beauvilliers favorably impressed with the counsel that Fénelon had given them in the *Treatise*, but within a short time—and in a way that may have been premeditated as part of their request for the work in the first place,[142] since Beauvillier was in the process of being appointed governor for the young Duc de Bourgogne—they passed it along to Louis's consort, the redoubtable Madame de Maintenon. As patron of her own special school for girls, she was also very favorably moved. The more remote result of the *Treatise*,[143] then, was that when Beauvillier was appointed by Louis on August 16, 1689, as governor for his grandson and petit dauphin (second-in-line to the throne), Louis, Duc de Bourgogne, he immediately saw to it that Fénelon was named as preceptor (and soon Claude Fleury as assistant governor). Bossuet himself was pleased at Fénelon's new honor; Tronson expressed joy mixed with a stern warning about the corrupting nature of the court at Versailles;[144] and Bausset tells us that "scarcely had the choice of a new governor and a new preceptor become public, than all France resounded with applause."[145] "A divine choice!" said the famous writer of letters Madame de Sévigné.[146] The future of the monarchy would be in good hands!

Fénelon had now become the private tutor to the young Louis, Duc de Bourgogne, oldest son of the grand dauphin Louis, child of Louis XIV and his late wife Maria Theresa. In due course, Louis's younger brothers Philippe, Duc d'Anjou (eventually Philip V of Spain), and Charles, Duc de Berry, would be added to Fénelon's responsibilities, in 1690 and 1693 respectively. The traditional expectation was that from the ages of seven to thirteen boys would be removed from the care of their mothers and turned over to male teachers for their formation.[147] The appointment of Beauvillier as governor and Fénelon as preceptor for the young Louis, as well as the earlier appointment of Bossuet to the preceptorial role with the grand dauphin himself, met with wide approval not only because of the standing of the chosen mentors, but because considerable apprehension existed, rightly, about the native potential of Louis XIV's heirs.

Indeed, it was recognized that these royal children were not necessarily promising prospects. Bausset describes Louis the grand dauphin and first heir as "a prince good and kindly mannered [*doux*], but with a character exempt from both virtue and vice, indifferent to good and evil, little aware of the value of glory, or of the sciences and the arts."[148] Saint-Simon characterized him as "a near voluptuary, but without discrimination" and as a "nothing himself, who counted for nothing in his long, vain wait for the crown."[149] And we will come to the petit dauphin in a moment! All the more reason existed, therefore, for detailed and close attention to their education, lest they grow to adulthood and be incompetent, jaded, and weak! As things developed, of course, the premature deaths of both dauphins, the eventual coming of a regency after the death of Louis XIV in 1715, and then the accession of the lackluster Louis XV were to bear out some of the worst fears. In the meantime, though, great hopes were vested in the eldest son, and then in that son's eldest son.

So Fénelon moved to Versailles to be part of the young duke's sizable suite, which would include Beauvillier, Fleury, and Langeron in due course as a "reader," and several other coaches and attendant gentlemen. He quickly proceeded to organize a program of study for his charge by tailoring the manner and method that he had formulated for aristocratic daughters to the needs of aristocratic sons, and, just perhaps in this particular case, a son destined to rule.

It would be difficult to overemphasize this last factor: it overshadows everything in Fénelon's care for the young Louis. This young man *may rule!* Indeed, we know that Louis XIV, ever mindful of the royal succession, was intensely anxious that his heir be up to the task. Having himself acquired the title "the Great" in 1679, in letters and memoirs he exhorts his successor to work tirelessly to develop all of the virtues necessary for regal greatness, the most important of which is the constant consciousness that "you *are* the King!" Sainte-Beuve, in his analysis of this material, rightly chose to emphasize the extent to which Louis expected the king to radiate "state," that is, "the true function of sovereignty,"[150] as a kind of personality trait. Louis spoke like a king, says Sainte-Beuve, "and that word 'glory' is ever on his lips."[151] This style shapes the manner, the methods, and the goals of a king, says Louis. It makes others tremble and keeps them at the grindstone. It ensures effectiveness and guarantees that France will have the respect from the nations that she deserves.

Let us then say that both Louis XIV and Fénelon loved France and wanted the same thing for Louis's heir, that is, true greatness in his leadership of the French people. But the obvious question was one of definition. Is this greatness to be described as "glory" and the "thirst for glory," or should it be construed on another and more spiritual basis as the pursuit of "pure love," as the construction of peace and justice for all of the peoples of the earth? Louis XIV will in due course treat this latter as a "chimera" and a pipedream. Nonetheless, it is the ideal that Fénelon attempts to instill into the young man who may one day sit on the throne.

In structuring the curriculum for his royal students Fénelon drew not only on his own writing, but on Fleury's pedagogical composition, *Treatise on the Choice and Method of Study*, as well. The central idea is that moral and spiritual truth is learned from the study of historical examples. Fleury's *Ecclesiastical History* would provide the core reading for sacred history, balanced by a solid diet of the classics, followed by selected historical treatments of modern times. Recommended literary texts are from the moralizing literature of the Hellenistic age, the wisdom literature of the Old Testament, and the works of the church fathers. There is a striking moral/philosophical emphasis as well in two extant letters from 1695 and 1696 to Fleury, where Fénelon outlines a curriculum and suggested readings for the young dukes.[152] Rhetoric and logic are included, as are readings in various political-legal histories of England, France, and the Low Countries, that is, those areas and peoples likely to be of special concern for a future king of France. While Fénelon is thus careful in his choices to measure up to the humanist ideal of incorporating material both old and new—he cannot be accused of being merely pious or antiquarian—there is a decided absence of contemporary *popular* literature. Any notion of "light" reading, we might say, is foreign to him. He is a strict classicist throughout, and he expects his charges to be so as well. Further, the emphasis is on learning to *think*, not on technical knowledge.

There is a famous sketch[153] of the total daily regimen for the three young men, written by one of Philippe's gentleman companions, Charles Auguste d'Allonville, Marquis de Louville, in which physical rigor (strict diet, very regular hours and schedule, highly structured exercise), the use of social isolation rather than corporal punishment as the penalty for misbehavior, and manly discipline learned in hunting are noteworthy. There is a real fear of making the young dukes foppish or delicate. "M. de Beauvillier is so convinced that a weakling prince is good for nothing— especially in France where princes have to command their armies in person—that all the risks which must be run in such a régime have never been able to deter him from his plan of action."[154]

We will see later that the Duc de Bourgogne ends up in Flanders with the king's army, doing his military "internship," but that he never became a "warrior" in quite the way that Louis XIV would have liked. Fénelon's later exhortations to him, in the Cambrai period, will be directed to the importance of doing his duty and shouldering his responsibilities, but there will always be a somewhat religiously obsessive and self-doubting side to his personality that will prove to be troublesome.

De Louville also describes the overall effectiveness of Fénelon's teaching methods. He succeeded in making the study of the Latin classics pleasant, interesting, and a source of creativity for his charges: "the Abbé de Fénelon has regulated their work with marvelous skill, adapting it to the age and future career of the boys."[155] Fénelon did not require scholarly precision from them but contended that "it was enough for a prince to know how to appreciate such things and judge of those who excel in them."[156] (This last, of course, is excellent advice for the leader who cannot be an expert in everything but knows how to pick people who *are* expert in a given field.)

The rise and fall of governments was a special area of focus, so that the young princes would learn statesmanship from a range of precedents. Fénelon's artistic playfulness—a natural "childlikeness," as it were—came out in the fabrication of dialogue situations, in which his young students could debate different points of view and work out their own reasons for favoring a particular position. As far as religion goes, "the aim is far more to make them Christians by inspiring them with virtuous feelings and removing from them whatever may set them a bad example, than by prescribing outward and difficult exercises which usually produce the opposite effect in children who are subjected to them, and which give them for the rest of their lives an aversion, or even a disgust, for piety."[157]

Now, the primary object of Fénelon's attentions as tutor, the developing character of the young Duc de Bourgogne, was a challenge. It is hard, though, to be objective about the nature of the challenge, since the principal descriptions come both from Saint-Simon on the one hand, who seems to have had a deep contempt for Louis, and from Fénelon on the other, who loved and nurtured him in a sacred calling. The former's description, an assessment contained in a letter supposedly requested from Beauvillier, approaches what we call "character assassination." He makes young Bourgogne out to be massively narcissistic (he has "an arrogance and haughtiness that passed all description"); he is frenzied, cunning, disdainful of criticism aimed at his many faults, uncontrollably angry at times, compulsively and rigidly religious, and utterly lacking in empathy and interest for others.[158] In Fénelon's view (as contained in a little essay entitled *Le Fantasque*—the "whimsical person"),[159] the young man comes off as immature, neurotic, and painfully self-critical ("often he huffs and puffs like a furious young bull, who, with his horns sharpened, beats the air, but when he has no pretext for attacking others, turns against himself"), but also charming, sensitively intelligent, and personable even in his thrashing about.

Probably both descriptions are accurate but reflect the differing perspectives of one who had a close relationship with the duke and one who didn't. It is a common experience that the sons and grandsons of massively authoritarian fathers, such as Louis XIV, who have high expectations for their heirs ("You are the King!"), are burdened with a crushing sense of inadequacy and failure. It is all the more amazing that Fénelon did such a good job, as was widely acknowledged.[160] Ramsay, for example, tells us that Bourgogne went from being the most impetuous and capricious of young men to being the gentlest, most compassionate, and tenderhearted of princes, dedicated to the well-being of the people whose care was his ultimate concern.[161] "Over and above the acquisition of knowledge, it was the 'Fénelon method' that produced marvels," says Melchior-Bonnet.[162] Bossuet himself, after an interview that he conducted with the young duke, came away[163] filled with "surprise and admiration" at the maturity of judgment inculcated by Fénelon, so much so that he predicted a highly successful reign for the young man, should he ever be the king.

The Literature of Instruction 1: Fables

What, then, was the magic? Some of it, at least, is contained in the kind of compositions that Fénelon produced for his young charges, as well as in the kind of guidance, primarily through letters, that he was beginning to provide for those who sought spiritual direction and trustingly opened their hearts to him. The magic was in the remarkable "care and solicitude" that Fénelon showed to everyone in his pastoral work.[164]

The first thing that he did was to charm his students with materials that captured some the best instructional techniques of the late seventeenth century.[165] No one was more popular for readers in the 1680s than the remarkable Jean de La Fontaine (1621–95), whose first two collections of *Selected Fables* in versified French had appeared in 1668 (121 fables plus introductory material) and 1678 (88 fables plus a dedication and epilogue), respectively. Modeled on the classical fables of Aesop and Phaedrus, as well as a multitude of medieval sources, these short, pithy, entertaining narratives in which humanized animal figures and their actions are the predominant means (but not the only means—some use human figures) of teaching a useful moral lesson enraptured their readers. La Fontaine dedicated the first collection to the grand dauphin Louis as the next king of France, and the second to Madame de Montespan, Louis XIV's first official mistress. A third collection would come out in 1693 (24 fables) dedicated to Fénelon's own student, Louis, Duc de Bourgogne, for whom La Fontaine appears to have had a special fondness. This last aspect of La Fontaine, combined with the fact that he moved in the same social-aristocatic and literary circles that Fénelon knew (the connections are complex), has led to tantalizing speculation regarding mutual aesthetic but also spiritual influences between the two men, but we do not know for sure.[166]

The general theme that La Fontaine develops is the idea that as human beings, whatever our pretenses, facades, rationalizations, self-justifications, huffing and puffing, and other assorted vanities, we are *just* human (with the implication: just *animal*) and all pretty much the same.[167] The purpose of the fables is to make us aware of this fact, so that, at least at times, we can transcend it by means of sound wisdom and upright ethics. As applied to rulers, this kind of teaching has a subversive element: the great ones of the world are often the blindest and most self-glorifying, and they are so at everyone else's expense. In one fable dedicated to La Rochefoucauld, La Fontaine uses the example of a flock of rabbits who are scared away by the sound of a gunshot, only to return and claim their turf as soon as the danger is past. Human beings are the same, says La Fontaine, when they put great energy into protecting their territory. "The interests of wealth, grandeur, and glory make the rulers of states, certain courtiers and people of all professions do the same. . . . Keep as few people as possible from sharing the pie, that's the rule of the game, that's the order of business."[168] The subversive implication might be: *wise* rulers will *share* the wealth!

It is no wonder that Fénelon, committed to the view that good education is moral education and that children thrive on narratives, was deeply attracted to La Fontaine. When he died, Fénelon paid him tribute as "another Aesop . . . through whom the brute animals, made to speak, do teach wisdom to the human race."[169] He produced a large number of Latin prose translations of La Fontaine's fables for the edification of his young charges.[170] And, most important, he also wrote his own *Fables* in French, of which thirty-six were eventually collected.[171] Chad Helms, in his recent introduction to a selection of these, shows that Fénelon's *Fables* can be conveniently classified into those that use animal protagonists as the central characters, those that describe the character of the ideal prince and his style of governance, and those that extol the "simple" life.[172] Indeed, one of the classical themes that Fénelon picks up from La Fontaine is the notion that civilization corrupts us and makes us complex and devious and predatory, and that we need to return to more basic values and ways. The idea belongs to the popular mythology of an ancient golden age, when the human race lived in primitive innocence and unbroken harmony. It also picks up as well on the biblical and utopian theme that when the kingdom of God comes, the lion and the lamb will lie down together: the unnatural viciousness of human society will be swept away, and nature in her purity will be restored.

As an example of a fable where Fénelon stayed close to his exemplar in La Fontaine, we might take "The Wolf and the Young Sheep."[173] A young sheep, naïve and inexperienced, is engaged in conversation with a wolf, who is sniffing around the edge of the flock, while the shepherd is relaxing with neighbors. The wolf assures the sheep that he only wants to enjoy some of the tender grass and that he personally subscribes to the philosophy that one should be content with a little. The sheep, touched by such a high ideal of brotherhood among the animals, wanders off, leaving the wolf to ravage the flock. The moral is that we are to be convinced by how people behave, not by their high-sounding claims to be virtuous.

Another instance might be that of the pigeons who live in harmonious community, until one of them, "disgusted with the pleasures of a peaceful life," becomes ambitious and embarks on a political adventure, which leads first to glory, then to an ignominious death. Ambition is vain and leads to destruction.[174] It is not hard to see a possible criticism of Louis

XIV's ambitious political machinations. These parables then tend to spill over into those that use the animal figures as a device for describing the virtuous ruler, as in that of the Two Lion Cubs, described by Helms,[175] where two cubs, one from the country and one from the city, are compared in terms of their suitability to be rulers. In the end it is the cub from the country, unspoiled by luxury and able to rule without tyrannizing, who is preferred.[176]

The underlying theme in Fénelon's *Fables*, where La Fontaine is the immediate literary inspiration while La Rochefoucauld is a more indirect philosophical source, is that what troubles human society, what makes people corrupt and ignorant, and what makes rulers ultimately unfaithful to their sacred charge from God is self-love—the stupid vanity in which the "glory" of the king is understood in a way that threatens to displace the authority of God with the pomp and self-delusion of a human potentate. And the vanity of the corrupt ruler is simply all human vanity writ large, although on a more destructive level. This is the idea that Fénelon drilled relentlessly into his young charges.

The Literature of Instruction 2: Dialogues of the Dead

Then we come to Fénelon's second teaching device, the *Dialogues of the Dead*, seventy-nine in all,[177] fashioned on the classical model of the satires of the third-century Lucian of Samosata and influenced by the 1683 popularizing of the genre by Bernard de Fontenelle (1657–1757) in his *New Dialogues of the Dead*. In this form of the literary-philosophical discussion, deceased persons, resident in the underworld and engaged at their leisure in sophisticated discourse, reflect on different moral and practical implications of their former earthly lives. The idea, at least in Fontenelle's formulation, is that these deceased now have the perspective and wisdom, no longer driven by earthly passions and ambitions, with which to make shrewd observations about human folly and perversity. By engaging in goodwilled disputation with one another, two historical characters, drawn either from antiquity or more modern times, can engage in some debunking of what passes for wisdom in the earthly sphere in order to articulate, as mouthpieces for the author of the dialogue, a deeper and more lasting insight. The effect is entertaining and pedagogically much more gripping than a straightforward moral essay.

For Fontenelle, the chief insight is that human beings spend much too much time deceiving themselves in the name of "reason" about their true nature, so that life is shot through with ridiculous justifications for unethical behavior, with religious obscurantism, and with senseless sexual passion dressed up as ethereal "love." We would do better just to "play the game" and not kid ourselves about what we're doing! Ambition, for example, may be foolish, but it "drives the engine" of human striving, and we would be diminished without it. In a more honest world, everybody could be more realistic and thus more human, women would be less oppressed by sexual power politics, and most of us would be better off learning to enjoy what we have, and, indeed, what we are, rather than hungering for something else. With such a perspective, Fontenelle charmed his own salon culture (his most avid readers) and anticipated the eighteenth century, but he also, in the eyes of Fénelon, helped to establish this particular form of the literary dialogue as an excellent teaching tool.

As the young Duc de Bourgogne and his other charges approached adolescence, Fénelon composed his own version of this type of dialogue in order to present moral issues on a more sophisticated level. Fénelon's raised-from-the-dead characters engage in the puncturing of human pretensions, the often absurd seeking after glory and fame through high public opinion, the illusions (and miseries) of the rich and famous, and the pomposity of much paraded virtue (which is actually a mask for self-love). There is a kind of "hermeneutic of suspicion" here, where the intention is to show that what presents itself in life as admirable and adorable is in fact just the opposite—and this can be demonstrated by intelligent critique. Thus, with such classical figures as Romulus and Remus, Pericles and Alcibiades, Alexander the Great, Hannibal and Scipio, or more modern examples such as the notorious Louis XI—all powerful rulers in their time and place—it can be seen that great men, often lionized by posterity, have routinely engaged in, or colluded with, injustice—despite all their noble statements. Their great vulnerability often has been their willingness to be manipulated by flatterers and then to imagine that they can secure an everlasting "glory" for themselves.

What forms a sharp contrast with Fontenelle, however, is Fénelon's determination to use the dialogues as a way of holding up a positive ethic of human goodness, in which bad leaders are exposed in their ultimately self-destructive vice and good leaders practice the virtues proper to their state: they put the needs of the people first; they firmly punish injustice and gladly reward merit; they listen to wise, not toadying, councillors; they recognize that faithfulness to duty is the only true source of immortal fame; they put peacemaking ahead of war-making; they recognize that generosity and good faith on the part of the ruler are the only secure basis for law or political stability; and so on. In other words, Fénelon uses the *Dialogues* to teach the young nobles the principles of statesmanlike leadership.[178]

Finally, he exalts the philosophy of Plato as the only real source of metaphysical truth, since what is good, beautiful, and true must be sought *directly and self-consciously*, as objective ideals, and thus he rejects the worldly paradoxicality of Fontenelle (ambition is both good and bad in its results), the calculated virtue of moderation in Aristotle, and the fence-sitting typical of popular philosophical skepticism. The ultimate mark of the great leader is that the "glory" he seeks, the ambition he pursues, is an unbounded actualizing of what is truly good for all of the people, not just his own but that of the whole community. If this is naïve, says Fénelon, a measured pragmatism is even more so, for it finally sinks in compromises. Let the young princes take note!

Finally, Fénelon's supreme pedagogical composition for his aristocratic charges, the *Adventures of Telemachus*, must be considered, but this work comes only in the period after he has spent time engaged with Madame Guyon, with the controversy over the *Maxims*, and thus with open debate about the nature of "pure love." We leave *Telemachus*, therefore, for a later chapter.

Beginning Spiritual Direction

It is during this time of 1688–90 that Fénelon begins his work of spiritual direction both in the form of letters and in individual meetings. Elizabeth Hamilton, Comtesse de Gramont, an Irishwoman married to a

French noble, was Fénelon's first long-term spiritual directee. In her case, Fénelon was giving guidance to a woman known to be passionate, sensitive to the prerogatives and standing of her family, contentious in personal relations, and religiously devout. In letters that Sainte-Beuve found to be eminently sensible for their "Christian Stoicism,"[179] Fénelon describes her as "a haughty and disdainful spirit," "with a long habit of self-indulgence" and with a "taste for refined living."[180]

All of his advice is directed to the cultivation of humility by accepting her own faults, being patient with those of others, and taking the blows of fortune not as personal insults or failures, but as opportunities for a closer relation with God. The opinions of others do not matter; she must use all of her daily moments to "practice the presence of God";[181] she must be diligent in her reading and prayers (without becoming scrupulous about it); she must accept the burdens of each moment or each occurrence as the cross God has sent her and not the one she has chosen; she must not yield to discouragement, which is only "the despair of vexed self-love";[182] she must cultivate solitude and time alone in the midst of a hectic life; she must realize that God often comes to us under the form of the irritating and obnoxious person who requires us "to die to self"; and we must realize that the process of being humbled by our own faults is the only thing that can make us forgiving and patient with others.

One particular theme, also echoed frequently in the correspondence with Madame de Maintenon, is the drastic need Madame de Gramont has for what we might today refer to as "downtime": "you greatly need certain free hours to be given to prayer and recollection. Try to steal some such hours, and be sure that such little parings of time will be your best treasures. Above all, try to save your mornings; defend them like a besieged city! Make vigorous sallies upon all intruders [the word is *importuns*—those who make demands on you], clear out the trenches, and then shut yourself up within your keep. . . . You are like a watch that needs constant winding."[183]

Humility will come, says Fénelon, with the practice of silence and recollection, with a deep sense of personal unworthiness coupled with absolute faith in God's goodness, and finally, with the recognition that the most powerful torments of life are also the greatest gifts of God's grace, when we turn to God with complete abandon. When God shows us an "irritated and severe face, [we must] let him do it; he never loves except when he menaces; for he menaces only to test, to humble, to detach."[184] In the same letter he reminds her: "If you seek God purely, you will find him even more when he tests you than when he consoles you." "God has touched you sharply," he adds elsewhere, "by humbling you; the loving doctor has put the remedy on the sick and sensitive part."[185]

Jeanne-Lydie Goré aptly comments on Fénelon's letters to Madame de Gramont that Fénelon is moving in the direction of a spirituality of "not-knowing," where interior peace is a "vigilant repose" in the bosom of God, where hope is in God alone and all passion has disappeared.[186] The core idea is that there is a letting go of the "me" that belongs to religious inquietude and its distracting power. At Versailles the lessons of Saint Sulpice about self-abandonment are driven home.

If Fénelon's advice to Madame de Gramont is intended to soften and calm a turbulent spirit, his guidance to two of the younger Colbert sons, both soldiers on campaign, has a regulatory character aimed at organizing them in devotion and behavior, so that they become models of manly discipline for their fellows. The analogy is with the acquisition of martial skills, learned by steady application and patient practice— not too much too precipitately. His urging to one of the warriors, the chevalier Antoine-Martin, is to be regular in prayer, but to take things one step at a time with brief meditation on Scripture texts "in a simple and easy manner"[187] and with a gentle, forbearing approach to distractions, which are inevitable. "There is no question of going quickly," he says, "but of going well."[188] "You must chew for a long time in order to digest properly,"[189] he says. It is better to do a modest amount conscientiously than to attempt too much and become discouraged. He compares their regularity in devotion to the laying of a foundation or the digging of a well, so that there is a deep abandonment of the self to God, just as one obeys orders without reservation. He repeatedly urges him to let go of the past with its debaucheries, to recognize that God is using this experience to prepare him for the future, and to avoid the anxiety and fretfulness of "disquiet" above all.[190]

But the end was to come soon. To Antoine-Martin he says, "I am thrilled to learn that your faithfulness with God increases, although you do not have the fervor of an intensely felt savor. This attachment to God, which is quite dry and quite bare, is indeed more pure. God loves you very much to lead you by the road which is rough, and where one must climb, without ever looking behind."[191] The Chevalier would be mortally wounded in combat three weeks later.

To another of the brothers, apparently[192] Jules-Armand, he wrote echoing St. Augustine, "Sir, do what you want, but love God. And let his love, brought back to life in you, be your only guide. I have often thanked him for having kept you safe from the perils of this campaign, wherein your soul was more exposed to danger than your body. Often have I trembled for you."[193] Jules-Armand would die in battle on July 1, 1690.

During the last months of his life as he suffered from a terminal illness, the oldest of the brothers, Jean-Baptiste, Marquis de Seignelay, his old superior during the Poitou mission, sought Fénelon's guidance. The tone of their lengthy letters is one of encouraging admonition to a man who had led, it seems, a somewhat dissipated life, but who had become religiously serious in his last days. To him Fénelon says, "The phantom of the world disappears; all that vain window-dressing will disappear soon; the hour comes, it approaches, it advances, and we touch it already; the charm breaks in, our eyes are opened."[194] His appeal is for a complete and unconditional turning over of his heart by the Marquis to God in a manner that is not dependent on "affective or felt love," where "the piety of relish and imagination" dissipates everything. There are constant warnings against bargaining and hedging and hesitation and holding back from God, because (apparently) the Marquis is a calculating and worldly man. In a way that suggests the growing influence of Madame Guyon on his thought, Fénelon increasingly emphasizes the importance of a complete letting go of the core of the self to God. The Marquis must see himself as a "nothing," that is, a mere creature and utterly ephemeral as such, while God is eternal and great and makes us great as we abandon ourselves to him. The key to humility—which the Marquis lacks and desperately needs—is the ability to see how small we are in comparison with God, and yet how large we are when we place ourselves in God's hands.

Everything that is not God is to become instantly contemptible. "A certain sentiment of condemnation against oneself," says Fénelon, "that one carries everywhere within the self, makes you sweet, humane, patient, modest, kindly, charitable. One thinks oneself blessed for doing good to the neighbor, and one thinks oneself unworthy of being served; one feels that nothing is owed to the sinner but confusion and pain. At the same time that one is abased in one's own eyes, one finds oneself great and capable of doing all things in God."[195] The only things that God cannot abide, Fénelon reminds Seignelay, are negligence and falseness. In his last letter, Fénelon urges him: "You have only one means of practicing virtue, which is to suffer with peace and sweetness; all of the other occasions of sacrifice have been taken away from you . . . [let your heart] nourish itself with God in secret."[196] Seignelay died in great peace (according to Madame de Maintenon) on October 25, 1690.

In addition to Fénelon's work of spiritual direction undertaken in the form of a voluminous correspondence, he also pursued it in the form of retreat addresses. It would be a good idea to take a quick look at a modest work, the *Talk on the Characters of True and Solid Piety*, which appears to fall in this period.[197] Gosselin contends that it was delivered "around 1690" at Madame de Maintenon's school at Saint-Cyr.[198] It is helpful to underline some of the central themes in this work,[199] so reflective of Fénelon's favorite pedagogical emphases and, at the same time, anticipatory of the impending influence of Madame Guyon.

What Orcibal calls the "precious prefatory note" of this work (included in the 1696 edition but removed later and not printed by Gosselin) says: "Many people today make a profession of being devout, such that one is at a loss to assess the situation of those who make up the majority of Christians. The problem is that since many embrace Christianity without rule and without light, it generally happens that they fall. And since greed drives their conduct, they make false beginnings and often distance themselves from the goal. This little work has been composed to remedy that disorder."[200] The problem, in short, is not the withdrawal from Christianity but the bad Christianity of disguised self-love. Therefore, he calls his listeners to a fresh self-examination and repentance.

His central theme, which will become a groundtone in all of his direction, is the importance of humility, because without it our piety will be no more than "vain confidence in good intention" that leads to "false conduct." We must "continually be on guard in order to prevent our self-love, which tries insensibly to compensate itself by means of amusement with little things, for the sacrifice it has made to God of big things; indeed, is there anything more deplorable than to see someone, who, after making the first steps towards perfection, looks lazily behind herself, and thinks she has done too much?" Nothing caters to our "disregulated inclinations" more, he says to the nuns of Saint-Cyr, than the fact that we wish "to do service to God as a security for ourselves." Fénelon tells his listeners that they must be ever vigilant for the tendency to make a "carnal politique" out of religion, so that we use religion as a means of self-righteous criticism and intolerance of others, or as a way to get the world's approbation, as something meant to cater to a person's peculiar mood or idiosyncratic "gifts," or as the social bond of an "in-group," where we practice the virtues only among our like-minded friends. For religion to be real, he says, it must make us charitable in the midst of our most brutal animosities, or it is a sham. If we wish for a "solid" piety, we must suffer for God's purposes, we must do so with joy, and we must be thankful for the opportunity to so align ourselves with the interests of God's glory, whatever the cost. Humility is the goal, and the cross is the way to that goal. Religion without profound costliness is no religion at all.[201]

And so we come to a major turning in Fénelon's career. Highly esteemed tutor to the king's grandsons and sought-after spiritual guide, as well as a respected and published author and a serious thinker, by the spring of 1689 he had entered into an intense correspondence with the notorious Madame Guyon. We see already how high he sets the spiritual bar for those over whom he is gaining influence. The essential thing for those who will hear him is the refusal to be seduced by the massive, all-pervading ethos of courtly and aristocratic life with all of its inducements to "falseness" and the consequent misery of "self-love." The antidote, learned in the traditions of the French school, is the "self-annihilation" of abandonment to God, the exaltation of God's glory alone, and the practice of virtues that reflect that perspective. The greatest danger for people of faith is false religion, the co-opting of religion by self-love; and the antidote is a deepened inwardness, in which communion with God is sought within the "real space" inside the humbled and abased self. The social implication is clear. Only under the leadership of such a spiritually, inwardly transformed nobility, where the love of God is primary, can France be a Catholic nation, a source of hope for the whole earth, not just in name but in truth.

Madame Guyon enters Fénelon's life just when he is looking for a way to go further, we might say, to develop a more explicit, more carefully worked out, more psychologically subtle understanding of just how the grace of God can claim the human heart and change it. The main drama is about to begin.

"I need for God to reshape and recast me in a mold."
—LETTER TO MADAME GUYON, JULY 26, 1689

"The clarification of [your views], far from scandalizing me, has strengthened me, and it has been completely necessary for me. I am well persuaded that there must be a great deal here that I don't understand with regard to very delicate and profound things, where experience alone can give the true light; but for the principal states of the way, I think that I understand your writings from one end to the other, at least broadly and in general, to the extent that I can reduce them easily to the true principles of the soundest theology."
—LETTER TO MADAME GUYON,
JULY 11, 1689

FOUR

Madame Guyon
THE CATALYST

1688–1695

Oc ne of the things we now know about Fénelon is that he absorbed and integrated ideas from many different sources. Raised and formed to be a pastor and a teacher, he was also a lifelong learner, quick to gather the insights of others, but always selectively and critically. We have seen him starting out with a solid grounding in the Greek and Latin classics, especially Plato, then moving to contemporary philosophical thought with Descartes and Malebranche, then aspiring to imitate La Fontaine and Fontenelle, who embody current literary chic, all of this shot through with the spirituality of the Sulpicians and the French school. Behind this spirituality stands the imposing colossus of St. Augustine, as well as the church fathers in general, and Scripture itself. Fénelon ceaselessly read, thought, formulated, and restated his views as he went deeper into these sources.

Now, already contained in this combination of influences was a sense of the "mystical" dimension in religion, a sense that God is to be sought and enjoyed in the immediacy of intimate, personal, deep interiority that transcends words, formulas, and outward observances, indeed surpassing all representation entirely. For French school spirituality this mystical dimension devolves specifically into the annihilation of the human "self," the active human agent, as the adoration of the goodness of God becomes the vital focus of religious experience. This is why Henri Bremond used the terminology of "theocentric"—God-centered—to describe this spirituality. God is sheer, intractable Mystery who can be surely known only because that God chooses to provide *given*, gratuitous experience for the human recipient. The paradox with Bremond is that this theocentric approach is also a "devout humanism," where what is known of God affirms and exalts human goodness and the means by which that goodness is expressed. Thus a spirituality of self-annihilation becomes, from the humanist perspective, a spirituality of self-affirmation. Part of Fénelon's work was to resolve this self-losing, self-gaining paradox in some way. What will become clear is that the human "self" that is annihilated is *only* the self of self-love: it is the self that I was before rising from my knees to welcome the self that I am becoming.

This project links up with, and reflects, a secular thrust as well. As we have seen, thinkers like La Rouchefoucauld, La Bruyère, and Fontenelle engage in a relentless critique of all of the vanity, posturing, and falseness of contemporary society. Human vanity and human pretension, they say, are absolutely corrosive of all motivation, and self-love is inevitable— and perhaps most of all when we are at our most idealistic, since it is precisely there that we can be most self-deceiving. There is the further idea that this self-love—which is a concept that stands for all of the regressive and destructive capacities of individuals and communities— inevitably precipitates us into long bitter moral struggles, wars of one kind or another that perpetuate themselves endlessly. La Rochefoucauld is pretty well convinced that self-love (that is, vanity) will normally, if not inevitably, triumph in human affairs.[202] This despair, or cynicism, or "realism," considers "pure" love an illusion, the never-never land of dreamers, but it is the quietist-mystical contention that pure love is not an illusion, *as long as our definition of it is wrought with sufficient care.*

In time Fénelon was to argue that if our love of God is to be "pure," then it must exclude everything "imagined, felt, or tasted which is illuminated or extraordinary," so that "we hold to God alone, in pure and naked faith, in the simplicity of the Gospel, receiving consolations as they come, and not stopping for any, not judging at all and always obeying, believing easily that we can be mistaken, and that others can correct us; finally, by acting every moment with simplicity and good intention."[203] It took, though, one more major input to bring him to this sharpness of focus.

The new infusion came at the hands of Jeanne-Marie Bouvier de la Motte (1648–1717), widow of the late Jacques Guyon and thus known as Madame Guyon. She is a major figure in her own right in the history of Christian spirituality, although most often paired with Fénelon because of their complexly close association. By the time she and he first met sometime in October 1688, she had been deeply formed spiritually by guides who were variably Franciscan, Carmelite, Capuchin, and Molinist-quietist, and she had already established a career as a known and controversial writer and teacher on the life of prayer. The principal source for her life story is her own *Autobiography*—which is itself a classic with its own rich history, comparable to confessional works by St. Augustine and Rousseau, and like them propaganda for her doctrines.

Raised in a cultivated and religiously serious household, married early to an older nobleman, mother of several children who died early, then widowed, she was constantly afflicted by illness, including smallpox that badly scarred her (a scourge sent by God, she believed, to relieve her of the vanity of physical attractiveness). She spent her intensely felt life looking for a religious vocation and experimenting with different possibilities, until she finally found her proper role as a lay spiritual guide and writer. Along the way, however, she landed in conflict with church authority in Italy and Savoy.[204]

At the time of her first meeting with Fénelon, she was living under official detention in the Paris area consequent to charges of leading a scandalous life and promulgating heretical doctrine. She had been examined by various theologians, including Bossuet, but a final and official verdict remained pending. Nonetheless, her reputation having preceded her among the court dévots, she was welcomed enthusiastically into their circle. Through the intervention of aristocratic women friends, including ultimately Madame de Maintenon herself, she was allowed to socialize at liberty with this entourage, whose gatherings included the charming young abbé Fénelon. Saint-Simon's characterization is famous: sneeringly dubbing this group "the little flock," for whom the "ambitious and smooth" Fénelon had become "the shepherd," he claimed that they had now become enamoured of Guyon's "passive way of prayer conducted gently 'without strain, without effort, without study, without artifice.'"[205] This "passive way of prayer" was the "prayer of simple repose" that we explored in chapter 1. But by using "passive" as part of his snide description of this prayer, Saint-Simon linked it with the heresy of Molinism, the implication being that such prayer is "lazy." And the term *passive*, as we shall see, will be a lightning rod in the ensuing debates about pure love.

Fénelon and Guyon had their first introduction at the Beynes country home of the Duchesse de Béthune-Charost (daughter of the former great minister Fouquet and the "great soul" of this devout circle, whose own daughter, Marie-Hippolyte, would become a Carmelite nun). The chateau, in addition to Saint-Sulpice back in Paris, was a favorite gathering place for the female members of the group, with whom Guyon had become especially popular, and allowed for relaxed, informal conversation. Most likely the Colbert daughters were all there, along with several priest spiritual directors.[206] The unspoken request would have been, "Please meet Madame, bon Père, and tell us what you think." As it turned out, after initial conversation, Fénelon and Guyon shared a coach-ride back to Paris. What a treasure it would be if we had a transcript of their conversation! He was cautious and wary at first (or, in his own words, "dry," "serious," and "cold" when first meeting people, but "warm and tender" inside)[207] because of her reputation for heterodoxy. But she pursued the acquaintance, wrote to him, and, after taking time to examine her writings, he decided to reciprocate. "His nature dry and calculating at first," says Louis Cognet, "revealed its complementary aspect: a childlike freshness, lively and spontaneous, maintained to the very end."[208]

Just exactly how to formulate the nature of their mutual attraction is difficult (and has led to massive amounts of speculative romanticizing), since it has to be surmised from the correspondence that rapidly accelerated after their first meeting, especially for the years 1689–90. Later interpreters have posited all manner of contrasts to convey the idea that they complemented one another in some fashion: he was cerebral and reserved, she more emotional and passionate; he was sophisticated and polished, she more down-to-earth and straightforward; he was more outward, she more inward; he was a son looking for a mother, she a mother looking for a son; and so on. There has also, of course, always been the hint of erotic attraction (he was thirty-seven, she forty), especially because in the *Autobiography* she uses phrases such as "spiritual filiation" and a "union increasing in a pure and ineffable manner" and "my soul has perfect rapport with his" to describe the early stages of their friendship, and there is constant reference in the letters to their "union"—which to a modern ear sounds suspect, but which was the standard language of mystical companionship.[209]

Louis Cognet suggests that Fénelon had become "cold" and "dry" in his spirituality and that she brought to him "a certain community in the inner life" and a more robust, less dry and cerebral "affectivity" that allowed him to renew spiritually.[210] Another way of looking at it is that he tended to be obsessional and at times excessively scrupulous and self-critical in his thinking, and she offered intelligent emotional support and wisdom that freed him for a less self-occupied, less fretful approach to inwardness.[211] I think also that, good Augustinian that he tried to be, he was still looking for a way out of the prison house of the sinful, self-loving human ego, *even at its virtuous best.* How can the "self" escape from the "self"? For all of his brilliant thinking and clarity of perception about the inner life, he needed an actual and sufficiently intelligent *mystic,* the real flesh-and-blood thing, with whom to dialogue, thereby getting him out of himself.

The correspondence is full and rich, and it is clear that they quickly established something like a peer partnership of spiritual direction, a relationship of mutual advice and correction on spiritual matters. "He offered many objections to me," she says at one point.[212] Each of them could be thoughtful and incisive, impassioned and sensitive, admonitory or consoling, commonsensical or subtle, in turns. They clearly respected and esteemed one another greatly as spiritually wise, and one senses that *that* was the main thing, if not the only thing. There is certainly a large element of opening their hearts to one another (at an almost oppressive level of insistence!), but it is in the manner, rightly pointed to by Goré,[213] of the male-female mutual mentoring typical of the period: Francis de Sales and Jeanne de Chantal, Teresa of Ávila and John of the Cross, for example, and numerous others. One would never describe their self-revelations in the letters as "inappropriately intimate," and yet their confidences are the deeply personal ("without reserve") admonishments and advice giving of friends.

Eventually Fénelon will become Guyon's defender in the charges of heresy with the argument that, saintly in her personal life, she was being willfully misunderstood because of exaggerations and clumsy expressions in her writing. But he was quick to add that, despite his spiritual friendship with her, the real issues at stake were ones of principle, of defending truth as such. At the height of the later controversy, Bossuet, enraged at Guyon, frustrated at his inability to separate Fénelon from her influence, and making use of the example of a notorious male-female pair of heretics from the early church, would accuse her of being "that Priscilla who has found her Montanus to defend her."[214] But the charge was ridiculous. The relationship was not only too formal for that, it was also marked on Guyon's part by a perfect willingness to be as affectionately critical of him as he could be of her.[215] He was eventually to say, once the fat was in the fire and he was on the defensive about the supposedly quietist ideas he had broached with Madame de Maintenon, that "in all of this the real issue is not [defending] Madame Guyon . . . it is really about me and about the depth of doctrine regarding the interior life."[216] Saint-Simon's opinion, cited by Melchior-Bonnet[217] and often repeated down through the centuries, that they became "spiritually amalgamated" is thus a kind of overstatement reflecting, perhaps, Guyon's effusive language as well as Saint-Simon's penchant for the witty turn of phrase.

Actually, the clearest statement of where he stood with her comes from Fénelon himself and is unambiguous. In one letter he says to her: "I am persuaded that you possess an eminent grace, along with the light of experience, for the ways of the inner life to an extraordinary degree, and I am quite convinced of the truth of the way of pure faith and of abandon—the way that you walk and that you help those to walk whom God has given you."[218] He esteemed and admired her. He then felt free to criticize her views on some things, including other people, as well as her unworldly incompetence in temporal affairs, "although I do not think you are ever mistaken about me." He could mistrust her judgment about many things, therefore, but never about *him in relation to God.* That was what mattered and it was what he needed, whatever people thought. Bremond tells us: "it was laughable for an archbishop to be directed by a woman, a contradiction of the natural order of things. We must relate this, however, to the Gospel-injunction to become as 'little children.'"[219] By his own words, then, we know that Fénelon claimed to have learned from her. It was learning about his own soul, but also about his soul in relation with God. What would that learning have been?

Molinos First

The short answer is that Guyon took him deeper into aspects of mystical teaching not necessarily identical with, but certainly by this time associated with, the ecclesiastically defined phenomenon of quietism. When Fénelon met her, Guyon was under royal censure and arrest for advocating ideas, especially in her books, perceived by authority as being akin to those of the Spanish priest Miguel de Molinos, who had been condemned at Rome (1687) on the basis of sixty-eight propositions dubbed "quietist errors" and believed to be found in his writings. One result of this condemnation and the enormous stir that surrounded it was that the term *quietist* was in the air and served as the brush with which to tar, with greatly varying degrees of justice,[220] a great many teachers and writers who, to some degree, shared in a common set of ideas.

Their arch-text was Molinos's book of 1675, *The Spiritual Guide (Who Disentangles the Soul and Leads It by Way of the Interior Road to the Possession of Perfect Contemplation and the Treasure of Inner Peace)*, a work with which Madame Guyon was familiar and some of whose ideas she seemed to perpetuate in her own publications, such as the *Spiritual Torrents*, the *Short and Very Easy Method of Prayer (Which All Can Practice with the Greatest Facility, and Arrive in a Short Time, by Its Means, at a High Degree of Perfection)*, and an early draft of the *Autobiography*. As Fénelon now acquainted himself with her work and inhaled, so to speak, its essence, he began to ponder the central tenets of Molinist quietism (although he later claimed not to have read Molinos early on, and, when he did, to be horrified at him) as Guyon had construed them. Let us, then, consider these characteristic emphases.

On the face of it, Molinos's spiritual teaching[221] in the *Guide* was premised on a traditional, popular, and uncontroversial distinction between the inner life of the individual and his outer, empirical person. The inner life is subjective, invisible, and knowable introspectively only to that individual and to God, while the outer life is objectively available to others for description and evaluation. The inner life is the life of the soul, and the outer life that of the body. During the seventeenth century people became intensely interested in this "inner self" even as the scientific understanding of the physical world made great strides. Immune to external observation, my inner life is uniquely "mine" and is understood as the arena of God's gracious activity in intellect, memory, and will. It is the place of moral valuing and decision making; it is the place where the individual can commune with God. The philosopher Charles Taylor reminds us that this sense of the "self" as an autonomous center and moral core to the personality with its own "space" gradually displaced the older view of the "soul" as a psycho-physical bit of the cosmic spirit in all of us and was, therefore, a hallmark of modernity.[222]

Two particularly important implications followed. One was the view that as individual selves we are constantly and privately faced with a fundamental choice of orientation, namely, whether to turn our moral energies back onto ourselves in the form of "self-love" or away from ourselves in the form of "other-love," that is, in the direction of God, the world, and the neighbor. A second implication, critical for Molinos's thinking, is the idea that the inner self as the preserve of autonomy is essentially inviolable by the outer world. It is the space where God can always be found in a powerful way, however helpless we may feel in the outer, exterior world.

It all sounds like Plato, of course. And like many seventeenth-century writers, Francis de Sales had already worked on this premise of the inner self and the "high point" of the soul, where God abides deep within us. There is a difference of tone, however, from de Sales that one notices right from the beginning of Molinos's *Spiritual Guide*. "Know that your soul is the center, the residence, and the kingdom of God . . . the divine fortress that defends you, protects you, and fights for you . . . [the] strong castle, which triumphs over your visible and invisible enemies," he says.[223] In other words, the inner self for Molinos is seen as *retreat* and refuge from an ugly world, a safe haven for disengagement from the world and its terrors and temptations. The interiority tradition of de Sales and Fénelon, on the other hand, moves in the opposite direction, that is, *toward* divine presence everywhere, starting with the discovery of God within the soul. The interior life is a refueling station, so to speak, for active discipleship in the world. By contrast, the *real* battles are fought deep within, says Molinos; because what is external is finally at best unimportant, or at the least, of merely secondary import.

In this retreat of the inner self Molinos wanted people to let go of anything outward, including the concrete representations and objects by which we ordinarily live. He wanted devout persons to practice the kind of contemplative prayer often called "abstract" or imageless, in which the one who prays no longer needs to strain after God by some sort of artfulness. The soul can relax and be succoured by the pure, wordless, totally nonmaterial presence of God. This, he said, is the prayer of "quietude and perfect contemplation such as few experience."[224] Most important, it is the means by which God teaches the soul to endure all forms of suffering, and not least of all that produced by the evil that sometimes is within the soul itself.

For indeed, according to Molinos, evil is everywhere and contaminates all human works, which are nothing but "vanity, satisfaction, and self-love" that "must be purified in the fire of tribulation and temptation so that they may become clean, pure, perfect, and agreeable to the divine eye." God uses this evil to draw souls inward to himself. Molinos invites the individual to "put her soul in the presence of God with perfect resignation through the act of pure faith" so that, as the wandering and anxious mind settles on God through "acquired contemplation," an interior state of alignment with the divine will ensues (called "infused contemplation"). In order to remain in the presence of God, only one act of resignation is necessary, never to be repeated. The endpoint is "mystical silence," whereby the soul steadies in a "perfect love," in which, all self-consciousness having been lost, every evil is quietly and peacefully endured "in continuous prayer and one continuous act of contemplation."[225]

Molinos mounts a strong argument that we are to be attentive to the condition of our own souls *before* attending to the welfare of others: "do not think that God favors the person who is most active; he is most loved who is most humble, most faithful, and resigned, and who best responds to divine approval and interior inspiration." A state of "holy inactivity" must precede action, so that room is left for the proper discernment of divine inspiration and vocation. When the individual falls into some relatively minor sin, she is encouraged by Molinos to be humbled by her weakness and to thank God that the sin was not any worse, thus avoiding the self-torments that are "the deceptions and golden whistles of Satan." Keep calm, ask forgiveness, let it go.[226]

Above all, says Molinos, be clear that there is an exterior perfection based on virtuous acts, holy deeds, and pious exercises that does not bring inner peace. Even more, such outward perfection may be quite dangerous, because it conduces to vanity and pride. But still more important, such exteriority does not bring the suffering of solitude, rejection, and persecution that is essential to real perfection. The soul *must* get to a place where "nothing new gladdens them, and no success saddens them," where exterior works count for nothing, where sensible feelings and spiritual counsels are discarded, and the negation of self-love becomes the key. There will follow a "spiritual martyrdom" and an "interior mortification" where "the truly humble person . . . suffers the trials of God, of men, and of the devil over all reason and discretion . . . exterior things upset him no more than if they were not."[227]

At this point, contends Molinos, the soul has become *passive* in the hands of God, ready to endure all that God sends and to be uplifted by God alone. "God is [then] likely to draw it [the humbled soul] up, elevating it without notice, to a perfect repose in which he gently and intimately infuses it with his light, love, and strength, kindling and inflaming it with a true disposition toward all kinds of virtue." "Loving Jesus has his paradise here in this interior retreat, to which we can rise while still existing and conversing on earth." The final state of the soul at this point is described by Molinos in the language of *nada*, where "the blows of adversity cannot reach" the inner fortress, as the soul "sleeps in nothingness" and "perfect annihilation" at "the mountain of tranquility."[228]

The intent and wisdom of Molinos's teaching was good and wise. There was nothing in his teaching that could not already be found in, for instance, the highly respected Spaniard John of the Cross before him. What brought down the papal condemnation were a number of specific points, however. In a recent assessment[229] of *The Spiritual Guide*, Bernard McGinn points to these: the view that imperturbable nonresistance to evil is sometimes the best defense; the idea of the "single, one act" of contemplative prayer; the simplification of love, prayer, and faith to a "single act" marked by indifference to reward; the emphasis on passivity in relation to God; the relativizing of external piety and spiritual disciplines; the language of the "annihilation" of the soul that seems to run counter to a Christian notion of created goodness. All of this can be summed up in the fear that constantly dogs quietist spirituality: the inner life is favored *at the expense of ordinary human obligation.* How can we really say that we love God if we do not love the neighbor at the same time and with equal seriousness? Molinos seems to encourage a piety in which there is an excessive disengagement from finite human existence. While the term is slightly too strong, there is, nonetheless, an air of paranoia about it.

While there is much modern agreement that all of this received exaggerated and unfair statement in the condemned propositions, it also had the effect of making Francis de Sales's language about "pure love," orthodox in that saint's writing, dangerous and problematic for others. After all, what is the valid distinction, say, between de Sales's "holy indifference" and Molinos's "holy inactivity"? Can love really be "pure" when we shift our mental focus away from our sins, maybe even stop actively fighting them? Can a state of prayerful communion with God be said to be "continuous" in any meaningful sense, or is the idea foolish fantasy? Here is some of the importance of the *Maxims of the Saints,* where Fénelon took up every one of these questions with great skill.

Bremond would have said that the core problem with Molinos is that his emphasis on the inner life is no longer a form of "devout humanism." Francis de Sales's emphasis on interiority *is* in fact a "devout humanism" because his interiority is meant to help us love the world, not fear and despise it. It will be the service of Fénelon to drive home the point that loving our natural selves and the world around us *precisely because God loves them and not as a form of self-glorification* is an important way of loving and serving the Creator-God. He will bend over backward later, while tussling with Bossuet, to argue that the sustained inward state of passive prayer is *not* exclusive of a continuing outward state of practical, upright discipleship, but in fact *demands* it.

What Fénelon does inherit from Molinos, at least indirectly through Guyon, is a deep sense for the darkness of mystical states. Francis de Sales has a certain "sunny side" to his spirituality, a buoyant optimism, that is one of his hallmarks and a great source of attraction. Not so Fénelon, who has by contrast a stronger awareness of the element of unavoidable misery and struggle in life, not least of all the life of prayer. For this reason he will pick up on Molinos's emphasis, again via Guyon, on suffering and then merge this focus with elements drawn from the French school and classical tragedy. But let us hear Madame Guyon first.

And Then Guyon

By contrast with Molinos, who favored the austere metaphor of the fortress in his analysis of the inner life, Guyon, in a manner that is pervasive in her writing, worked with a different set of deep metaphors. Her images for the soul seeking to love and be loved by God are those of intimate dependence first and, *only then*, passive helplessness second. The soul is the passionate and clinging bride of the bridegroom, the unquestioning child of the ever-caring, ever-present heavenly Parent, and, in one striking poem, an earthbound swallow, seeking to rise to the sky from a world "filthy as dung."[230] Most of all—at least so far as Fénelon was concerned—she made great use of the image of the soul as a baby nursing at its mother's breast, or the toddler held in its parent's arms, or "the harmless and undesigning child"[231] roaming the world. We have seen the relational imagery in Francis de Sales as well, whom Guyon read early on, but she developed its implications more luxuriantly and certainly more sentimentally. To the extent that she relies on Molinos, Francis de Sales is a counterbalance.

She tells us at the beginning of the *Short and Easy Method* that the "way of Simple Love and Pure Adherence" in prayer is open to everyone and that "nothing more is intended by it than to invite the simple and child-like to approach their Father, who delights in the humble confidence of His children" since Jesus loves "simplicity and innocence." This simplicity of a child is the heart of prayer, and "prayer," she says in the *Autobiography*, "is the only way to Heaven," so long as it is "prayer of the heart, which everybody is capable of, and not of those reasonings which are the fruits of study, or exercise of the imagination." The essential activity of the "heart" in prayer is love: "none can exempt himself from loving; for none can live without a heart, nor the heart without love."[232]

Those few words capture her central spiritual project. The *Spiritual Torrents* was written to describe the experience of rapture that arises from intense closeness with God; the *Short and Easy Method* was written as a spiritual guide into that same experience; the *Autobiography* was her apologia to her critics; and a short work entitled the *Abstract*, prepared initially for Fénelon, is her schematic outline of the stages of mystical ascent to union with God. We can certainly say with a recent critic[233] that her work was "not the 'pure gush' that her more maladroit friends claimed to see in her," but that it was *mystical*, that is, a product of personal experience that tends to clothe itself in metaphors that may be over-expressive, exaggerated, incautious, and loaded with implications unintended by the one who uses them. Louis Cognet claims that, despite her tendency to overstatement, she was in fact "an excellent theoretician of the theopathic state," that is, of the form of suffering entailed in closeness to God.[234] Indeed, her evocative use of language, rich with possibilities, is precisely what attracted the humanist Fénelon to her and precisely what made her so intuitively insightful with regard to his spiritual struggles.

Guyon's principal tool and prime technical implement for the life of prayer, and thus for knowing and loving God, is the inward-turning, inward-operating "prayer of simplicity." Like Molinos, and Francis de Sales before him, she urges souls to rise above a reliance on the artifices of meditative prayer, where our senses become "dissipated" with a multiplicity of distractions.[235] Much like the ceaseless reiteration of the Jesus prayer in the Eastern Orthodox *Way of a Pilgrim*, the prayer of simplicity overcomes the jumble of voiced prayers with many words in order to become *a single point of focus within the soul*, outwardly silent and inwardly mindful of the presence of God. In a famous phrase, everything else is "allowed to fall away [*laisser tomber*]," robbed, so to speak, of its psychic valence as just so much distraction—whether this be the accumulated and emotion-laden baggage and stimuli that fill one's memory, or the present temptations that lead to habitual and willfully corrupt behaviors. Then, as the soul lets go, it yields to a state of abandonment, a kind of free-floating relaxation into the divine "holding." There is a "feeding upon" the divine presence and a "swallowing" of what this presence offers, in which the mind is steadied, focused, calmed, but also enflamed with the passion of unqualified loving gratitude.

We will learn later from her conversations with Fénelon that the technique of such prayer varies, but often, as a reaction to formalism and in the mode of the "child," it will take the form of many short, brief, ejaculatory, unpremeditated cries to God in the course of ordinary ongoing activities. Fénelon will, in his letters of direction, often speak of the importance of yielding to one's *attrait* in prayer, the attracting pull of God's spirit in some particular direction. Today we might speak of "spontaneous flow" in prayer, where a sustained and energized rhythm finally leads to insight and then enhanced self-control. The important thing is to be able to break free from structure, when appropriate, but always returning to the structure, so to speak, as a base. In any case, the implication is that simple prayer, practiced faithfully, moves the individual toward a mental "steady state," passive/receptive and increasingly unconscious, rather than being a conscious series of discrete, temporally bounded acts or speech formulations. The distinguishing mark of this steady state will be "tender affection," in which "a pure and disinterested love, as seeks nothing from God, but the ability to please Him, and to do His will," will predominate.[236]

But second, and absolutely central to the dynamic by which the mind is empowered to turn to God, she said, is the experienced misery of life when it is separated from God by sin, this separation being comparable to the pain felt by a lover toward the beloved because of some infidelity, or "a feeble child, sorely bruised by repeated falls." In the *Autobiography* she everywhere describes this misery in terms of the tormented conscience, painfully aware of the least fault, not least of all *at moments of high virtue and "natural" goodness*, and then, she says, "at this time it is of great importance to know how to make use of this pain, and on this depends almost the whole advancement or retardation of souls." The essence of sin is self-love, and the consequence of self-love is that when sinners make a serious effort to approach God, dryness and emptiness, "a purgatory, amorous yet at the same time rigorous," must be the result.[237]

And there is the key, for Fénelon, to much of her thought: spiritual dryness and its pain are the signs of grace, indeed, *are* grace at work in the soul. Dryness is the way to love. It is why he can say later that "privations are the bread of the strong." The experience of dryness, *rightly understood*, has the effect not of producing an insatiable craving or despair, but rather a liberating sense of conscious detachment from desire and its satisfaction as the central need of the soul. *Desire itself* is not eradicated as something evil, but rather it is freed to rise to its final destination (recall her use of the swallow image above).

In the tradition of Guyon, it is when I discover that *I* am my problem, with all my little wants and wishes, and I realize that I must get this *me* out of the way in order to find God, on my knees, that the real work begins. Part of the *me* is the thrill, the felt pleasure, so to speak, that I am always seeking from God. The devotee comes to see that the hunger for God must become a hunger for what God wants, not what we want, and that if you yearn for a life with God, it must be on God's terms, not your own. The spiritual fruit of this shift in the soul's orientation is what Fénelon calls "dry peace," which is the renunciation of the normal concomitants of satisfaction, but also freedom from insistent cravings as well. Such a transformation of human desire must be painful, must be filled with suffering, which is to say that "God gives us the cross, and then the cross gives us God." The suffering that brings us to God as helpless infants is sacrificial, beautiful, necessary, gracious. The result is the abandonment of self, the reduction of the self to nothing (called in French *néantisme* or "nothingness-ism"), in order to be reborn with God.

She went on in this vein to argue that as the soul moves into the bliss of child-parent relation with the all-nurturing God, as it withdraws within and pulls away from the sensory world of outward experience, the "potent magnetism of the center itself," that is, the attractive power of God, takes control, and the soul moves to a paradoxical state of voluntary passivity.[238] That is, the soul freely chooses a state of utter receptivity to God, and this state becomes stable. There is no "deadness" here, but rather the aliveness of actively willing not to will, to be in complete surrender with a "tender love" for God. As the soul begins to suckle at the divine breast, or, alternatively, basks in the light of the rising sun, it enters the condition of "mystic rest," or repose, in God. Another telling image from the *Autobiography* for describing the soul's rest in God is that it is "as a wife seated near her husband knows it is he that embraces her, without saying to herself, 'It is he,' and without occupying her thought with it." Prayer is now simple, continuous, and silent, and "sin seems so far removed from the believer at this point that he is hardly even aware of it." Indeed, the consciousness of sin continues to exist only in the sense that anything that impedes closeness with God is abhorrent, so that even the remembrance of sin and its consequent remorse is discarded.[239]

She further contended that as the state of repose in God becomes prolonged and finally habitual in the life of the adept, there is such a conformity to the divine will by the human will that "He takes from you all your own workings so that *His* may be substituted in their place." "As soon as the milk of divine grace flows smoothly, we have nothing to do but, in repose and stillness, sweetly to imbibe it; and when it ceases to flow, we must again stir up the affections [return to meditation] as the infant moves its lips." In the process called "disappropriation," she says in the *Autobiography*, the soul, submitted to the divine Love, is purified of all "restriction, unlikeness, and '*ownness*,'" that is, ceases to have a sense of possessing its own separateness and distinctness from God's will. She acknowledges that the "self nature," the selfish and carnal/worldly side of the person, continues to exist, but only as a kind of pinprick and reminder that total abandonment to God must be repeatedly embraced.[240]

Furthermore, like Molinos she contended that the antidote to sin is not confrontation, but an ignoring of the temptation, or, if the sin is committed, a relinquishment of remorse, in order to turn back toward God afresh. The "giving up of self" must be total, since "everything else is a lie. God is All; you are nothing." In the annihilation of self, "prayer [becomes] a dissolving and an uplifting of the soul. The warmth of love, this melting, this dissolving and uplifting causes the soul to ascend to God . . . in a consuming fire of love in [its] inmost being, a fire of love for God." She insists that in all of this the soul remains active, but *only* by God's leading, and in a way that is the antithesis both of laziness and of self-initiation at the same time. She spoke here of a "continuous, inner act of abiding [that] begins to take place within you," which is a "passive consent" on the part of the soul to all of the suffering entailed in the required purification. "The thing called *activity* is, in itself, opposed to union . . . because God is an infinite stillness."[241]

— So, to Fénelon's everlasting credit, once he had met Guyon and had had a chance to assess her ideas, at least in a preliminary way, he knew he was dealing not so much with a theologian but with a practical religious genius. Guyon had managed to extract from her own conversion and struggles a psychology of inner experience, which she then elaborated into a technique of spiritual guidance. In this process she seemed to have brought the quietist doctrine within the bounds of orthodoxy in an attractive fashion. Thus, after some careful reading and some sustained conversation, Fénelon decided that there was an eminently trustworthy foundation to her spirituality, as long as one was clear that her gift was *literary* but not doctrinally precise expression.

She was definitely a breath of fresh air in the stifling, stilted atmosphere of the court. And her troubled, tormented personal situation made her *real*, as we say. She was not doing academic theology—although, as we will note, she could theorize. We do not know how quickly or in what order Fénelon perused her writings, but there are indications early on that he read her biblical commentaries, especially the one on the Song of Songs where she develops her mystical teachings on the relationship between the soul and God as that of two lovers, and an early draft of her *Autobiography*.

She also prepared a *Summary* or *Abstract* of her thinking on the "states," as they are called, of the soul as it moves into closer, mystical relation with God. It is in Fénelon's critical comments on this work, in the letter of August 11, 1689, that we will see his own view of how he absorbed and began to rework her ideas. But before we view how he pushed back against her thought—and push back he did—it is important to appreciate how he metabolized it. He immersed himself in her writings, started a vital correspondence with her, began his tutorial labors with the young dukes, and became an intimate of the royal household at Versailles all at about the same time.

Saint-Cyr: One More Twist

It is precisely at this point, where Fénelon and Guyon are forming a close relationship, that the context starts to become more complicated. The increase came from the redoubtable Françoise d'Aubigné, Marquise de Maintenon. After being for some years Louis XIV's mistress and consort, as mentioned, she became at some indeterminate point in a secret ceremony his (unannounced and morganatic) second wife. As a participant in the circle of dévots, she had become an enthusiastic follower of some of Guyon's ideas, and she was beginning to appreciate Fénelon as well. She saw both of them as admirable and skilled spiritual teachers, and, with Fénelon already serving as preceptor for Louis's grandson, she wanted their help with her special and deeply beloved project. This was the organizing and running of Saint-Cyr, an elite boarding school adjacent to Versailles, created for the daughters of aristocratic officers killed in battle, and staffed by a specially recruited women's religious order, the Dames of Saint-Louis.[242] Maintenon functioned as the grand patron of this thoughtfully progressive institution, which "would be an indelible work for forming perfect young women, the future spouses and mothers who would bear the children of the Christian France of tomorrow."[243]

It would be hard to overstate Maintenon's personal and emotional investment in Saint-Cyr: she considered the young nuns of the faculty "her dear daughters," and she used the premises of the school as a kind of nest, her place of personal retreat. A special piece of music had been composed, so that it could be played whenever she visited a class for a royal inspection. But there had been problems with discipline and good order at the school, and she needed the best help she could find. We know that by the early months of 1690 she had enlisted both Guyon and Fénelon as helpers in this endeavor. In addition to seeking some degree of personal direction from both of them, she approved their special role as adjunct spiritual directors for selected members of Saint-Cyr's faculty and student body. Indeed, in time Fénelon's influence would be pervasive.[244]

All of this was very well, but it also was a situation of crossing lines of authority, where a powerful lay patron of a convent school, the local bishop with canonical authority, a women's religious order with its own hierarchy, and various individuals such as Guyon and Fénelon invited to offer direction would eventually operate at cross-purposes. Opportunities for dysfunction were legion, and in due course Guyon and Fénelon were both caught in the middle of a hothouse atmosphere of gossip, intrigue, and miscommunication. This is a partial help in explaining why Maintenon first loved Guyon and Fénelon, respecting their teaching and needing their help, but then, when things blew up, became bitterly disappointed and enraged with them.

The Impact of Guyon

With this increasingly embroiled context in mind, some consideration of what Fénelon was taking in from Guyon and from the quietist-Molinist background to some of her thought is in order. How did the quietist teaching sit with him, particularly in Guyon's form? The answer is that it had a powerful appeal, especially where it was consistent with, or even coincided with, and finally sharpened, what he already knew and believed from de Sales and the French school. Guyon had managed to create "an extremely profound theory of mystical purification" by means of which Fénelon "entered the way of annihilation . . . realized by the spirit of being a child."[245] J.-F. Marquet adds the related idea that Guyon's theory drew much of its energy from an intense vision "of the love of God under its aspect of *tremendum*," that is, God's love not as beautiful and comforting but as overpowering and humanly annihilating.[246] She thereby drew together threads of French school spirituality represented particularly by Benedict Canfield with elements from the Spaniard John of the Cross, as well as from the Rheno-Flemish mystics such as John of Ruysbroeck. This was new territory for Fénelon. He wrestled with these ideas and partially absorbed them, but he also partially critiqued them.

According to her *Autobiography*, the integrating event of Madame Guyon's spiritual journey, which then provided the central theme in her teaching—to which Fénelon responded with great enthusiasm—was a "mystic marriage" with the Child Jesus on July 22, 1672, immediately after the shattering death of her father and her first daughter. In the spiritual contract she made with God, she pledged herself "to take for my spouse Our Lord, the Child, and to give myself to him for spouse, though unworthy." "I asked of him," she said, "as dowry of my spiritual marriage, crosses, scorn, confusion, disgrace, and ignominy; and I prayed him to give me the grace to enter into his dispositions of littleness and annihilation."[247] Her course was set, then, within the inextricably tight bond of marriage to the Child and the inexpressible suffering entailed. Not long after there followed a seven-year period of total deprivation of her human faculties, a state of complete enfeeblement, with a sense of being utterly bereft of God, with a deathlike quality,[248] followed by later quasi-monastic vows of poverty, chastity, and obedience to the Child Jesus. The emphasis placed on the parent-child relationship with God in her writings grew out of her personal experience. Here is the hook for Fénelon.

For Fénelon, newly immersed in the rituals, affairs, intrigues, and social pressures of the court of Louis XIV, where looking good and acting smartly are the greatest values, there is no greater spiritual danger than falseness, or, as we say, just "going through the motions." Even worse would be to use religion for merely personal advantage (as we know some did by feigning devotion after it became popular because of a somewhat deepened religious seriousness on the part of Louis XIV). The main problem is not *no* religion—which is bad enough—but *corrupt* religion, which is much worse. Saint-Simon, as well as La Bruyère (two of the best-known contemporary observers) constantly note the pervasiveness of religious hypocrisy among the aristocracy and at court, and they, of course, treat this hypocrisy with withering contempt.[249] What Fénelon then wants as a pastor, more than anything else, is spiritual sincerity and truthfulness, for people to be *real* in their faith. He wants faith and love, not posturing and calculating. The practical challenge is one of formulating spiritual teaching for those who are serious, for those, in the language of the time, who seek *perfection*, and to do so in a way that is accessible and attractive. Recalling, then, that Jesus himself had said that no one enters the kingdom except in the way of a small child, the central idea of the Guyon-inspired deepening of his spirituality will be that we must learn the "simplicity of a child" in our relations with God, for only *then* will faith and love be "pure."

From the very beginning of their correspondence,[250] the references to becoming like "children" and acquiring "simplicity," both with God and with one another, are omnipresent for Guyon and Fénelon as nodal centers for clusters of ideas and concepts. Bremond has helped us to see the background.[251] He contends that within the spirituality of the French school the need for a true devotion to God, in which human pretense, pride, and egocentricity are laid aside, was captured by emphasizing the importance of adherence to the Word Incarnate in the Child Jesus. In the terminology of Bérulle, the infancy of Jesus is the first "state" of the incarnate Lord, with which the believer must identify. This state, representative of the self-emptying of God in the Incarnation, bespeaks a human reality, that is, the neediness and utter dependence of the small child. Through this evoking of childhood experience we are reminded that children cannot survive except by looking to adults who shelter and care for them, but also that it is by charm and lovability, by sweetness, that they secure this adult care. This aspect of devout humanism then became with the Sulpicians the doctrine that "except ye adhere to my state of Infancy," says Jesus, "ye shall not enter the kingdom of heaven" (Matt. 18:3).

Childhood is now equated with the loss of self in death, complete helplessness, as well as the passivity and receptivity of being in a subordinate, powerless position. The child must be self-abandoned to the care of the higher power, so that, says Bremond, "the austerity of this doctrine is at once transformed into gentle sweetness; abandonment takes the place of annihilation, 'simplicity' that of self-ignoring."[252] So, strictly speaking—Fénelon somewhat pushes back here—the renunciation of the self in order to become a child is not self-*cancellation*, but rather the recovery or rebirth of a *purified* self. It is precisely here that the effusions of Molinos, but especially of Guyon, must be disciplined by clear thinking! For the humanist Fénelon this language of radical change must be handled skillfully or its tendency to extravagance will bankrupt it.

So, what is the "simplicity" of a graced "child"—a hunger that Guyon understood and to which she ministered—for Fénelon? Essentially, it is this decision to go "within," to make a deep commitment to interiority in the search for closeness with God by turning away from an entangling and primary investment in the "outer" world of daily cares, tasks, and responsibilities (the "adult" world, we might say). And this is *not because the outer world is unimportant or contemptible, but because it normally operates in terms of the dynamics of self-love.* The outer world is *not* simple, because it requires one to play roles, to maneuver, to engage in customary and ritualized behavior of all sorts, to make moral compromises, to become enmeshed in social and political structures that by their falseness, artificiality, and constant demand for accommodation cause one to lose God. One way to say this in modern jargon might be to argue that the *opposite* of being a child is narcissistic grandiosity, the sense of being "special." This is the tendency to define our sense of self in terms of something unrealistically big, outsized, and wonderful in the world, as well as to see ourselves through the admiring eyes of others. It is a kind of bondage to the perceptions that (we think or we hope) others have of us. It is to imagine that I am "everything," when, in fact, says Fénelon, I must realize that I am "nothing."

We should recall how hard Fénelon worked to develop the "simplicity" of the inner life for his young royal charges, so that they would not be vulnerable to the constant flood of fawning and manipulative flattery at Versailles.[253] La Bruyère's description can serve: "A man who knows the ways of the court is a master of his gestures, his eyes and his face; he is deep, impenetrable; he pretends not to notice injuries done him, he smiles at his enemies, controls his temper, disguises his passions, belies his heart, speaks and acts against his real opinions."[254] "Shrewdness," played well but never overplayed, is the name of the game, and hypocrisy is the order of the day, says La Bruyère! What a trap for all of us, but especially for the powerful in worldly terms. The "simplicity" of the "child" in his inner life with God, says Fénelon, is precisely the antithesis of all this.

Another way of describing the opposite of "simplicity" would be "self-conscious technique," that is, the utilization of traditional means of devotion in a methodical, carefully regulated, "correct" way. Some of the most distinguished interpreters of Fénelon have suggested that his spiritual practice prior to the influence of Madame Guyon was just that way.[255] He would have relied heavily on vocal prayers, meditative reading, material images that stir pious affections, prostrations for mortification and contrition, the use of the Breviary at set daily times, and so on. At different times he prescribed all of these practices—for himself as well as for others. He then suffered "scruples," anxiety about the correctness of his practice, and then "dryness," or the disappearance of the satisfactions, or "consolations," that these traditional practices are supposed to provide. As he would say later, valuable though all of this is, it should lead to a progressive loss of the "me" in devotion, and the problem is that frequently it does not, but even perversely increases it.

A Relationship Marked by "Simplicity"

The behavioral correlate of being a "child" is "simplicity." Fénelon and Guyon worked at this in their relationship. The challenge for both of them was one of not compromising with the ethos of the court and its self-protective falseness.

Thus, a number of behaviors can be labeled "simple." In his first letter to Guyon Fénelon urges her to be completely obedient in submitting her history, as well as her ideas, to the judgment of the authorities, hiding nothing about herself and maintaining a disposition of openness, while carefully protecting the privacy of others.[256] In many letters he repeatedly urges her not to worry about being a nuisance, not to engage in an artificial circumspectness, not to yield to "willful reserve" in revealing herself to him, but to be perfectly straightforward and forthcoming with whatever is in her heart. The phrase "without reserve" is everywhere in their correspondence as the manifestation of "abandon," so that the ultimate sin, it is implied, is to "hold back" through motives of "worldly prudence" in their candor with one another and with God.

Such straightforwardness will include, of course, her honesty in scolding him when *he* fails to be simple: "Whenever you find me being too wise," he says, "tell me to be simple." In an important letter in early 1689, after their relationship had sufficiently ripened, he agreed to her request to call him "her child" (a request about which she was apparently troubled, although in the *Autobiography* she refers to "the true maternity" in which the "children" given by God are "united with me in charity."[257] He urges her to "follow freely the bent that God gives to your heart" and "to open yourself to that consideration [calling him "child" in token of his degree of spiritual maturity] without any reserve and to help me by it to enter into childlike simplicity."[258]

In some cases, where the opposite of "simple" is "reflected upon" or "self-conscious," Fénelon realized that he was not being simple precisely when he analyzed his behavior or deliberated about it in a guarded, or cautious, or self-critical way (that is, in the form of "reasonings" leading to incertitude). The goal by contrast should be an interiorly unguarded, "supple" spontaneity in which God can speak immediately, and in the moment, to the individual soul, ready to hear and ready to respond in obedience, because the conscious need to "screen" what the Holy Spirit is saying has been transcended. The way Fénelon will say this in mature formulations is that God's will can begin to replace our own, when our reliance on "perceived" marks of grace is discarded and we trust God to move us interiorly, constantly, unfailingly.

As Melchior-Bonnet says,[259] "simplicity" and "peace" for Fénelon have the status of the "signature of God" on the soul: peace, which is "dry, astringent, deprived of the felt joy of God's presence," is the outward mark of inner simplicity, where "the positive, free, response of the finite creature to the glory of the infinite God" can have room for the "play" of the child of God. Then God's love, pure love, provides the motivational energy and direction for our activity of pure love.

So it is that Fénelon uses "simple" to capture an element of innocence, as in his human, nonculpable need for amusements: "sometimes when I'm alone, I play like a little child, even in making prayer. It happens sometimes that I can jump and laugh when alone, like a fool in my room."[260] Indeed, it becomes clear that both Guyon and Fénelon appeal to the image of the "child" as a way to break through to immediacy in experience, to bypass the tendency of our observing, sometimes critical, ego to short-circuit the energy and richness of this present moment, when God is *here* right now—and absolutely nothing else matters. Sometimes, too, "simple" is the opposite of a narcissistic prickliness and sensitivity, in which the difficulties in dealing with other people are always seen as a personal insult or affront, rather than a God-given opportunity for deeper understanding. Here "simple" becomes almost equivalent to "humble," lacking in self-importance, and, *therefore*, truly patient with others.

But we also discover in the early correspondence between the two spiritual masters that "simple" becomes a code word for consistent, even, steady, almost unchanging as it pertains to our spiritual dispositions, that is, our mental states in relation to God. Lack of simplicity suggests a kind of effort of my thinking ego to distance itself, because of something unpleasant or unsatisfactory, from what I am actually feeling and experiencing in this present moment. It is what happens when the analyzing mind gets in the way of the heart flowing free, *either positively or negatively*. In that first letter to Guyon he advises her to *stick with* the disposition God has given her at the moment, to honor it, difficult though it may be, and not flee from it. Elsewhere, she urges him to remain quiet in the midst of "repugnances," perhaps feelings of disgust or animosity toward some behavior, in the conviction that as he lets go of his own will to engage in some aversive response, God's purposes will be revealed in and through the very experience of these. Likewise, constant "importunities" from other people are seen not as miserable burdens to be minimized, but as gracious opportunities to be embraced. *What is* is good within divine providence (this is quite different from saying: *What is* is what God *wants*). Nonreactiveness can be outward, for instance, with no behavioral response, such as retaliation, but also inward, with no emotional response, such as getting angry at what or whom you don't like.

What then emerges is the fact that *dryness and distraction* are the dominant disposition, as in Fénelon's frequent complaints of an increasing sense of tedium and apathetic listlessness in ordinary affairs and relations: "sometimes I feel nothing in my heart for God to the extent that I find myself dry, empty, and occupied with trivialities."[261] But Guyon has the interpretation that is precious to Fénelon: "the heart attracted to God has only disgust for that which impedes its joyful play . . . the one who loves perfectly is completely dead to self. Being in an essential union [with God], the soul is in a state of possession which cannot be interrupted by the encumbrance of creatures." The point is that the prolonged, not just passing, dryness and distraction are intentional, providential, necessary, because they are the essential hallmarks of the soul detaching from enmeshment with the external environment and moving in the direction of a childlike clinging to God. But God is not warm and fuzzy, we might say—God is a raging forest fire and the divine presence is scorching and desiccating. The dryness *is* gracious, as long as (*pourvu que*—"provided that" is a frequent qualifier for Fénelon) we do not despair utterly.

Their correspondence is full of many variations on this theme, which is the chief contribution that Guyon made to Fénelon—the constant reminder that mystic "repose," the peace of the heart that rests in God, must be cruciform if it is genuine, and that this cruciformity has degrees and stages that can be mapped. Further, these stages can be, in modern parlance, operationalized, that is, formulated as a practical program of mystical growth. Its application, though, requires a high degree of discernment and skill on the part of the teacher, not least of all because, as we saw with Molinos himself, the ability to maintain such a quiet state is premised on the willingness to let stimuli coming from the *outside* (including thoughts from one's rational mind, as well as temptations of every kind) "fall away," recede from one's awareness, so that one "falls back" into God. Today we might say that distractions—and everything outside is a distraction—must be *gently* ignored. Let us, however, acknowledge a paradox in the language being used by Guyon and Fénelon (if it is not actually a contradiction!): if I am to resist being "distracted" by the world around me, does this mean that I am disengaged from it, don't care about it? How can I not be "distracted" by my children, while refusing to ignore them? The psychological answer, I believe Fénelon would have said (and as we shall see), is that my attention to them will cease to be *anxious*, and thus will come from a trusting calmness (a "quiet") deep within me.

Let us also admit that this combining of the theme of the cross with that of the child, although it is absolutely central, is counterintuitive, since we do not normally think of children as suffering.[262] In fact, the "child" in Guyon's language is not "childish" or infantile. The agony of love, if it *really* is love, is extreme, since this is about the adult becoming a child again, and *that* entails the letting go of one's own ego, which eventually will prove to be painful on a number of levels. We see from their correspondence that Guyon helped Fénelon focus, ponder from various angles, metabolize, and integrate this truth into the structure of his thought. And this is an absolutely critical point.

Guyon will teach Fénelon by means of a kind of cognitive reframe that the dryness and deadness he experienced in the inner life, the lack of *goût*—of relish or delight—from all of his traditional practices, are precisely the marks of one who is drawing closer to God in being reduced to nothingness, where self-abandon is the endpoint and God awaits. Dryness only *seems* to be a dead end, when it is actually the beginning of a new start. As he will say later in my favorite aphorism: "Privations are the bread of the strong."

A few examples will serve. In one place he says, "I continue to feel together with dryness and distraction a great deal of peace in prayer. I have a presence of God which is sweeter and easier." Elsewhere he has a meditation on Isaiah 54, in which he notes that the church is "the rejected and sterile spouse" marked by a "sterility full of tribulation," precisely so that she can attract others to the letting go of self that is a sharing in God's grace. In a remarkable image he speaks of the way that God "breaks all of the branches by which my spirit seeks to take hold . . . in the midst of waves . . . and which plunges me again into the obscure abyss of pure abandon." And there is his description of a frustrating experience that led to self-laceration and then self-release, an experience in which he believed that he had been hardhearted toward someone in need: "I feel myself so dry and languishing that I'm like a boat with no oars or sails, with my heart pulling at me and my face sweaty; not that I'm making interior efforts, but because the majority of exterior things are painful for me, since God pursues me, not leaving anything for natural movement, which he has withdrawn from me, so that the taste of peace in prayer diminishes. Sometimes I amuse my senses a little, in order to steady myself in a simple, easy recollection; and indeed, far from being troubled by this sensory amusement, it on the contrary makes me more peaceful. *I'm like a child who has been given a toy to keep it from running about, and that enables it to have food and rest with the nurse."*[263]

Now, I mentioned earlier that in due course Fénelon "pushed back"—critiqued—some of Guyon's ideas. It is important to see this for two reasons, one substantive and the other circumstantial. The first is that as a theologian he felt the necessity of toning down overstatement, and sometimes misstatement, in her teaching. The second is that his criticism should completely lay to rest any opinion that he was unduly influenced for the worst by her. The extraordinary thing here is that a man, Fénelon, who has allowed himself to be a "child" with "mother" advising him, suddenly bites back, as it were. In truth, though, he had in no way abdicated his sharp intellectual capacity. So, let us hear what he had to say in a pointed, yet withal gentle, way.

The critical letter is the one from Fénelon to Guyon on August 11, 1689. He is responding to the *Abstract* of her teaching that he had requested. The tone is businesslike and scholarly, even. He summarized and synthesized her doctrine on the "states" of the soul in mystical ascent—that is, of the soul as it increasingly becomes a simple child in the arms of God—and he raised two critically important questions. Precisely as he treasures but then critiques her thinking, we are reminded of Bremond's statement that Fénelon found "her experience to be good and rich, full of edification, but she wrote too much, a hundred times too much, and was too incautious. What mattered was that she was full of Spirit!"[264]

At the outset of the letter he states matters politely. He indicates that he wishes her to know how he understands her thought and where he is still confused, but this latter statement is a way of saying "where I have substantial reservations." He is clear that the first degree, or state, of the soul's approach to God is that of the active mortification of the exterior senses, particularly in the form of a progressive reduction of multiple prayers to a single, sustained, inner prayer. The second state is that of "passive faith," "passive" because God is allowed to take control by removing all pleasure, all relish, from the inner life of the believer. This begins the time of "dryness." The third degree is that of a general deprivation, in which the "gifts," or marks, of faith are gradually removed by God, thereby leaving the believer with no reassurances that his faith is intact and functioning. This is where faith becomes "bare" or "nude," so that even the prior dryness, which could be seen as a sign of gracious activity, is gone, being replaced by emptiness. This is where the believer ceases to have faith in faith, so to speak, and now has nowhere to turn except toward God.

The fourth degree is that of death, in which God "disappropriates" (Guyon's word) the soul from itself by removing all sense of its having a will or mind of "its own." All "natural" movement by the soul is gone. The result is that everything that God chooses to impose on the soul is accepted completely—because it is completely acceptable. This is what Fénelon means when he says that nothing is now "repugnant" to the soul, because, being dead to itself, it no longer has the will to offer any kind of resistance to God or to what God presents, and thus it no longer experiences sentiments of disgust, aversion, or the like. The fifth degree is that of resurrection, where the soul, dead and denuded, begins to receive in an utterly passive way all the new impressions that God wishes to work in it.

In this fifth degree Fénelon introduces a subtlety. It is as if he is saying to Guyon, "Now, wait a minute here." He argues that the "passivity" with which the soul receives God's new impressions is an "active passivity," by which he means that the soul elects to endure, to receive, to undergo, to be "supple" to all that God sends by way of transformation. In the fourth state the soul had been disappropriated of its "own-ness" by remaining totally and passively inert to the deprivations imposed by God (we would say: the soul "just took it"), but now it embraces the suffering God sends (we would say: the soul "takes it in and digests it" or "works with it"). Nonaction has indeed been replaced by action, as the soul moves closer to God. Fénelon is ever mindful of the fact that the Council of Trent had said that the free human soul *cooperates* with sanctifying grace. In this way, Fénelon began to introduce crucial qualifications into Guyon's language about the passivity of the soul, and these distinctions would prove to be critical in the debates to follow. Suffering still has to be endured as the supreme form of being God's child, but now *creatively*.

The sixth state is that of complete transformation, in which the soul's will is entirely replaced by that of God; the soul's heart, as it were, beats with the "heart" of God. The annihilation of the "self" of the soul is finished. The action of the soul has become completely divine, because it *cannot* sin. This is what Louis Cognet means by referring to "practical impeccability" in Guyon's description of the beatified soul completely reposed in God's loving arms. The soul is now "pure" with the purity of God.[265]

Then Fénelon produces his two explicit concerns. The first is that it is confusing to speak, as Guyon does, of the "disappropriation" or loss of "selfness" on the part of the soul as long as any purification remains to be done. Thus, even in mystical "death" there is still a real degree of self left to the soul. While it is this self that carries a remaining element of impurity in the soul, nevertheless this self is part of the soul's nature as spirit, not a mark of sin or corruption, like rust on metal. This is an Augustinian way of saying that as long as we are mortal and live on this earth, there must always be some element of "selfness" in our nature, or we would cease to exist; having a "self" is essential to our created nature. It is also a way of saying that free will, thus moral responsibility, remains intact even in the most "passive" state. The fact that Fénelon chooses to push back against Guyon here will always preserve him from unfair charges of heretical "angelism," that he believed we could be morally perfect, or morally "above it all," on this earth. As long as we are human and mortal, the *propensity* to sin will exist, and we are sinners.

The second objection is even more interesting. It is all very well to speak of the "darkness" of bare faith, but this darkness, he insists, is not blindness, seeing nothing at all. The obedience of faith will always be reasonable, he says, never a cascade into irrationality and madness. "Fanaticism and extravagant enthusiasm" are out of the question, he contends, because faith is always faith *in God*, which means for him that there are sure signs of revelation, such as Scripture, which one can trust, no matter what. The "obscurity" and "darkess" of faith pertain to the "mysteries" revealed in Scripture, spiritual truths that transcend human reasoning but that are not arbitrary and nonsensical. This, again, is a stock Augustinian argument, one that Augustine used forcefully against the Donatist separatists. We submit to authority because that is a *rational* thing to do. "Pure faith," then, says Fénelon (here he believed himself consistent with John of the Cross), is the soul's vision of the truth of the Gospel, truth spoken by God and thus always ultimately more than the human intellect can grasp, but never less than it can grasp.

Thus, faith always possesses its proper certitude, even in the darkest of dark nights, and it is by this that we know that it is *God, even though "hidden,"* who is leading us and not a concoction of our own fantasy. Part of what always remains unclear is whether *I* am being faithful to God's way, but never whether *God* is being faithful to me, or the way that he has laid out. Although we must learn to be indifferent to our salvation, to leave *that* matter in God's hands, we can never be indifferent to the possibility of illusion or gross sin. It is precisely here that Fénelon "covers himself" against charges of quietist immorality and "illuminism" (special revelations given by God to privileged individuals). He also sidesteps the view known as "fideism," which says that Christian belief is *solely* a matter of believing without recourse to the structures of human reasoning. His concluding statement is that a purified soul "will have all of the clarity and all of the certitude that are necessary for an upright conscience, and that all that it does is the purest reason; it lacks only 'reflective' [i.e., analytic-rational] clarity, which is what nature wishes to have in order to support its own virtue by a movement of self-ness." Guyon took all of this, we might say, "on the chin," but she did so gracefully by offering clarifications and modifications, considering herself well instructed.

Within the week following this letter Fénelon would be appointed preceptor to the Duc de Bourgogne, and, along with Guyon, would be fully swept into the vortex of Versailles. This relationship between Guyon and Fénelon was in no way damaged by their frank exchange of views. Guyon acknowledged the force of Fénelon's concerns and sometimes raised counter-objections, sometimes backpedaled, sometimes stood her ground with sharpened formulations. Polite and respectful as the conversation was, the "mother" and her "child" could quickly exchange roles. That was what made the relationship *mutual.* When the time came for Fénelon to defend her views forcefully, he would always be defending what she *intended* to say, and always with his own restatements.

"Whoever does not love does not accomplish anything, though seeming to accomplish everything . . . love true and pure is the fulfillment of the law. This pure love is the living and interior law."
—LETTER TO THE MARQUISE DE MAINTENON,
MAY 25, 1692

"Crosses are necessary for you; and God, who loves you, won't let you go without them."
—LETTER TO THE COMTESSE DE GRAMONT,
JUNE 17, 1692

✦

FIVE

Madame de Maintenon, Saint-Cyr, and the Question of "Pure Love"

1689–1697

By the beginning of 1690 Fénelon was ensconced at Versailles, functioning as preceptor to the Duc de Bourgogne (and later his two brothers), as teacher and spiritual guide along with Guyon at Saint-Cyr, and as an increasingly popular director for a number of the devout members of the court (most notably the Beauvillier, Colbert, and Chevreuse families, but also others, such as Madame de Gramont). Perhaps most significant, he was moving into the role of personal advisor to Madame de Maintenon.

This period would proceed through a growing controversy surrounding Guyon, an increasing debate about quietist ideas culminating with the Conferences of Issy in 1694–95, an ensuing and ever more acrimonious struggle with Bossuet on how to understand the Articles of Issy, and finally the publication by both Bossuet and Fénelon in 1697 of major works intended to defend their different understandings of mystical spirituality—Fénelon's work being the famous *Maxims of the Saints*. In the course of these developments Fénelon would be raised to the episcopate as archbishop of Cambrai, would continue the debate with Bossuet after the *Maxims* appeared, and would finally be silenced with papal censure in 1699. This is a convoluted, multifaceted, and almost maddeningly complex time for the student of history.

But it is also the period of Fénelon's mature teaching, that for which he is best known. This is contained in his letters, particularly those to Maintenon, but also in the two collections drawn from letters and addresses, partially assembled by admirers during his lifetime but only posthumously completed, the *Manual of Piety* and the *Instructions and*

Advice on Various Points of Moral Teaching and Christian Perfection.[266] Much
of this material is impossible to date precisely, but the general view is
that it emanates from this time when Fénelon's influence at court was
at its peak.

During this period much of his guidance, aside from his tutorial work,
was directed primarily to women of the court and women in religious
orders, which is to say, women living within the constraints of rigid
social and ecclesiastical codes and rules. Theirs was a situation in which
the tension between a prescribed and potentially stifling structure on the
one hand, and the need for some kind of room for individual autonomy
on the other, is enormous. These were cultivated women determined
to *do their duty as they understood it and as God had given it to them* at whatever
personal cost, but the hunger was to do it *intelligently*. The challenge
was to develop spiritual practice that renewed and refreshed and that
truly glorified God, within severely imposed parameters. Under such
conditions, the development of true freedom in the inner life becomes
crucial, so that a person's soul does not disappear, so to speak, behind a
façade of social constraint.

Advisor to Madame

Fénelon's actual relationship with Madame de Maintenon was quite
informal.[267] Officially, he functioned as preceptor to her second step-son,
but unofficially she made use of him as a helpful personal consultant, this
being done with the approval of her actual spiritual director and the chaplain of Saint-Cyr, the priest Paul Godet des Marais (soon to be bishop
of Chartres and thus with episcopal/canonical authority over the clergy
at Versailles, which is in the diocese of Chartres). Early on in Fénelon's
introduction to Versailles dévot circles, she was "charmed" (her word) by
him, finding him wise and sensitive, and so sought him out for advice.

There have been countless assessments of Françoise d'Aubigné, this
woman of Calvinist roots, wife and then widow of the poet Scarron,
governess to Louis XIV's first son, then mistress ennobled as the Marquise
de Maintenon, and finally wife and mainstay to Louis.[268] Suffice it to say
that she had, in Louis Cognet's words, "a complex personality and that

she seemed sometimes to have had real aspirations to the interior life."[269] Although it is sometimes argued by biographers that she was a cynical "climber" or, more charitably, a street-smart woman in a patriarchal society who was not afraid to make good use of her opportunities, her correspondence with Fénelon suggests that she was sensitive, sincere, and well intended, while also being insecure and, once aroused, ferocious. With men she tended to be cunning, with women domineering. Clearly aware that much at Versailles was façade and pretense, thus exhausting as well as treacherous, she yearned for spirituality that would sustain her. Attracted thus to Guyon's teaching on the central importance of self-abandonment as the way to a true inwardness, but also to Fénelon's ability to calibrate that ideal to her unique circumstances, she turned to him in particular. In the letters written to her by Fénelon, one is struck by the intimacy with which she opened herself to him. Although he did not hesitate to be sometimes complimentary, he was for the most part candid, confrontational, and direct, even occasionally rough, in response to her varying needs for support, encouragement, correction, and admonition.[270] In return, she gave him affection, respect, and loyalty—at least for a time.

By contrast, for all of the high esteem in which Fénelon initially was held by Madame de Maintenon, he seems to have been a failure from the outset with Louis XIV himself. There is a famous anecdote from a later memoirist that tells the "substantially exact" story in a witty fashion. "This lady [Maintenon], enthused with the spirit, graces, and eloquence of the abbé de Fénelon, obliged the King to provide a private audience for him, hoping that this Prince, charmed by the abbé's discourse, would take him into his confidence, and would make a straight line toward God with such a good guide. At the designated time, the abbé de Fénelon was brought into the King's chamber, and thinking that he would find the same dispositions that Madame de Maintenon has, he spoke at length without letting up; he did not stop to think that this Prince, who was an absolute monarch, put less value on flowery discourse and more on a certain timidity or awkwardness, which he would only have attributed to respect and which would have been more successful in such an important one-on-one encounter; the King seized on a pause and said: 'M. l'abbé, when I have something to say to you, I will let you know,' and in the area where he was walking [later] with Madame de Maintenon, he said, 'I have just met l'abbé de Fénelon. Isn't he your advisor, Madame? He will never be mine."[271] Orcibal cites d'Aguesseau's speculation that Fénelon may have tried a little too hard or that something about him made Louis uncomfortable. My guess is that husbands are rarely comfortable with other men who know too much about their wives, and that Louis was sensitive. Eventually, he became infuriated with Fénelon, but only after the scandal of the *Maxims*, and especially after the criticisms of his leadership with its lust for glory in *Telemachus*.

The amazing thing—in light of all of the conflict to come—was that Maintenon so treasured everything that Fénelon wrote to her. And I use the word "wrote" advisedly, because even though they lived in very close proximity, most of the communication was elaborated on paper with all of the epistolary conventions required for formal prose. She saved all of his letters, wrapping them together with a red ribbon in what is called her "secret little red book," which survives to this day. Much of this material, excerpted from other copies, found its way, in addition, into the two large collections the *Instructions and Advice* and the *Manual of Piety*.

The spirit of his teaching for Maintenon, which he would elaborate in countless ways, can be set out in the form of two prayers from the *Manual of Piety*. The first prayer frames the big picture: "Lord, you are the God of all nature; everything obeys your voice: you are the soul of every living thing, and even of what is not alive. You are my soul, more even than the soul you have given my heart; you are nearer to me than I am to myself. Everything is in you: my heart . . . is in you, and not in me. . . . O my eternal portion, there are no consolations here below, not inner pleasures, nor extraordinary lights [spiritual gifts] that I want . . . it is you, and you alone, for whom I am hungry and thirsty."[272] And then the second prayer voices the spirituality of the French school in the way that Guyon reinforced for Fénelon: "I worship you, baby Jesus, as you lie exposed in the manger. I love nothing more than your being a baby born in poverty. O who will give me the gift of being as poor and as childlike as you? O Eternal Wisdom, brought down to the form of a baby, take away my vain and presumptuous knowledge and make me a child with you." Fénelon followed the latter prayer with a conclusion: "Most of us would prefer to die with Jesus in his agony than to see ourselves lying in swaddling clothes alongside him in the cradle . . . it is torture to no longer be counted as anything, like children." Seek God alone, and do so with the spirit of a small child. Fénelon's task with Maintenon was to determine just how to hold her—proud, powerful, and insecure—to such a high calling!

Initially he utilized the image of the "child" with Maintenon as a way of challenging her to be honest, open, real, gentle, persevering, light-hearted under stress, and generous with the needs of others as well as her own. It is a way of helping her to take herself less seriously. His desire for her, he says, is that she have "a perfect childhood, with him who became a child for us, [since] if we do not seem to be like him in that state, we will not be truly renewed." "A little of childhood in the arms of God, and of childlike joy, in the midst of the most serious cares, gives us our wisdom, and heals us of everything," he adds early on in 1690, urging her in her dealings with Louis to act "with simplicity, liberty, joy, pleasingness, without precaution and without reflection [that is, conscious calculation], like a small child." "I pray to Jesus Christ," he says, "that he will give you the heart of a child," so that by grace God will "enlarge your heart like the ocean." He even coins a neologism, "to become small" (*apetisser*), where one is "docile to all of the impressions of grace," to capture some of what is entailed in this spiritual childhood.[273]

We can only imagine how any of this would have resonated with Louis, if Maintenon had decided to share it with him. One irony is that this language of the "child" can sound very much like a certain lighthearted, agile, flexible personal style, free of self-conscious self-importance—qualities we modern folk tend to value in leaders! What Fénelon was doing here with his aristocratic directees, especially Maintenon, was to "road test" his spiritual teaching, in order to see if it could be taken out of the hothouse of special mystical relationships, as with Guyon, and made viable, even compelling, for Christians "in the world." Louis XIV was apparently less sanguine about this business of becoming a "child" again than was his spouse, since it probably sounded child-*ish*, maybe self-indulgent, to him. Louis took himself *very* seriously!

We know from the letters that Maintenon constantly moaned to Fénelon about the swarm of sycophantic, dishonest schemers around

Louis. Take it all with a grain of salt, says Fénelon. "Be free, gay, simple, a child," he advises, and then cautions: "But be a sturdy child, who fears nothing, who speaks out frankly, who lets herself be led, who is carried in the arms; in a word, one who knows nothing, can do nothing, can anticipate and change nothing, but who has a freedom and a strength forbidden to the great. This childhood baffles the wise. God himself speaks by the mouth of such children." The way to handle all of these phonies is just to be honest and straightforward. But there is a twist to his counsel, when we note that it occurs in the context of his exhortation to Maintenon that "she suffer less and love more." He will not let her moaning function as a form of self-pity. "Nothing is more false and more indiscreet than always to want to choose what mortifies us in everything." In other words, being surrounded by a horde of sycophants goes with the territory and is your load to carry. Handle it gracefully, don't dramatize, and don't feel sorry for yourself! He has no patience with a self-chosen, self-manipulated, and finally self-serving set of spiritual practices, however pious they may seem, if they have the effect of pumping up the *moi*, the ever-present human ego, in its relationship with God. "We would like to enter," he says, "into pure faith, and always to keep our own wisdom; to be a child, and to be great in our own eyes. What a fantasy of spirituality!"[274]

Now the distinctive mark of the Fénelonian spirituality begins to emerge. It is the point at which we first begin to see him as a spiritual psychologist. This spirituality of the Child Jesus is a direct challenge to all of the pseudo-religion of Versailles, especially in the wake of Louis's own religious deepening under Maintenon's influence. Fénelon warns her: "you have at the court people who seem well-intentioned . . . take care, for a thousand people would make themselves 'devoted' to please you." But the *real* enemy is within, lodged in her own breast. He underlines how much she defeats herself, as well as Louis and the realm, if she allows herself to become false in *her* religion—which is precisely what will happen if she does not get her self-loving and sinful self, the *moi*, out of the calculation. "The 'me' of which I have spoken to you so often is still an idol that you have not broken. You wish to go to God with all your heart, but not with the loss of the 'me': on the contrary, you seek the 'me' in God." "All our faults," he says, "come from still being attached and curved back onto ourselves . . . it is the 'me' which wishes to put virtues in its own service."[275]

Renounce then, he says, without hesitation this unfortunate "me." She is constantly tempted to put God at her disposal even in the most serious practice of devotion. This is easy to do in a situation where everything and everyone tends to flattery and the inflation of her ego. But it is deadly and counterproductive in the end, just another manifestation of how "askew" the world is, where "good is combined with evil, evil operates with force . . . and evil even wishes to pass as good." "Corruption in humankind is like water in the sea."[276] This last conveys to us a claustrophobic sense of how overwhelmingly suffocating the environment of the court with its rigid and overstructured social codes must have been. We know as well from Fénelon's early letters to Guyon that that is what he himself felt, and that the typical consequence followed. Fénelon was often "supple, cautious, refined, ambitious," conducting himself with suitable political polish, but also "restless, conflicted, often in spells of interior dryness" as well, "a man of the interior life living in a gilded palace."[277] And this was exactly the dilemma faced by his aristocratic directees.

Looked at from this perspective, the spirituality of the Child is *liberating*, an escape from the shackles of cultural slavery for a free inner life, and, possibly, with radical consequences for outward behavior, even social and political life, as well. At one point, Fénelon writes to Maintenon, "You must remember what God can do in a moment with the vilest and most unworthy creature, how God can call back what we have damned even in ourselves . . . so that even this vile person is made precious in the sight of God."[278]

It is no surprise to discover that the substitute for the "me" in a cleansed spirituality is "pure love." "True goodness of the heart," he says, "consists in fidelity to God and in pure love." But what does catch us a bit by surprise is the claim that "pure love" is precisely *not* "the generosities and all the natural tender acts, which are only a more refined self-love, more seductive, more flattering, more lovable, and by consequence, more diabolical." Rather, it is to love with a love "perfect, infinite, generous, active, compassionate, consoling, equal, beneficent, and tender as God himself. The heart of God would be turned into yours . . . the true love of God loves the neighbor generously, without hope of any return."[279] This is to say that Fénelon will not let Maintenon think of "pure love" as some sort of conventional kindness writ large, a "Lady Bountiful" magnanimity to one and all. *That* would be a huge temptation for Maintenon, even more than for most of us. *That* kind of love—call it ordinary philanthropy—is usually a monument to the giver.

What Fénelon now does is to challenge Maintenon to go *inside*, because it is here that the real enemy resides, and it is only here that the shift from self-love to pure love can happen. Making the shift cannot be simply a matter of technique, of using this or that prayer. It must involve a radical change of perspective. Facilitating that change is the purpose of the whole body of thought contained in Fénelon's spiritual direction from 1689 onward, refined from his collaboration with Guyon, and (somewhat) codified and systematized in the *Instructions and Advice*. How can these powerful aristocrats with great temporal responsibilities (the duties imposed by God!), burdened by a ceaseless flow of business (often from "importunate" clients), expected to maintain a social front at all times, constantly tempted to self-indulgence and grandiosity, isolated and lonely in the midst of intrigues and manipulation, and finally held to account by a severe God (as well as their human constituency), possibly find inner peace and stability? It is in response to this kind of human struggle then and now that Fénelon, having absorbed and adapted Guyon, is at his best.

To begin at the most practical level, Maintenon seems always to have been operating under enormous stress. She suffered from a whole range of (at least somewhat) psychosomatic complaints, including sleeplessness, joint pains, dietary irregularities, and general nervous prostration. Thus it is that Fénelon is always quite traditional with his starting advice for newly serious Christians: get into place a benign "rule of life." Get a better balance of work and rest in motion, get enough downtime, eat sensibly, get proper medical care (and do what the doctors say!), and so on. We know it all, and Fénelon showers his directees with such admonitions. This is a way of getting back into control, of constructing boundaries, when one's life has been out of control and unbounded. One of Fénelon's favorite words for this unboundedness is "dissipation," being scattered and fragmented. With Maintenon in particular, he grinds away at the issue of creating a balance between her own needs and those of others. The issue is one of being accountable to God for the good use of the time that one has been given. "There is a time for everything in our lives," he says, "but the maxim that governs every moment is that no moment should be useless. Every moment must enter into the order and progress of our salvation. Every moment must be accompanied by duties that God has allotted with his own hand, and of which he will demand an account. For from the first instant of our existence to the last, he has never designed for us a barren moment, nor one that we can consider as given up to our own discretion."[280]

What may also surprise us is Fénelon's claim that the kind of overfunctioning that he sees in Maintenon is a sign of pride. If ever there were an indication that the "pure love" of God does *not* exclude proper care for oneself, it would be here. There is the need for rest, for refreshment with one's intimate family (but also for solitude), for reading and study, for maintaining proper diet and healthy habits, for getting enough sleep, et cetera. There is the need for regular time for peaceful and prayerful recollection. Fénelon gives Maintenon the constant advice to avoid needlessly stressful activity, whether it is particular devotional exercises or unproductive time with tedious people, or taking on more tasks than can reasonably be accomplished with available resources and time, or pushing herself to the limit so that no one can criticize her. Nothing is wiser than the decision to make time for such refreshment: "it is thus that at the feet of Jesus Christ we heal secretly all the wounds of our hearts, we wipe off all the bad imprints of the world. This even helps our health, because, if a person knows how to make simple use of these retreats, they rest the body no less than the spirit."[281] Nothing is more contrary to the will of God for us, says Fénelon, than the kind of regimen, driven by human anxiety about the future, in which we demonstrate how little trust we have in God and how inflated our need to shore ourselves up has become.

The paradox here is that *lack* of control in our lives, no proper rule, is a manifestation of self-love but so is *overcontrol*, religious practice infected with "me." What will happen in either case, Fénelon warns, is that, displeased with our performance, we will become discouraged by our "faults" and merciless toward those of others. When we attempt to "push" piety, when we do not operate with the childlike simplicity, the death to self that Fénelon advocates, we will find that religion has become a monster of our own creation. This plays out for Maintenon in the form of either enduring all of the headaches of her demanding life, but doing it in a self-depleting and hateful way (that is, being out of control), or establishing a set of spiritual practices that simply compounds the problem by making her prideful (too much control). For instance, she could simply bite her lip and push herself even harder in tolerating intolerable people (while despising them), *or* she could increase the number of penances she performed by way of contrition for her negative attitude! He warns Maintenon, "This disdain of the wretchedness of others is a wretchedness which does not recognize itself enough," but also "the more perfect we are, the more we get along with imperfection," including our own imperfection.[282]

Likewise, there is a passage in a letter to Madame de Gramont in which Fénelon eloquently generalizes on the universality and destructive results of the "me" in human relations. "There is no peace," he says, "in hoping in oneself, where we live at the mercy of a mob of avid and insatiable desires, and where the 'me,' so delicate and so sensitive to everything that touches it, never knows how to be content. . . . Touch it with the end of your finger, and it thinks itself scorched. Join to it the crudeness of a neighbor filled with imperfections of which he himself is unaware, and then join to it our neighbor's revolts against our own faults—a revolt no greater than ours against his—and there you have the children of Adam . . . each half of humankind made miserable by the other half."[283] The social implications of self-love, of the "me," thus infinite, call for the radical solution of pure love, of the cross.

This is where the dark side starts to appear. Since the "me" is the problem, advice alone is never enough. The assumption is that we grow only by means of crosses, which comes very close to saying that failure is the only teacher and the suffering imposed on you the only trainer. Getting a spiritual discipline in place is always a work in progress, since our present state of humility and simplicity and compassion is always deficient, and crosses provide the working energy. But the question is whether they will be the ones that God wants—and thus grace-filled— or the ones that we want. The latter type puff us up, says Fénelon, and become grand sacrifices that we make, while the former *abase* (Fénelon's word) us often by their mundane quality, or the clumsiness with which we embrace them, or the feeling of utter helplessness that we have to endure while struggling with them, even as we find enough strength to hang in there and to grow. "The crosses that we make for ourselves by overanxiety about the future are not the heaven-sent crosses . . . [in fact] the future is not ours . . ." he wrote; "we may never have a future, or, if it comes, it may be completely different from all we foresaw."[284]

An important term that Fénelon uses with Maintenon for the heaven-sent crosses is that they manifest themselves as a "subjugation" (*assujettissement*), a burdensome binding and constriction in our lives that "takes the wind out of our sails," so that God can fill us ("enlarge our hearts") with a fresh breeze. In a letter to Madame de Gramont, he says, "You endure those who importune you, you are subjugated, you are harassed; but God is doing this, and that suffices. . . . The only question is that of being faithful, patient and peaceable, in the cross of the present state, that one has not chosen, and that God has given according to his designs."[285] Self-chosen crosses breed a certain smug pomposity.

So, the purpose of a rule in our lives is to get us into the mode of listening for God's direction rather than our own. This is why Fénelon constantly cautions against "far-fetched mortifications" and austerities and exercises of every kind that, unless carefully watched, become sources of scrupulosity and pride. Be quiet, listen, be open, attend carefully to the inner bidding, let yourself become "supple" to the leading of the Spirit as God shows the way, "abandon" yourself to that leading one step at a time. Each of us needs just enough structure to follow this kind of guidance, but not so much that the structure becomes an end in itself. If the structure enables us to maintain an "unstrained" (that is, without *empressement*, another important term for Fénelon) posture of expectant readiness for what God will send and what God will provide, knowing that this will happen under the form of the cross, that suffering will be entailed, and that another layer of self-love will be stripped away, then the structure is doing its job.

What then happens when we take time and start listening for God? From a behavioral perspective, the first thing is that, having discovered the interior realm and its power, we start to get our lives together by pulling back from all destructive investments in worldly goals and pursuits. This covers a lot of territory for Fénelon, some obvious as in the rejection of gross sensuality, but some much more subtle since a great deal of seemingly virtuous and well-intended and applauded human behavior is infected with self-love. We might say it has a narcissistic, "look at how wonderful I am" quality, sometimes manifesting as complacent or smug self-congratulation (looking in a mirror and liking what we see), sometimes as overweening arrogance or self-righteousness (the trap of powerful people like Maintenon), and sometimes as a self-preoccupied, self-critical anxiety (as in scrupulosity and perfectionism, Fénelon's personal traps).

This is where we see Fénelon constantly advising Maintenon to slow down, take a break, get some time for herself, pull back from micromanaging Saint-Cyr, and pay more attention to her physical and mental health. We might have difficulty in seeing all of her manic level of activity as self-love, but Fénelon is convinced that it is, precisely because it implies a kind of self-initiated self-improvement program, *rather than* humble submission to the program of transformation that God desires and graciously enables. Here his advice to her is that "you must pre-eminently sacrifice the 'me' to God . . . so that you no longer seek out reputation or the consolation that comes from verifying to yourself that you have fine qualities and good sentiments. You must die to everything without reserve, and not even possess virtue with reference to self." Differently stated, in order to get the "me" out of the way, the will must be purified by nothing less than a death.

The underlying contention is that when we go inside, what we discover is the "heart," which in fact is the *will*, the working moral core of the person and the source of all desiring. Fénelon goes so far as to say that "we have nothing of our own but our will; all the rest does not belong to us. Disease takes away health and life. Riches are snatched away by violence. The talents of the mind depend on the condition of the body. The one thing truly ours is our will. And it is of this that God is jealous."[286] Having looked deep inside ourselves, we are brought face-to-face with the great energy of desiring that we have the freedom to direct. If, sick and tired of vanity, we decide to turn this desiring toward God, as God desires, then we orient ourselves in the direction of the "child" who will now live by the cross, and true discipleship has begun. The first act of that new life will be complete submission of the human will and its self-love to the divine Will and its pure love.

Pressing Maintenon Beyond Her Limits

But now the struggle begins in earnest. In Guyon's teaching, supported by Fénelon, once Maintenon had decided to go deeper in her relationship with God and the journey toward pure love, the times of dryness and interior agony would be inevitable. For Maintenon much of this pain would take the form of being faithful to her demanding schedule with its hordes of suppliants, tolerating all of the emotionally draining infighting of the court, being constantly vulnerable to exhaustion and illness, and, most of all, propping up Louis in her role as faithful spouse and confidante, while, at the same time, learning to do without the "worldly," "natural," "merely human" rewards that self-love ordinarily confers. Fénelon regularly exhorts her to remember that she cannot be self-satisfied with her own virtue,[287] cannot in any way congratulate herself on clever successes or hard-won victories, cannot savor the pleasure of dealing harshly with those who "importune" her (when they so richly deserve it!), but she must take all of the burden of this as a *gift from God*, believing that God is transforming her, "enlarging" her heart, in the process. She cannot play the victim or imagine herself a saint. Surely, one of the most painful points—that she cannot, must not, take satisfaction even in her own virtue, her "natural" goodness, for to do so is once again to fall into self-love—must have rankled.

Further, when Louis treats her poorly, she must consider this as a "cross" and not lapse into self-pity or despair. There is also the loneliness of this process, since Fénelon frequently reminds her that she must not take too many others into her confidence, not allow herself to have weak moments in which she ventilates a little too much with anyone, not allow herself to be publicly enraged in moments of utter frustration. Indeed, he sets the bar very high for her when, shattered by Louis's decision to join his army at Mons in the Low Country in March 1691 and expose himself to great danger, she was frantic with worry: this "rough road" that God has you on, he says, is "an inestimable blessing . . . and it would be a great misfortune if things were otherwise," since now she can "practice quietly the patience, humility, detachment, and a little of the abandonment that you have spotted from a distance, but that has now drawn near to you."

Fénelon thus makes the radical claim, to be echoed by many later writers, that each moment is a "sacrament," however brutal and punishing in nature ("sacramental," indeed, *precisely because it is brutal and punishing*), in which God is present as both a cross and a resurrection, as suffering and as the enabling grace that teaches compassion because of the suffering—all of this in each single instant of life. He says to her, "Madame, I desire with all my heart that the depression you often feel will serve to make you die to all self-will . . . when you are in a state of almost continual subjugation, so that you are constrained, despite yourself, to do nothing . . . the depth of the heart is saddened, dried out, and discouraged; but it is this very discouragement, provided that you do not succumb to it, that purifies the heart. One does the will of God in doing nothing, one shatters one's will—but as a consequence does a great deal, although appearing to do nothing."[288] As things turn out, this is to set the bar impossibly high for the spirited and lively (*vive*) woman that Maintenon was reputed to be, however much she claimed to be enthralled with his teaching and that of Guyon, especially when he advised her to step back from her beloved Saint-Cyr and to let others run it. This, combined with Louis's growing antipathy toward him, may have set the wheels in motion.

The kind of detachment and indifference advocated by Fénelon in the practice of love would have required Maintenon to make some changes that she was not willing, or could not, make,[289] and Fénelon refused to coddle her. There seem to have been two points at which he was pressing Maintenon beyond her limits. One involved her relationship with Louis, and the other involved her relationship with Guyon and thus with Saint-Cyr. The former came to a head later on with the *Maxims* and *Telemachus*, but the latter erupted sooner, as trouble broke out at Saint-Cyr with regard to matters of discipline among the faculty and the students. At the center of the difficulty were members of the community who were in close touch with Madame Guyon and Fénelon. One nun in particular was the flashpoint: Madame de la Maisonfort, teacher and director of studies, a cousin of Madame Guyon, and Maintenon's personal choice to become the leader of Saint-Cyr further down the road.[290]

Born in 1663, Marie-Françoise-Silvine de la Maisonfort had indeed been handpicked and brought to court by Madame de Maintenon especially to be part of Saint-Cyr and, Maintenon hoped, to be the individual who would run the school and make it prosper after its patroness was long gone. Now, as an unvowed member of the Dames of Saint Louis, Maisonfort shared in the common prayer and discipline of the order but at the same time enjoyed a considerable measure of personal freedom. Her spiritual director was Godet des Marais, both before and after he became bishop of Chartres, but at her request Fénelon was allowed to be an advisor as well. In addition, her father had been Madame Guyon's uncle, and Guyon was allowed to meet with her, as well as a few others in the school, from time to time.

Madame de la Maisonfort was highly intelligent, articulate, and outspoken—virtues that are not always welcomed in communities where obedience and submission to authority are prerequisites—but she appears also to have been emotionally unstable, moody, and impulsive.[291] She had a hard time yielding to the direction of her female superiors, chafed at some of the details of prayer and discipline required by the community, and complained directly to Maintenon about her unhappiness, as well as to Fénelon.

Madame de Maintenon wanted to attach Maisonfort to the community by monastic vows—and indeed Maisonfort took simple vows at the end of a novitiate in March 1692 and then solemn vows in April 1694—but there was a great deal of storming and handwringing around both occasions, as Maisonfort doubted and hesitated.[292] Maintenon pleaded with her, and we have a series of letters in which Fénelon counsels her to "sacrifice your will to that of God" as represented by her superiors, to practice docility, to stop all of the "reflecting" (anxious and scrupulous second-guessing), to hold nothing back from God, to stop asking for special treatment (such as sending letters to Maintenon). In short, he told her to *settle down and follow the rules*.[293] Indeed, the amount of uproar that was generated around Maisonfort, and then around some other of the nuns as well, seems to have been quite considerable. Maintenon was to complain in due course that Fénelon was inviting these ladies to enjoy the freedom of the children of God, when they had not yet become children (i.e., obedient)!

— The chain of events is complicated (as always in small, tight communities). Part of the problem was that some of the nuns were looking to Guyon for inspiration. Introduced into Saint-Cyr by Maintenon herself, because she brought a certain "sweetness" into the spirituality of the community, Guyon and her *Short and Easy Method* had fascinated some of its members.[294] Fénelon had become quite popular. But a spirit of insubordination simmered. Finally Maintenon lost all patience, and she reacted by taking steps, with Godet des Marais's approval, to have the Dames of Saint Louis brought under the structure and discipline of the Augustinian Order. This was in August 1693, and Maisonfort and the others submitted. There was peace briefly, and Godet and Fénelon together composed a discipline for the community. But then an incident in which the restless Maisonfort insulted Godet in front of Madame de Maintenon occurred. She accused Godet of being rigid and obsessive about details and appealed to Fénelon's authority for justification. Not only was Maintenon mortified by such insubordination, but, in addition, Godet, after finding that a number of the nuns were reading Guyon's books, recommended to Maintenon that Guyon be dismissed. To put it bluntly, the situation was a mess, and Fénelon's head would be on the block next.

Godet also discovered in conversation with Maisonfort that she attributed some of her resistance to following the community rule to Fénelon's insistence that her outer practice of prayer must be concordant with her inner state. Indeed, Fénelon had been inclined to be patient with her by affirming her "general dispositions to prayer" and tolerating her discomfort with outward disciplines. Godet asked her, as Fénelon himself had done repeatedly, to stop spreading the latter's ideas to other members of the Dames. In other words, after a period in 1692 in which Maintenon herself had been urging the nuns to be more cautious in their use of ideas from Guyon and Fénelon, momentum was building during the last months of 1693 and early 1694 for seeing Fénelon's teaching, ambiguous and dangerous in content but also impossible to contain in a closely knit and gossiping community, as the ultimate source of discontent, rebelliousness, and unrest.

As Maintenon and Godet conferred with one another, the bishop admitted to increasing concern about Fénelon. The crunch came when Maintenon shared with Godet what would be Fénelon's last letter to her, that of May 7, 1694, as well as her whole collection of letters from him (her "secret little book" with a red ribbon) and Godet critiqued a number of passages. She then passed this critique to Louis-Antoine de Noailles, then bishop of Châlons, and to Louis Tronson, Fénelon's universally respected mentor at Saint-Sulpice, for their comments. In short order, in November, Fénelon sent Tronson an *Explication* of his teachings with Maintenon. It gives us a first glimpse of how he was beginning to give systematic shape to his ideas and how he would defend them, if need be.

Final Communication with Maintenon

In this for-the-time-being final letter (there would not be another until September 1695, and only fitfully after that) to Maintenon, and as he had done many times earlier, Fénelon struck at what he regarded as her self-love, manifesting itself in rage and frustration at some turn of events that she could not control. In this case, as in others, subjected to what she considered mistreatment and unjustified criticism, she took refuge in a sense of her own goodness and uprightness. He then points out to her: "You do not cling to the grosser goods and honors, but you do hold, perhaps without seeing it, to your own sense of self—to being in good repute with people of worth, to friendship, and especially to a certain perfection of virtue that you wish to find in yourself, and which takes precedence over all other goods: this is the greatest refinement of self-love, the consolation of every loss."

Godet, in his comments,[295] was in substantial agreement with this statement—that a smug satisfaction with one's own virtue is simply self-love—but he then had trouble with Fénelon's further admonition to Maintenon that the true perfection of virtue is "to see it in herself as being completely in another, without any complacent feeling that it is hers rather than another's." This advice is part of his general position that we are to let everything about ourselves, good and bad, "fall away,"

so that it is not "ours" any longer and is inconsequential (the French is
qu'importe—what does it matter?). We avoid the religious hypocrisy of self-
righteousness on the one hand, when we are good, or, on the other hand,
the despair of self-condemnation (anxious scruples), when we are bad—
both of which are forms of self-love.

Godet in his critique made it clear, however, that he missed the
point by offering the ham-fisted comment that "true charity has for a
rule to love one's own perfection first of all," and then by engaging
for the remainder of his commentary in a sustained exhortation to the
discipline and rule of daily, unending moral improvement, "the solid
practice of virtue," in the Christian life. He also expressed confusion
about Fénelon's comment when the latter said to Maintenon in this same
letter: "You will be, please God, always very virtuous; but God wishes
for souls to whom He gives a great deal, a disappropriation of his gifts,
a smallness, and a death without reserve, that an infinity of penitent
and very virtuous persons do not know." What Godet tended to hear
in such a statement was a discounting of the value of moral endeavor,
as if it simply doesn't matter, whereas, as Orcibal points out,[296] Fénelon
is trying to separate morality from religion, to make it clear that the
approach to God *cannot* be essentially a matter of human virtue, for then
religion would be about us and not about God.

And so Godet (let alone Maintenon) did not understand Fénelon's
"theocentric" intentions, because the fear of moral laxity would, for them,
override everything. What they cannot see is that, above all, God wants
me to "die," not to be well-behaved and of sterling character. In a letter
to Godet,[297] Madame de Maintenon said, "I am much chagrined that God
wishes me to separate myself totally from the abbé de Fénelon." On May
12, 1694, Godet concurred.

Before long, however, Fénelon came out fighting, and the whole
ensuing drama of the Conferences of Issy (with which we are about to
deal) was in part a struggle to vindicate himself. But first, in the *Explication*
that he sent directly to his beloved mentor, Tronson, in November 1694,
he addressed the questions raised by Godet regarding his advice to
Maintenon. His strategy was to take a number of the passages marked as
questionable by Godet in the letters to Maintenon (passages that appear
now in parts of the *Instructions and Advice*, primarily 22, 23, 24, 26, and

33), and to demonstrate that, taken "in a good sense," they are entirely consistent with the teaching of the best spiritual writers, primarily Francis de Sales.[298] He cites passages from de Sales to justify the concept of spiritual childhood and the intimate relation of the soul to the heavenly Father; the concept of spiritual simplicity in which we "know nothing, but know everything" by entrusting the future to the providential care of God; the idea that pure faith begins when we stop trusting in both the exterior and interior "gifts" or "graces" we have received from God and start trusting *only* in God alone; the teaching that we are to cease to put any trust in our virtues or even to be mindful of them but only to focus on our imperfections and how far we are from the perfection God wishes. He refers to de Sales also for the views that we are to let our virtues "fall away," insofar as they are "ours" and thus a source of pride, and for the more radical idea that there comes a time when God "strips away" our virtues so as to induce the humiliation, and then humility, that are so central to true faith. For the idea that there are, and have been, many pious persons who are obtuse to the nature of pure and disinterested love, he has no trouble referring to multiple orthodox writers who say much the same.

In order to clearly distinguish himself from so-called quietist thinking, Fénelon makes the strong point that when he speaks of the rejection of spiritual "gifts" by the devout person, he means those that are consciously perceived and felt "sensibly," and thus are potential objects of prideful self-love and false assurance, but not the unconscious sanctifying grace that is the essence of the work of the Holy Spirit and of a relationship with God. He is also clear that in his use of "detachment" and "disappropriation" there can be no question of losing God as such— as if the ultimate sacrifice were to cut free even from God—but rather of casting off everything that *self-love* claims as a source of strength or satisfaction.

In his conclusions he contends that in his description of what God wishes of us, he has reduced it to trust "in his providence over events, in the written and inviolable law governing virtue, and to certain interior qualities that God has given conformably to his law, so as to make us more simple, smaller, more dead to the sensuality of the flesh and the pride of the spirit." He allows for no "willful attachment to the least imperfections," and he insists that his teaching is only "for very pure souls that are very advanced in death to self." He also insists that in his instructions to Maintenon he purposely stayed away from "passive prayer" and only encouraged some relaxation of overreliance on a multitude of spoken prayers, much as Francis de Sales would have advised as well.

This *Explication of Some Expressions Drawn from the Letters of Fénelon to Madame de Maintenon* is a strong, robustly assertive document in the marshalling of authorities and the careful clarification of the traps Fénelon believed himself to have avoided. Clearly Godet was outclassed, and it is doubtful if Maintenon ever fully grasped what was at stake, although Fénelon insisted that he was only trying to help her with ideas about which she was apparently eager for enlightenment. The open question involved just exactly what is possible, and desirable, for these "very pure souls" who are seemingly ready for a "more advanced" level of perfection.

~ As things boiled to a head at Saint-Cyr, Guyon's situation was coming to a climax as well. Exasperated by the long delays, she had continued to push for a final determination on her ecclesiastical status. Her aristocratic supporters put pressure on Harlay in Paris for a definitive adjudication of her case, and one part was finally brought to closure after examination: the charges of immorality against her were dropped. But the doctrinal question, to everyone's frustration, hung fire. Louis and Maintenon, therefore, decided to take matters in hand by secretly convening a board of commissioners, who would examine Guyon's writings in detail and submit a report. They considered a number of possible candidates for this assignment—individuals whose judgment would be wisely respected—and thought first of certain theologians of Jansenist sympathies, particularly the famous Pierre Nicole. But these were clearly hostile.

Probably it was Fénelon himself who recommended Bossuet, with Guyon's approval, partly because of their old friendship and partly because he was seen as "not opposed to the interior life."[299] Bossuet accepted the invitation but stipulated that all deliberations would be kept secret from Harlay (he and Bossuet were church-political rivals) and that Guyon first turn over, all of her writings and letters to him for his own personal analysis. Madame de Maintenon was entirely in agreement with this arrangement, since she had already been utilizing

Bossuet's intervention at Saint-Cyr for conversations with the nuns and an independent assessment of the rebelliousness in the community. As early as September 1693, she had asked Bossuet "to cause Fénelon to return from his errors and his prejudices on behalf of Madame Guyon."[300] In her own mind, the good Fénelon had been tainted by the disruptive and untrustworthy Guyon.

— So it is that during the last months of 1693 and the early months of 1694, while the situation was blowing up at Saint-Cyr, Guyon's friends continued to look for other examiners to join Bossuet in his review of her work. A lively correspondence went on between Guyon and Bossuet as he sought explanations and she offered clarifications. What eventually emerged from the exchange was a crystallizing for Bossuet of his central "issue" with Guyon—which was her novel jargon for describing interior states, particularly her use of "passive" to characterize the higher states. Bossuet confessed to a major difficulty here, for, he argued, in one's relation with God "there is always a very free, very quiet, very inward act of the will, marked by free consent, without which prayer does not accrue Christian merit, which is at the same time both our merit and a gift from God."[301] We may recall that Fénelon had earlier expressed his difficulty to Guyon about her use of "passive," and indeed this concept will play a central role in the formulation of all of the critical issues.

By midsummer 1694, as the time for the meeting of the examiners at Issy, outside of Paris, approached, and as fresh correspondence between Bossuet and Fénelon moved into high gear, it was clear that three issues would dominate the conversations: the nature of pure love as "disinterested," the meaning of the concept of "states" in the life of prayer, and the question of whether the claims for a passive dimension in prayer are viable and well grounded in Catholic tradition.[302]

Bossuet was at a disadvantage. Part of the problem was that he was not expert in many of the writings of the mystics—a deficiency that Fénelon would try to remedy with a barrage of excerpted material—but part of it, too, was that he approached Guyon with a lack of sympathy for the experiential, personal quality of her spirituality by engaging in an excessively intellectual, even rationalizing dissection of her writings.[303] The whole idea that love can be "disinterested" implied for him that we would never ask God for anything in prayer, not even for the power to resist sin or for the grace of perseverance in faith. The problem is that by raising such an objection, he is assuming that if we do not ask God for something, that means we do not *need* it—but the assumption is fallacious.[304]

Or Bossuet assumes that "passivity" in prayer implies an absolute absence of action of any kind—a conclusion that is also quite false, however much it appeals to common sense. Or he assumes, rather like Godet des Marais, that if we do what God has told us to do, such an act cannot really be evacuated of spiritual worth through our being "interested" in our own spiritual welfare. And so on. Cognet offers the thesis that Bossuet "ignored the problem posed, however maladroitly, by Madame Guyon: this is the possibility of the legitimacy of an attitude in which the soul . . . preoccupies itself consciously and exclusively, by way of a psychological method, with loving God only for God's sake, and forgets itself entirely, to the point that even its interior acts are no longer perceived."[305]

Thus, in March 1694 Bossuet's judgment was that Guyon must reject all of the bizarre, visionary, "passive," extreme spirituality of her life's experience, suppress her writings, and submit unconditionally to the authority of the church.[306] Louis XIV is supposed (apocryphally) to have said, "L'état, c'est moi," but Bossuet might well have said, "L'église, c'est moi"![307]

Finally Louis and Maintenon, with the advice of Beauvillier and others, decided that the board of commissioners would consist of Bossuet, Antoine de Noailles, the bishop of Châlon (and eventual successor to Harlay in Paris), and Tronson. At the latter's instigation (since he knew full well who was *really* being evaluated), Fénelon was to be included as an advisor. Based on their final decision, Louis would then determine what restraints, including possible incarceration, would be imposed on Guyon.

This board of inquest would, at its several meetings (called *conférences*), convene at Tronson's place of residence, the country house of Saint-Sulpice, in the Paris suburb of Issy-les-Moulineaux, beginning in late July of 1694 and ending in March 1695. Its decisions would be final in the *affaire de Guyon*. Fénelon repeatedly swore to Bossuet his complete submission to its decrees, since they were both quite aware that it was his own work as well that was being judged.

He quickly began the process of submitting his own defensive statements to Tronson, as well as inundating Bossuet with texts and references from the recognized mystical writers of the church. The central battle of Fénelon's career had now begun. The Conferences of Issy, its decisions, and Fénelon's reaction will lead straight to the *Maxims of the Saints* and his lasting legacy.

"Even when we have faith, we may not have any degree of charity."
—MAXIMS OF THE SAINTS, OPENING EXPOSITION
(TR. HELMS, 216)

"Quiet your spirit and listen to God. You will see that this interior silence is not idleness, but the cessation of our disquieted thoughts, in order to receive a simple and tranquil spirit, and a will pure and supple for the impressions of grace."
—LETTER TO SR. CHARLOTTE DE SAINT-CYPRIEN,
DECEMBER 15, 1696

SIX

From Issy to the Maxims and Beyond
FÉNELON AT HIGH NOON

1694–1699

As the examiners at Issy began their work of poring over Guyon's writings, meeting with her, and deliberating about the soundness of her ideas, Fénelon started sending to Bossuet "memoirs" that he hoped would serve two purposes. Ostensibly, as summaries of historical material, they would be a way of educating the examiners, particularly Bossuet, on the subject of mystical prayer as it had been practiced and explained by recognized Catholic saints. But they would also demonstrate that certain of Guyon's ideas, while aggravating to Bossuet, were well supported in orthodox tradition despite her sometimes exaggerated forms of expression.

Fénelon's thesis was that mystical prayer as taught by Guyon is not a "novelty," not something spun out of whole cloth by a demented brain and never seen before, but, on the contrary, a spirited and forceful evocation of what the church had always taught and saints have always known. This is a huge claim—but one that makes sense in Fénelon's historical and polemical context. The charge always being hurled against the Protestants (recall Fénelon's own *Ministry of Pastors*, and Bossuet was an expert at this kind of apologetic) was that their practice and teaching did not exist in the early church and, *therefore*, was utterly invalid. Nothing delegitimated an idea faster than to say that it was "new" and unheard of, and nothing gave it more credence than to say that it was "ancient" and that reputable authorities from the past supported it.

And so Fénelon set out, initially from behind the scenes, to prove the case, having been careful to make an express declaration that he himself would abide by whatever decisions the commissioners would make and that in his own teachings regarding passive prayer he had only restated the views of Cardinal de Bérulle himself. In his response to Godet des Marais's critique of his letters to Maintenon he was at pains, we recall, to show that his ideas (criticized by Godet) are already found in the beloved Francis de Sales, but now he draws from a larger range of writers from the patristic church all the way down to the "spirituals" such as Teresa of Ávila and Balthasar Alvarez from the recent past. In a letter of July 28, 1694, to Bossuet he says, "I am sending you, Monseigneur, a part of my work, while waiting for the rest to be completed. . . . I am making extracts from books, and pieces of analysis on passages, in order to save you the trouble of gathering the relevant texts [*épreuves*]. . . . I only want to show you, without prejudicing the case, what I believe I have read in the works of several saints."

It appears that the work that he submitted to Bossuet initially was the *Memoir on the Passive State*, along with the smaller *Treatise on the Authority of Cassian*, and possibly the short piece entitled *Annihilation*.[308] It seems to have been about this time also[309] that he attempted to enlighten his former mentor with a compilation entitled *The "Gnostic" of Clement of Alexandria*.[310] Clearly Fénelon's intention in these compositions was to swamp Bossuet with "authorities." The strategy was understandable, even though in due course Bossuet was to dismiss much of this material as idiosyncratic, over-interpreted, or plucked out of context. What is most interesting, though, is the way Fénelon construes the texts, thereby giving ever-greater coherence (that is, "system")[311] to his thinking.[312]

It is in these "memoirs" that Fénelon first begins to synthesize his core thesis, and he does so, as Goré has eloquently argued, by gathering up the whole classical tradition of apatheia or "indifference." The roots are, as mentioned, in the Greco-Roman classical sources, but basing himself on Francis de Sales primarily, Fénelon gave it a fresh formulation as the heart of Christian contemplation.[313] For ancient philosophy the detachment of pure indifference is the wise person's response to the inexplicably dark and overwhelming nature of fate, because it is the one zone of freedom left to each human being. It is in the abandonment of all things, in detachment from those goals dictated by our "passions," that we find inner peace and a kind of release from the chains of a deterministic universe. In Christian hands, as we saw with Francis de Sales, this ideal will become that of "holy indifference," the inner posture of the soul that focuses on God by detaching from all that is not God—all that is worldly, sensual, natural, external, transitory.

The second-century Clement of Alexandria, for Fénelon, already anticipates seventeenth-century mysticism with his contention that the inner life of the mature Christian must come to reflect the "knowledge" (*gnosis*), or wisdom, deeply embedded in every soul and reclaimed from the obscurity of corporeality by Jesus Christ. It is a wisdom forgotten by "carnal" and worldly people, as well as immature Christians, who are afraid of God or try to use God for limited and selfish purposes. In fact, says Jesus, if we wish to follow him and to enjoy the blessings he confers, the blessings of true reason, we must learn to love God by practicing the apatheia of indifferent love. We must withdraw from investment in all that is carnal in order to contemplate God with the eye of the soul, as the Truth, the logos of the universe, in a spiritual, incorporeal, and disinterested way. Then Fénelon turned to the *Conferences* of the fifth-century abbot John Cassian, who, as he instructed his community of monks[314] in the practicalities of Christian discipleship, advanced the idea that in contemplative prayer, as heart and mind turn increasingly to the indifferent adoration of God, something like a stable state, a "perpetual prayer," gradually emerges. This habitual union, says Fénelon, "is that pure love that prays to and contemplates ceaselessly the well-beloved. It is that contemplation of amorous regard of which all the mystics speak . . . it is the contemplation of a fixed and enduring state that no interior activity can interrupt," and yet at the same time, "it is not a kind of ecstasy that prevents the ordinary activities of life."[315]

What Fénelon thus claimed to find in the tradition of Greek Christian culture, culminating in Cassian and then passing down through a variety of authors, is the view that "perpetual prayer" is a "state, [an] immobility of the soul always pure and detached from all that is not God, always evenly tranquil, whether the spirit breathes with distinct communications or not, always faithfully passive so as to be sharply alert for God's working. [It is] a habitual disposition, which allows for the kind of interaction with God in which the soul vacates itself, so to speak, and then returns to itself in order to view what God will reveal to it of the divine activity, without there being any cessation of the passivity."[316]

This "passivity," this "perpetual *state*" of prayer, this inner and detached contemplation is a way of talking about what *comes*, and *might happen*, when we turn to God—*if* we earnestly seek perfection, and *if* God imparts a special measure of enabling grace. The clear implication, for Fénelon, is that we *should* seek this higher contemplation, if in fact we yearn for perfection (maturity), because God wants to give the necessary grace. This mystical prayer is thereby "normalized" as a desirable possibility for everyone.[317]

In the *Memoir on the Passive State* Fénelon argued that the ideas of "pure love" and "the simple and passive prayer by state" are interlocked, mutually defining realities.[318] "One is the love that the mystics call pure, or abandon, and that St. Francis de Sales calls holy indifference; the other is the simple prayer, or passive prayer by state." He goes on to describe this state as one of total focus on the goodness and glory of God, so that any kind of willed act on the part of the adoring soul is excluded, including pious acts of thanksgiving or praise, which normally bring some kind of pleasure or satisfaction to the soul that offers them. This is a radical way of saying that self-will, and therefore self-love, have disappeared while the soul is focused on God. Part of this is that the soul no longer operates in terms of discrete acts of any kind, because all such acts require an element of self-consciousness ("reflection on the self"), and in this sense it can be said that "I will nothing and know nothing"— that is, I am *passive*—while in this special state of adoring prayer.[319] Then comes the even stronger statement: "One is not indifferent to God's will, which is one's own will; nor as a result can one be indifferent to his law or the precepts of his church. But one no longer has a will in the measure that the will of God declares itself interiorly or exteriorly: his will has become ours." Echoing St. Augustine, he claims that the soul in the passive state is in the mode of "adoring consent" to the divine will.[320]

In the mystics, says Fénelon, holy indifference, abandon, passive prayer, and contemplation by state are all essentially equivalent. He is quite clear—and he tries to put Bossuet at rest on this—that *moral* imperfection will still mark the life of the Christian, thereby necessitating moral struggle, and that any attempt "which turns prayer into a corruption of morals" is abominable. He gathers a number of authorities to support his case[321] and concludes that this concept of the passive state describes the human soul "in the simplest, most direct, manner, the manner most supple and free from hesitation and *admixture with its own movement* [italics added], for cooperating with grace." This is the state, he avers, in which without doubt the prophets and apostles operated. This is the true and hidden ministry of Jesus Christ, completely given over to the love of God, and in no way in contradiction of the Law. But also he stakes the claim that all loving contemplation, in the final analysis, is a passive prayer, because "passivity means wanting what God wants," and *only that.*[322]

In these essays, Fénelon thus put his cards on the table, in a way calculated to appeal to Bossuet and then to the other examiners as well, as clearly but also as precisely as he could.[323] Another way to say it, though, is that he tried to stack the deck in his favor by snowing Bossuet.

Facing the Examiners

How did they respond? First of all, Bossuet took charge of the proceedings and quickly became the dominant examiner. Second, we know from a complex correspondence that Guyon was treated roughly, particularly because of some of the more graphic passages in her *Autobiography*. These texts confirmed Bossuet in his belief that she was "diabolical." Nonetheless, she was careful to keep Fénelon unimplicated in her trials and prepared on her own an elaborate and well-researched set of *Justifications*. But inevitably Fénelon and his ideas formed a kind of horizon and backdrop to her own arguments.

Bossuet moved deftly. On the one hand he smoothed things over between Maintenon and archbishop Harlay, who, feeling that his authority had been ignored, moved to issue an official censure of Guyon without waiting for the results of Issy. On the other hand, he began the process of counterattack with Fénelon. In a work entitled *Tradition of the New Mystics* he argued,[324] with some justice, that Fénelon was reading back into Clement of Alexandria latter-day understandings of the gnosis/wisdom of Christian faith rather than discerning ancient meanings. Most significant, though, he began to introduce his own oversimplified version, dubbed "new mysticism," of what Guyon and Fénelon had been saying about the nature of passive prayer.

Louis Cognet calls this oversimplification "an outrageously schematic understanding, hardened to the point of becoming a caricature."[325] The essence of Bossuet's claim is that the "new mystics" teach the idea that the person who is passive in prayer operates in the mode of a "single continuous act of contemplation," which never needs to be renewed, which is always a single, undifferentiated state where nothing happens (it is all "state" and no "act"), and there is no interruption. Any kind of differentiated consciousness of God or of Jesus Christ ceases. "It is a sort of complete inaction," says Bossuet, "and [thus] something that is utterly foreign to true Christianity." Cognet calls this caricature an example of Bossuet's "intellectualist and pragmatic" mentality expressing itself in a minimalist understanding of Clement of Alexandria (Clement, says Bossuet, is simply teaching the good habits of ordinary Christian discipleship) by contrast with Fénelon's "mystical exegesis," which is a maximalizing view (Clement teaches the full-blown interior mysticism of "perfection," says Fénelon).[326]

One thing, though, that is remarkable about Bossuet's orientation is that he stuck to it doggedly, even after years of discussion. In the period after Issy, while he and Fénelon sparred, he insisted in his *Instruction on the States of Prayer* on interpreting the passive state in prayer as a "ligature," a condition in which the human soul is bound, literally "tied up" by the power of God, and is completely helpless. Bossuet was willing to acknowledge that such a thing happened for a very few extraordinary souls but believed it had no place in ordinary Christian living. By contrast, Fénelon insisted that the passive state, *properly understood*, is not powerlessness but empowerment and thus has a central place in daily discipleship. That point would be driven home by the next turn of events.

Sudden Elevation in Medias Res

In January 1695, Bossuet rendered his personal verdict on Guyon, and she, by her own request, soon went into retirement in a convent in his diocese to await some sort of judicial sentencing by the crown. But then, as that piece of the drama drew to a conclusion for a time (in due course she would end up in prison at Vincennes and then the notorious Bastille), another big piece suddenly was set in motion, a "gift" from Louis XIV that Fénelon would call "the greatest that anyone could receive from another man."[327]

The first official notice of the death of the much venerated Jacques Théodore de Bryas, archbishop of Cambrai—which happened to be the wealthiest see of the kingdom—came on November 18–19, 1694. Under the rules (called "Gallicanism") of the French church, Louis would name the successor and, unless the pope strenuously objected (which was unlikely), that cleric would be the next archbishop. After some church politics had been processed (including some machinations involving "seniority" among the clergy), Louis announced on February 1, 1695, that "he would be naming as archbishop of Cambrai an abbé that would surprise everyone, but also that everyone would approve." On February 4 he indicated his choice: the abbé Fénelon.[328]

The reasons are complex. We know that, whatever his reservations about having Fénelon as his personal advisor, Louis approved of and was grateful for the quality of the work Fénelon had been doing as tutor for his grandsons. There is also the fact that although he was an aristocratic priest entitled to church emoluments (guaranteed income), Fénelon had been slow, because of modesty, to acquire these and was overdue. There is further the suggestion that, disliking the fact that too many bishops idled at Versailles and became nuisances, Louis wanted to support the Counter-Reformation emphasis (from the Council of Trent, but not always honored) on "residence" for bishops, that is, that they actually reside in their dioceses and function as local pastors most of the time.

Fénelon had been an outspoken advocate of that Tridentine ideal, but it also allowed that for three months out of the year a bishop could be elsewhere—and in Fénelon's case these would be three months in which he could be at Versailles as a royal tutor. It also seems to be the case that by naming him to Cambrai, Louis avoided the possibility that Fénelon would be available for nomination (which some friends hoped) as the archbishop of Paris when that politically powerful position became vacant (which it did very soon, and it went to Noailles). Maintenon's feelings are not clearly known, although there has always been the suspicion that she favored Noailles for Paris. So, the reasons were multiple. In any case Louis was right—everyone *did* enthusiastically approve.

Now the game changed at Issy just a bit. "Up to this point he had been treated courteously but somewhat condescendingly, especially by Bossuet. He would henceforth be anointed with the same sacred oil as the other bishops, a successor of the apostles as they are. From this date, therefore, the commissioners agreed that they should allow Fénelon to join their group as an equal."[329] Indeed, in due course Bossuet uncanonically (it was not his diocese) but at Madame de Maintenon's request (because she wanted to make a show of "peace" between the two men) and in her presence and that of the Duc de Bourgogne and an admiring female community would be Fénelon's chief consecrator in the chapel of Saint-Cyr on July 10, 1695.

The mandate of the Issy examiners in the meantime had not changed—to pass judgment on what seemed erroneous in Guyon's teaching and *by implication* that of Fénelon as well—but now Fénelon had to be included in the formulating of the conclusions, the "articles," produced by the commission, and he had to sign them and agree to abide by them. What complicated matters was that the examination of Guyon's *writings* and public teaching at Issy was all mixed in with Bossuet's more individual assessment of her as a person—the state of her soul and her spiritual soundness. What was to separate Fénelon and Bossuet on a very profound level was that the former, while agreeing on occasion that Guyon's writing had marks of exaggeration, overstatement, and misstatement, also insisted that as a person and spiritual guide she was reliable, sensible, and wise. Bossuet, by contrast, came to the conclusion that because of her exaggerations she was demented and saw everything in her writing as wrong to the core. On the one hand, Fénelon made every effort to keep these two agendas separate and thus repeatedly averred that the *real* issue in the debate about Guyon was the true nature of mysticism, its essential principles, not the status for better or worse of one woman. And for a time, but not indefinitely, he was able to maintain this high ground.

But it was starting to become clear that Bossuet would not have it: for him everything about Guyon, both her person and her work, equated with false mysticism, and Fénelon's insistence on being loyal to her would eventually make him seem false also. The idea that the higher level of contemplation—that labeled "passive"—excludes reflexive and discursive acts, thereby making it possible for the believer *meritoriously* (that is, with free will intact) actually to be indifferent to salvation, was hard for him to swallow. His analysis of the nature of charity, that is, love of God, weighted the factor of "indifference" in a way that diverged from

Fénelon's views by limiting its application to worldly vanities only and not heavenly rewards.

Bossuet further insisted that the unitive states of prayer described by the mystics, Fénelon's "passive states," are nothing more than "a disposition and habitual, perpetual preparation for doing nothing that would displease God and for doing what would please him."[330] Cognet calls Bossuet's thinking at this point "the victory of anti-mysticism" and argues that in the final analysis "the formulas of Bossuet in the ensemble were triumphant."[331] Fénelon would insist later that he had signed the Articles of Issy only because Bossuet promised to compose agreeable interpretations of what the articles meant.[332] In fact, that never happened.

Operating on the defensive, Fénelon conceived his task as one of toning down Bossuet's position and patiently arguing for modification in his formulations. The other commissioners worked up a statement of thirty articles, Fénelon responded with his own "counterproject" in thirty-three articles, and the final result, after the haggling, was a series of thirty-four "Articles of the Conferences of Issy," issued on March 10, 1695, and signed by the four commissioners. The first thirty articles were primarily the work of Bossuet and Noailles, while the last four were included as a concession to Fénelon. The purpose of the articles, in Gosselin's words, was not only to indict "reprehensible" ideas in Madame Guyon's writings, but also "to oppose to the errors of the new fashion of mysticism [*mysticité*] some doctrinal maxims intended to prevent the abuse that was being perpetrated on the basis of the exaggerated expressions often encountered in mystical authors."[333] Politically the purpose was to make peace between Bossuet and Fénelon. For this reason the articles have the form, not of an indictment of Guyon personally, but of a generalized and orthodox understanding of mystical prayer. But the whole product was a whitewash and endured the fate of most such efforts: failure.

The Final Articles and Their Impact

The Articles of Issy[334] were produced by churchmen (primarily Bossuet and Noailles) who were trying to quash with a twofold strategy a movement (quietistic spirituality) that they perceived to be disruptive of the orderly discipline and teaching of the church. And yet that movement was too well grounded in the whole history of Christian experience (the attitude of Fénelon and Tronson) to be simply dismissed. Thus, it was a touchy business.

Their first thrust, therefore, was to emphasize what is obligatory normally, ordinarily, and generally for "every Christian, in every state, although not at every moment." Every Christian, including those in the higher states of contemplation, is required to maintain always the "distinct" exercise of works of faith, hope, and love; to have explicit, not just *implicit*, faith in *all* of the attributes of God, as well as in *each* member of the Trinity; and to have explicit faith in Jesus Christ as the divine mediator. In the true worship of God the focus can never be completely "abstract" or finally separated from particular representations of Christian revelation. Further, every Christian must engage in the fight against sinful desiring; must continually seek remission of sin; must engage regularly in standard acts of piety such as reciting the Creed and the Lord's Prayer, going to confession, and so on, or engaging in suitable "mortifications," so that the "doing" of "acts" of faithful living is in no way diminished or discounted in favor of a "higher" piety in which one might no longer need to will not to sin.[335]

In the same spirit of cautious churchmanship, their second emphasis was on the danger at worst, the optional nature at best, of "extraordinary states." The tendency for the believer to look to "special" inspirations for guidance is forbidden, as is the overvaluing of exceptional states of prayer or imagining that the interior life consists only of such states. The faithful Christian is reminded that self-conscious awareness of one's obligations, one's spiritual gifts, one's spiritual state is a good and necessary thing, as long as one avoids a sinful self-love in doing so and gives God the glory. "Indifference" as a spiritual quality is affirmed only with regard to earthly consolations, *never* with regard to salvation. "Perpetual prayer" is defined, in Bossuet's terms, as "a habitual preparation" for doing good and avoiding bad, never as a unique, continuous, uninterrupted "act." "Extraordinary spiritual paths," when they happen, must always be subject to the authority of the bishops. Extraordinary contemplation of the type endorsed by Francis de Sales must be affirmed so long as it does not obviate more ordinary practice by appealing to "the pretext that the love of God [implicitly] includes them in some manner."[336]

The real "give" to Fénelon is in the last articles, where it is acknowledged that there are truly great spiritual persons who manifest superior levels of perfection by continuing to love God despite being convinced of their own damnation. Part of the excellence of such persons consists of loving God in all of the "rigor" of the divine justice, knowing that such rigor may entail a withdrawal of any sense of the divine love from the soul. There is an acknowledgment that some perfect souls, operating on the "impossible supposition"—namely, that even though God, seemingly, has damned them they will love him because he is God—may at a high level of perfection make the disinterested sacrifice of their own salvation (called the "conditional sacrifice of salvation" because salvation is foresworn *only on the condition* that such is God's will). But there is the insistence that we must not allow such souls to acquiesce in such a mistaken belief. Finally, there is the acknowledgment that some "perfect" souls are led by God in a way that diverges from the way of "beginners," "each in his own way, by a different set of rules," and that the perfect understand the Christian virtues at a higher level.[337]

So, with these last concessions and some change of detail in the earlier articles, Fénelon was willing to sign. Bossuet rubbed it in by tacking on a later coda of his own, unsigned by the other commissioners, regarding the passive state in prayer, insisting that it is, as mentioned above, a "ligature of powers," that is, that the soul in such a state no longer has free will or any mind of its own.

A brief period of truce followed, in which Fénelon seems initially to have been content with the articles,[338] although each endured some criticism from supporters for compromising. In letters that shortly followed to Madame de la Maisonfort and to Charlotte de Saint-Cyprien and then in a more detailed *Explication,* examined and approved by both Tronson and Noailles, Fénelon clarified his understanding of what was implied in the articles. Bossuet for his part, in a directive to his diocese dated April 16, 1695, the *Ordinance and Pastoral Instruction on the States of Prayer,* laid out *his* understanding of the implications of the articles. It was gradually to become clear that the two men were moving in different directions in their interpretations.

Since these developing divergent views would, in 1697, result in the two definitive works of this phase of the quietist controversy—for Fénelon

the *Maxims of the Saints* and for Bossuet the *Instruction on the States of Prayer*—
let us consider the key ideas that build up to this climax. The essence is
straightforward, although the details become convoluted. Fénelon stands
for an understanding of the spiritual life in which interiority is construed
in terms of inner conditions or "states," formed through intimacy with
God and then generative of outward behavior. Bossuet tends to come
from the opposite direction: interiority is the inner distillate of the moral
results of discrete "acts" of faith or practice, of how we behave. There
are contemporary derivatives as in the contrast between cognitivism and
behaviorism in psychology.

Take, for instance, the basic Christian conviction that we are saved by
grace: is that conviction, *properly speaking*, a constantly repeated, constantly
reinitiated assent by the will and the intellect (Bossuet's view), or is it a
settled condition, a moral/spiritual orientation, conscious or unconscious,
sustained with a person's "heart" (Fénelon's view)? If it is both, is the
second higher and more desirable? The question is: on which side of the
divide does mysticism, rightly understood, fall?

In order to legitimate his view of mysticism, Fénelon engaged in ever
more careful distinctions, so that what is false or merely "novel" in current
mystical practice could be winnowed out. In a letter to Madame de la
Maisonfort of March 1695, he is exquisitely eloquent about why it is that
he values true mystical prayer so much. The purpose of such "passive"
prayer, of such "passivity" in general, is to help the devout person break
free from the "bad" sense of self, that is, the self-love, that propagates
"complacency or anxious disquietude" in prayer, where "forced" acts are
constantly taking place. The admonition, thus, to drop "self-reflection"
in prayer is not intended to discourage a "good" self-awareness, in which
one is intermittently conscious of what *God* is doing or presenting in one's
life, but precisely to enable the kind of patient listening and responding
that can occur only when a self-forgetful, unstrained "state of repose" or
"simple prayer" occurs. This is why focusing on one's eternal salvation
as the ultimate gift from God only *increases* disquietude, shifting the
emphasis (nonanxious) from what God is wanting to give me to what I
need (anxious) from God. "Although the reward which consists of eternal
blessedness can never be truly separated from God's love, these two can
still be separated in our motivations." When I rest with God, having been

"drawn" by grace into a disinterested, passive state of loving and simple regard, *then* God empowers the "simple and peaceful" actions that are the fruit of quietude and that are *always* the outward marks, so to speak, of the real thing. These actions are "distinct," says Fénelon to Maisonfort, but not "forced" and are tailored to the circumstances and exigencies of the individual. True mystical prayer, "if it is genuine, far from turning us away from simple acts in the principal occasions of daily life, is, on the contrary, the pure source that produces and facilitates such actions."

In a later letter to Charlotte of Saint-Cyprien (March 10, 1696) Fénelon produced a skillfully composed[339] resumé of the main points in his understanding of Issy. He was careful to send it only after first showing it to Bossuet, who approved. In laying out "the principal aspects of the doctrine of the interior life . . . in abridged form and in haste," he urges this Nouvelle Catholique convert, now a Carmelite nun, to understand clearly what it means to be a "small child" with God: it is "the simplicity of candor, of straightforwardness, of a unique rapport to God alone, of sincere defiance of self in everything," where, he says, "you must never think yourself advanced, because you are scarcely so . . . you must let yourself be judged by others, even though they have no great insights . . . you must never compare yourself to others . . . you must forget yourself, not at the expense of vigilance, which is essentially inseparable from the love of God, but only with regard to the anxious musings of self-love."

Having thus described the mindset of a proper interiority, he articulates its devotional core: "the act by which we adore spiritual Being—infinite, incomprehensible, unable to be seen, felt, tasted, imagined, and so on— is fundamentally the exercise of pure love and pure faith." He tells her to "keep at it, by which I mean renew it ceaselessly [and thus, *not* in a single, continuous, uninterrupted act] in a simple and peaceful manner. Don't leave it off for anything else that you might seek out perhaps with inquietude and inner urgency, contrary to the direction that grace takes in you." This is "true faithfulness of the soul, which, in its deepest peace, prefers listening to the interior spirit of grace above anything else."

In this same letter, he is at pains to emphasize that contemplative prayer for Christians is always in and through Christ, sometimes dependent on a sensory meditation on his life, or his Cross, or his words, but that "it is not necessary always to have an actual picture" or "a felt union with him" in mind. Sometimes souls will think they have lost him, but at such times of "testing" they should know that he is only hidden, so that they might rise above "sensually tasted, mentally held" possession. The great insight of the mystics, Fénelon insists, is that they realize that *anything* less than God himself, however excellent, pious, virtuous it may be, quickly becomes "a seeking after one's own consolation and one's own interest in the enjoyment of God's gifts." The greatest danger comes with the greatest gifts, because in the very moment that a gift from God becomes an instrument for the propping up of self, its valence is reversed—and a positive becomes a negative. His programmatic statement follows: "the activity with which the mystics find fault is not real action and the co-operation of the soul with grace, but rather anxious fretting or a forced fervor that seeks after God's gifts for its own consolation. The passive state, on the contrary, is a state simple, peaceful, disinterested . . . where the soul is 'exempt from the anxieties and urgings of self-interest.'" And so, the "last purification of the soul" is "the rarest and the most difficult," and yet, he would insist, it is the high calling to which we all are called.

Bossuet must have been pleased, because at this point Fénelon was being careful to resist even the faintest suggestion that mystical prayer and pure love, rightly understood, would accommodate quietist, Molinist distortions. There is also the implication, as Fénelon would repeatedly insist now and later, that there was no fundamental disagreement between himself and Bossuet on "the interior ways." However, we know from his private commentary, or *Explication*, of the Issy Articles, produced sometime in early March 1696,[340] that as he rankled at the severe and increasing condemnation of Guyon and the increasing pressure, especially from Maintenon, to issue a public censure of her person as well as her teaching, he was also engaged in efforts to show that the Issy articles needed qualification.

To take just one example, Chérel points to Fénelon's dissatisfaction with article two of Issy, in which the claim is made that the good Christian "always does distinct acts of faith." Yes, said Fénelon, that is true, but such acts must not be done in a "perceived," self-aware way. The point is that it is still all too easy for self-righteousness to rear its ugly head. In just such a manner was Fénelon beginning to pick away at what he saw as dangerous imprecision in the articles.

To Tronson he explained his situation with regard to Guyon and her status by stating that "the whole mystery boils down to my not wanting to speak against my conscience, and not wanting to heap useless insult on someone whom I have revered as a saint so far as all that I myself have seen."[341] Although he stayed silent in public, he made private pleas to Maintenon on March 7, 1696, and to Chevreuse the next day on behalf of Guyon, emphatically swearing his loyalty to Issy and Bossuet, but also contending that Guyon was being mistreated and misrepresented throughout the whole process.

Clearly some sort of psychological slippage was occurring for him in this incongruous situation: he could not *both* defend Guyon *and* take the position that he and Bossuet were in deep agreement. It is probably the case, I think, that he began to see that he had compromised too much, that in his yielding at Issy to Bossuet's insistence on the dangers of false mysticism and in tolerating the seemingly willful misconstrual by Guyon's critics of her ideas, the true nature of "pure love," both in theory and practice, was being at best obscured and at worst eviscerated.

In his own mind, at least, he was perfectly confident that he had tradition, in this case Thomas Aquinas and the medieval "schools," on his side: perfect charity, which is "perfect" or "pure" because it is completely disinterested, gathers up into itself all other virtues, so that the virtue of hope, normally reflective of the natural human desire ultimately for beatitude, is itself "supernaturalized," that is, becomes a hope for what God desires and not what we desire. Another way to make this point would be to say that the *valence* of hope, when subordinated to love, changes: it rejoices in the fulfillment of God's purposes and not our own.[342] Justice had yet to be done to this idea, seemingly subtle at an abstract level but critically important, Fénelon thought, when translated into daily discipleship. He would spell it out in the *Maxims*.

In the meantime, Bossuet served up his views. In the *Ordinance and Pastoral Instruction* already mentioned,[343] he published the Issy articles for the enlightenment of his diocese and made it clear that several errors contained in the writings of the "new mystics," of those "who seek in prayer sublimities that God has not revealed and saints have not known," had been flushed out and condemned. He detailed these errors as the belief that in the prayers of the perfect, contemplation of the humanity of Jesus Christ is no longer necessary; that there is a "false and disinterested generosity" toward God in which we no longer ask him for anything (including salvation); that contemplative prayer requires the cessation of all distinct acts, including those commanded by God, based on free will; that in prayer one may cease to exercise the mortifications required for the practice of Christian virtues; and finally that the practice of "extraordinary" prayer in contemplation in some way excuses one from the ordinary disciplines and practices of the community. At the conclusion of the document Bossuet indicated that by the Articles of Issy the works of Michel de Molinos, of François Malaval, and of Madame Guyon (although she is not mentioned by name, only the titles of her books) are hereby condemned. On that note Bossuet, followed by Noailles and Godet des Marais in similar documents to their respective jurisdictions, began his post-Issy assault on the "new mysticism." But he was saving his biggest guns.

The pressure on Fénelon to come forth with a public disavowal of Guyon intensified, especially since he had signed the Articles of Issy, thereby *seeming* to have rejected her. On the contrary, his reading of Issy was that an affirmation of core elements in Guyon's teaching had been clearly stated in the all-important articles thirty-one to thirty-four. Since he remained adamant in his refusal to disavow her and the public scandal was increasing (why does Monsieur de Cambrai not condemn that horrible woman?), Bossuet attempted a (seemingly) reconciling move—which would, in due course, backfire. He proposed that they produce a joint work, interpreting the Issy articles for a wider audience, showing their agreement and putting the disputes and bad feeling to rest. The plan was that he, Bossuet, would take the lead with an initial treatment that he would then submit to Fénelon for his input and approval.

Fénelon agreed to the plan, and Bossuet commenced grinding out the composition that became the *Instruction on the States of Prayer*, a work that seems to have started in a conciliatory spirit but that by degrees became in its final form a full-scale, merciless assault on Guyon.[344] Addressing the work to Pope Innocent XII, he rolled out every argument, every text, every polemic he could possibly conceive in order to kill this monster of Molinist/Guyonian quietism once and for all, while offering at the same time his own construals of the principal orthodox mystical writers.

In July 1696, Bossuet sent the *Instruction* in draft to Fénelon, just as the latter was leaving for Cambrai, in anticipation of gaining his approval. It was not to be. By his own statement Fénelon, after an initial glance at the work, immediately saw that Guyon was the target. In Melchior-Bonnet's phrase, the situation now went from "insult to confrontation."[345]

What enraged Fénelon was his perception of a mindlessly and rigidly literal reading of Guyon along with an absurdly gratuitous critique of her person. He sent a furious letter to Chevreuse on July 24, 1696, with a list of the false charges he believed Bossuet to have trumped up against Guyon's books, and then summarized the same material for Madame de Maintenon in a long, plaintive September letter. Feeling that enough was enough, and after ranting at length about Bossuet's gross over-reaction to exaggerated, incautious, and colorful language in Guyon's work while ignoring the saintliness and rectitude of her character and her wise spiritual direction of others, he announced to Maintenon that he had begun a work that would serve as his own public interpretation of Issy. The book would be, he explained, a defense of true mysticism, something "much too unknown to the majority of scholastic doctors" and, therefore, ripe for proper explication with a suitable marshalling of authorities.

Having refused his approval to Bossuet's *Instruction*, he now felt duty bound, he claimed, to offer his own exposition of core mystical principles, of "the system of interior ways," in a strong, clear, and precise manner. He told her that he had been careful to show a first draft to Noailles and Tronson and was fully assured (!) that Bossuet would be comfortable with it. His hope was that "all of the pain of wounded, sensitive vanity [*vains ombrages*] would be dissipated" as he offered to the world an "authentic" declaration of his views. He would be making use, he told Maintenon at the end of November, of "proper things for reducing to silence the hardest critics" and "the people with damaged sensibilities [*les gens ombrageux*]."[346]

A whole drama of timing then followed, in which Fénelon's friends (particularly Beauvillier and Chevreuse, supporters of Guyon and eager to see Fénelon vindicated), approving of his intentions and knowing that Bossuet might beat him to the punch with his own about-to-appear book, moved quickly to have the *Maxims* published. Tronson and Noailles, who had a chance to scan it ahead of time, recommended some abbreviation and tightening. Tronson, always prescient,[347] raised the issue that later would be the sticking point: is it fair to say that all the virtues, particularly love and hope, share the same single goal, the glory of God, or is it better to say that love and hope have different goals—the glory of God in the case of love, human salvation in the case of hope? Tronson thought the latter and that Fénelon's move to absorb all virtue into love, where the glory of God becomes then the *only* object, was unwise.

Sure enough, Rome balked on just that issue. Nonetheless, before Fénelon could demur, Chevreuse had the book printed and it appeared on February 1, 1697, far enough ahead of the official publication of Bossuet's *Instruction* on March 15 to have time for independent impact and to upstage the inevitable debates to follow. Fénelon's new work was, says Louis Cognet in a marvelous phrase, "a redoubtable war machine."[348] The die had been cast, and the battle had been joined.

Fénelon versus Bossuet: Who Is the Heir of St. Augustine?

Bossuet was especially surprised, stunned, and hurt by the preemption. The result was that the two books were to function as position statements in an exchange of blows that would continue for the next year and a half. In an increasingly polemical, often repetitive series of critiques and rejoinders Fénelon and Bossuet each claimed to represent the true voice of the church's tradition on the subject of mysticism. The public loved the virtuosity of the swordplay (although some were lost in the technicalities or considered the whole matter too abstruse). Church leaders were polarized and scandalized. Louis and Maintenon were infuriated at the continuing uproar. And finally, after being drawn in by all parties, the pope intervened. So, we ask the question again: what was really at stake in this convoluted debate about "pure love"?

The essence of Bossuet's constructive argument in the *Instruction*,[349] and the spirit of the work, is captured in the "conclusion" at the end of the last chapter. Having polemicized at length against the "excessive exaggerations"[350] of the false mystics, his chief thrust is aimed at the whole idea of a passive "state," continuous, unchanging, and never needing to be repeated, that the mystic claims to enjoy in the presence of God. Bossuet contends that the false teachers represent this state as one of utterly indifferent love in which the mystic is relieved of ordinary Christian responsibilities, duties, and expectations because the essential nature of such prayer, operating at a suprahuman ethereal level, enables him to transcend such requirements. Such passive prayer, as Bossuet describes it, is, in the language of the Issy articles, "extraordinary." The term tends to be pejorative, since it denotes for both Bossuet and Fénelon a kind of unregulated, chaotic spiritual state subject to demonic illusions and fanaticism. And having then proceeded to lay out his own understanding of the orthodox mystics, particularly John of the Cross and Francis de Sales, by offering a clarification of their views on the nature of passive prayer or the "prayer of quiet," he comes to the point.

"The fundamental commandment for a Christian is clear," says Bossuet: it is to love God totally, because "the whole Christian life tends to pure and perfect love."[351] Fair enough, Fénelon might have said, but "the devil," is, as we say, "in the details." Bossuet goes on to explain this commandment in a very specific way, because he chooses a biblical text that slants the interpretation. At Deuteronomy 6:4ff., Moses, speaking to the people of Israel as they are about to enter Canaan, tells them that they are to love the Lord their God and obey him "for" God has chosen to bless them and their forefathers with a rich land and much abundance. Thus the divine goodness and the divine demand are inextricably coupled. The clear implication, says Bossuet, is that the God we are commanded to love is precisely "God for us"—that is, the God who wills that we unite ourselves to him in love and gratitude for many blessings but who also makes it clear that we are to express our gratitude by obedience to his commandments. Love, thus, is a function of gratitude and obedience. "The chaste and pure object of our love is a God who wishes to be for us . . . so that the motivation to love God as the God who wills to be for us is what pure love is." In other words, we are to love God for his goodness in loving us, and we are to express that love in orderly lives. Love for God is loving God for what we are given. The problem with the "new mystics" (that is, Guyon), thinks Bossuet, is that this is not good enough.

Bossuet's intention, of course, is clear. His view is that the concept of "love" makes no sense except in a context of mutual *quid pro quo:* love by its very nature is an exchange of benefits. There is an adamantine bond between the commandment to love God and *the desire for favors, as well as gratitude for favors,* as the basis of that love. At a later time, blasting away at unreal notions of "indifference" in the nature of love, he said it this way: "the essence of love is that it always wishes to possess its object, and human nature is such that we *necessarily* wish to be happy."[352]

For Bossuet, certain implications follow. Loving is just part of the fabric of living. Thus the true love of God is the goal of *every* state of the Christian life, and we see that this state called "passive prayer," or for that matter anything "extraordinary," is quite unnecessary for attunement to that love. The second is that love is behavior. *Actions*, the actual doing of "explicit" deeds of piety, or loving-kindness, or self-assessment, are inseparable from *being*, that is, from "states" of the soul, however exalted, before God. These may not be "suppressed or suspended" by appealing to false ideas of an imageless, undifferentiated, continuously withdrawn type of prayer, the one exception being those unusual conditions known as "the binding of powers," where a very few mystics, such as Francis de Sales's famous associate St. Jeanne de Chantal, lose all control of their human will in times of intense contemplation.

Finally, for Bossuet, we must never think of obedience to God's commandments as being "interested" in any valid sense of that word. The hope for salvation or beatitude, a hope that we actively pursue through obedience, is not a self-interested disposition, as if it were "selfish" to desire these lofty ends. In modern parlance, Bossuet would say that we are "wired" to desire certain things, and that the real question is not whether the desire itself is good or bad, but whether we engage in the pursuit at the expense of others, or not. True love, Bossuet would say, is like a faithful spousal relationship in which faithful love for a partner is expressed when one is "urged on by the chaste desire to possess him." What could be more pure than to love God in the same way? And yet, Fénelon might have said, there is something unsettling about the idea that we should "possess" God in the way that we might a human partner!

The Maxims

Fénelon, razor sharp and poised at this point, moved quickly. He reviewed Bossuet's arguments and proceeded to expose his misreading of the orthodox mystics as well as his tendency to confuse quietist errors with the real thing. Using in the *Maxims* a structure of "false statement — true statement," he proceeded to show that not just Bossuet but all the "anti-mystics" (including the Jansenist Pierre Nicole in his 1695 *Refutation of the Principal Errors of the Quietists*) launch their thunderbolts at all manner of "false" mysticism. They then fail to appreciate the "true" mysticism consistent with the dogmas and traditions of the church. Indeed, his criticism of Bossuet in a letter of February 9, 1697, just after the publication of the *Maxims*, was that operating from a recent and superficial acquaintance with Francis de Sales and other mystics, he was ill prepared to separate out the true from the false in understanding these writers correctly.

Fénelon saw that in order to overcome these ill-founded criticisms, especially those of Bossuet, he had to come forth with a set of more finely honed, "more precise,"[353] and at the same time more transparent formulations. The language of the mystics often *is* misleading, if not dangerously inflated,[354] and it is much too easy, given the clearly heretical nature of Molinist doctrine, Fénelon thought, to misconstrue mysticism in Bossuet's way as at best an elitist doctrine for a very few chosen souls, while for most of us it is a dangerous escape from the realities of human nature, the ethical requirements of the Gospel, and the ordinary structures of legitimate authority. Fénelon set out to clear the air once and for all with a clear statement "of the system of interior ways."

The intellectual challenge, as Fénelon saw it, was to place the insights derived from Guyon and others firmly within a well-defined mainstream, and the best way to do this was to adopt a schema derived from Scholastic-Aristotelian theology, in which all created things strive in the direction of their proper "perfection." Since the essence of human spirit is to love what is most lovely, that is, God, all human loving strives in this perfect direction, even though in actuality it may not, and often does not, reach it: that is, its "potential" does not become fully "actual." "Pure love," then, is the end and perfection of all loving, that for which we are made, and it is particularly the mystics, such as Richard of St. Victor and Bernard of Clairvaux, who worked out a series of stages by which the human spirit can ascend from imperfect to more perfect levels of love.

⌐. This is the schema adopted by Fénelon that he used for the rest of his life in defending his ideas. He later reformulated this structure in the language of the medieval Scholastics, such as Thomas Aquinas, arguing that the glory of God is always the *final, ultimate* object of love, whereas human salvation is its *formal and proximate* object. In other words, one loves God in the *form* of seeking one's salvation, but for the *purpose* of being transformed, so that motivated by the divine will as the operating force within, one learns to love God with God's own love.[355] It is the distinction between my loving you in order to get something from you, versus my loving you in order to be changed into some more ideal being. Being human, we get to the latter by way of the former; but the mark of maturity, Fénelon might say, is that we become less reliant on the former as a necessary mechanism. Love becomes less dependent on desire.

In the "system" of interior life as practiced by the mystical saints of the church, Fénelon tells us in the opening discourse of the *Maxims*, the soul that desires to love God will, as it matures, move through five stages of ascent to God, each state marked by greater indifference (and thus, more "perfect") as the motivating force.[356] At its lowest level, the love for God is entirely selfish, based on the desire for earthly good and the fear of earthly bad. At its highest level, this love, now entirely disinterested and void of all self-referential motivation, is focused solely on the glory of God as its end. Several levels of "mixed" love, where varying degrees of self-interest and disinterest are simultaneously present in the one who loves God, come between the extremes.

The highest level of love is, of course, the level of most concern precisely because it is the one to which all of us should aspire, but it is also the most problematic for description since it contains the inevitable paradox: the loss of self is the gaining of self, to lose oneself in loving God is precisely to find oneself. Although there is nothing essentially new here, since we already know that love for God, if the individual wishes to be mature, must progressively eliminate self-love as a motivating force, what *is* new is the use Fénelon made of the graded structure between the extremes. With this series of stepping-stones, he could show that different levels and forms of practice are acceptable and appropriate for the Christian who is "on the way." No level of love is inherently evil, just imperfect or immature, waiting, as it were, to move forward in ascent to a higher level as and when the individual is ready to take that next step.

Part of what happened was that Fénelon was taking with all seriousness the claim of his critics that, in appropriating Guyon, he had broken with tradition. Absolutely critical, therefore, was an increasingly self-conscious use of Augustine as a warrant, partly because Bossuet was doing the same, and partly because Jansenist critics such as Nicole had accused him of being disloyal to the great Augustine. Bossuet, for instance, in his *Instruction,* made steady reference to Augustine and the third-century Cyprian of Carthage for the idea that "abandonment to God" has nothing to do with so-called passive prayer but simply refers to what is ordinary and normal for every Christian: the act of trusting God's grace, rather than our own works, as the means of salvation *at the same time that* we continue to make every human effort to live holy lives.[357]

Fénelon, on the other hand, insists in the *Maxims* that Augustine is quite clear about "the selflessness of love concerning salvation," although it is true, he says, that loving God "can never exclude conformity with God's will which desires our own salvation and which wants us to desire it as well—with him for his glory."[358] On the question of the passive state he declares that he will proceed only with the "utmost caution," since "all interior paths lead to pure love as their destination, and, in life's pilgrimage, the highest of all degrees is the habitual state of this love . . . [which] is the foundation and roof of the whole structure." He wants to anticipate "all possible dangers," but his bottom line is clear: "the love of God alone, considered in and of himself and without any mixture or commingling of selfish motives or of fear or of hope, is pure love: perfect charity."[359]

Fénelon could now move forward with a twofold strategy that he honestly hoped would work with Bossuet. By means of his hierarchy of the levels of loving, he could allow to his critics many of the practices such as explicit acts of faith, devotion to the sacred humanity of Jesus, repeated and self-consciously willed acts in response to divine commandments in Scripture, and the like that they insisted on as being essential to Christian discipleship. But he then argued insistently that these belong, *insofar as they are self-interested,* to the lower, less mature levels of Christian practice. That is, they have the character of what he calls "mixed love" at the intermediate levels, which is a blend of genuine love for God with ordinary human self-seeking and thus some degree of a fearful and mercenary spirit. Such love is also dependent on sensuous, pleasure-producing imagery in the approach to God, because it requires "payback" from God in the form of various satisfactions in order to sustain itself. But here is the twist: there is a massive difference between "God, inasmuch as he is perfect in himself and without relation to me, and God, defined as my possession that I want to try to acquire."[360] The essence of what it means to move from immaturity to maturity is to learn that lesson. The duty of the competent pastor is never to push souls to grow until the time is right. "It is necessary to limit oneself to letting God act and to never encourage pure love except when God by the workings of an inner anointing begins to open a heart to this word, which is so harsh to souls still attached to themselves and so liable to scandalize them or to cast them into anxiety."[361]

So far so good, we might say, and my guess is that Bossuet, though edgy, would have moved in step with Fénelon through the first four of the *Maxims*. The fourth in particular would have appealed to him, because there Fénelon is clear that the virtue of hope remains intact *within* the virtue of love, since they both have God as their object, even though their motivation is different (hope has self-interested motives, but love does not).

Beginning with the fifth, however, Fénelon began to work his second strategy, implicitly at least, with the idea that at a higher level of the soul's structure it begins to operate by means of contemplative prayer in a "state" of holy indifference, and this indifference is a mark of a change that has occurred, namely, that the soul is starting to work not by its own will but by means of the divine will. In this state, says Fénelon, the will wants "not wanting," that is, it aims to transcend its natural dynamic. The sure sign that grace is beginning to work in the soul is the cessation of cravings and longings of all sorts: the will "lets go" of its own natural energy in order to open up space where God can enter. Such a soul, he says, can then be available to want only what God wants, and since that includes salvation, to want *that* also—but contrariwise, if God's will was (or at least, seemed to be) for damnation, then to want *that* as well.

Be it noted, moreover, that this "not wanting" happens only in the "higher level" of the soul, while the "lower level" may do business as usual, feeling every normal human emotion and desire. This idea of the two levels to the soul—a higher that functions on a transcendent plane and a lower functioning in terms of our psychic/physical nature—goes back through Francis de Sales to Augustine, but it serves as a way of saying that the soul can be focused on God and on the world at the same time, the only question being which focus shall be dominant. The mark of maturing is that the higher level is progressively reining in the lower level. The agonizing Jesus Christ himself "happy on the cross," that is, in the higher part of the soul where intellect and will are located, while in great suffering in the lower part where are situated imagination and sensation, is the supreme example.[362] Fénelon's intention is clear here: he has found a way of saying that in mystical prayer we do not become automatons, and "holy indifference," rightly understood, cannot mean apathy to ordinary human needs.[363]

But, nonetheless, this is the kind of talk Bossuet considered "extravagant and exorbitant," even though Fénelon insisted that it is found everywhere in the tradition and that it is only, as Francis de Sales intended, a logical, even if incautious, restatement of what it means "to love God alone." In other words, indifference means just that—*indifferent* pushed all the way beyond mere resignation, which is a simple turning over of everything to God—so that the active loving of God as God *does not preclude our daily immersion in the strains of ordinary human turmoil.* Fénelon makes the point that "abandonment" to God, that is, the embracing of disinterested love, is not a "brutish indifference" to everything, as if nothing mattered in this life (the false view), but the willingness to follow God when there are no rewards in doing so—to follow God, we would say, purely because God is lovable. Bossuet, of course, would have added, "because it is commanded," thus leaving the door open, Fénelon thought, to self-love or spiritual smugness (I'm doing what I've been told to do. Aren't I good?). The soul that abandons itself to the indifference of loving God suffers profoundly and never ceases to struggle with sin, even while it loses all spiritual consolations and ceases to be conscious of its own virtue in the form of "selfish reflection" on its "direct acts."[364]

If Bossuet was obtuse to, or rejecting of, Fénelon's twofold strategy, then his complaint makes perfect sense. All of this expects too much of people, he said, and it simply demotes natural human loving; while it may be descriptive of the lives of souls in heaven, it can never characterize sinful human beings living in the midst of a complex world. Quite the contrary, Fénelon would say, it only shows what God is capable of doing with our "natural" (always imperfect, even when "innocent")[365] human loving, with our hopes and dreams, with our potential for goodness when we go inward and turn these over to him for purification and transformation.

Fénelon is at pains to explain that this higher level of perfection must not be confused with "hearing voices or seeing visions" (that is, "illuminism") or with the spiritual pride or arrogance of those who feel superior to everyone else. Indeed, Fénelon worked with an everlasting paradox: those who *really* are spiritually superior never know it, never think it, never act on that basis—but *we* know it and are edified. The supreme example here, Fénelon contends, is the Christian who, absolutely convinced that she is lost, "does not even indirectly agree to cease loving him [God] for one instant."[366] That is the point of becoming a "child" who cannot conceive of *not* loving the parent. This is what Bossuet could not grasp.[367]

The psychology of quietist spirituality comes out again in Fénelon's sustained effort to affirm, on the one hand, all of the traditional corporal disciplines that guard against sin, while contending, on the other hand, that it is the right use of these disciplines in the right spirit that is essential. The trouble with so much practice is that it is done in a spirit of anxiety, lacking trust in God, and ultimately fearing punishment. Thus, it becomes an instrument of self-love, a form of "indiscrete and hasty zeal." He says of those who are growing in pure love that "they fight tooth and nail against sin, but this struggle is peaceful because the spirit of God resides in peace. They resist in the presence of God, who is their strength. They resist in a state of faith and love, which is a state of prayer." Here he articulates a softened form of the Molinist/Guyonist "laisser tomber," that is, letting temptations "fall away" by ignoring them and thus robbing them of power.[368] As Owen Chadwick once observed,[369] this strategy of "death by attrition" for temptations makes perfectly good sense for obsessive-compulsive people—most of us—since in many cases the faster and harder you fight or run, the faster and harder you are defeated and fall.

Vocal prayer is good, says Fénelon, but silent prayer is better; the use of meditation with images is good, but contemplation based on immediate communion with God is better; discursive and discrete actions in prayer are good, but it is better when you let God take control of what happens; talking "actively" to God is good, but listening "passively" is better, because the listener is letting God's grace work and is getting out of the way, and so on. In passive prayer, Fénelon contends, there is an "ebb and flow," by which the soul moves in and out of God, never in a fixed, lasting, unchanging way (imagine an elevator moving up and down between the levels of the soul), but in an alternating rhythm of relaxation into God followed later by loving human response.[370]

Then he summed up the daily morality of pure love. First of all, it entails a responsible use of worldly wisdom for unworldly ends. The Christian must live in the present moment, using what is at hand, but trusting to divine Providence like a "little child." Natural pleasures may be freely enjoyed but never in a way forbidden to others by divine command. All of the virtues are to be practiced assiduously, but without the interference of distracting, often complacent self satisfaction or self-awareness. Living in pure love implies that one's soul is open to divine leading at every moment, and there ensues a certain freedom from the restraints of set structures such as regular times for prayer or prescribed mortifications and penances.[371]

❦ In this last he was, of course, on dangerous ground, because he seemed to be saying that "more mature" Christians do not have to play by the same rules, but what he actually meant was that maturity precludes scrupulosity, legalism, and overreliance on structure, precisely because the mature Christian is living in more direct communion with God. One way, perhaps, to say this is that the mature Christian "uses" the rules instead of being "used by them." But this is a risky train of thought, and Fénelon would be misread here. Even though Bossuet hated this kind of talk, he would have been, and actually was, just as quick to denounce legalism in religious practice. Fénelon then went on to make it clear that this "communion" of the mature soul with God is an accomplishment of grace, that is, something God gives and that remains dependent on God, not the expression of some kind of flawless perfection ("original innocence") in human terms. Everything here depends on wise pastoral care by the clergy directed to persons who are in a suitable condition to profit from mystical teaching, because nothing is easier than to be deluded into a false spirituality that makes a travesty of pure love by imagining that it is easy, quick, or already accomplished. The "perfect" are always just beginning.[372]

So, there we have it. Fénelon laid out his vision of the spirituality of pure love, setting an elite standard as high as eternal perfection itself, but simultaneously struggling to affirm all that is necessary, obligatory, realistic, and practically possible for all persons at whatever stage or level of development they may be. "Be where you are," he would say, "but aspire for more, and never just 'settle' for less." I called Fénelon's two-fold strategy "dangerous" because it hovers on an elitism in the negative sense of the word—something of which Bossuet accused him—but he was careful to avoid that by insisting that what Henri Gouhier calls his "dualist structures"[373] (higher and lower levels of the soul, conscious and unconscious) pertain to all persons inherently and are not the special agenda of superior individuals. There is grace here for large hearts and minds, but judgment as well for those who operate with a more constrained, perhaps more cynical, vision.

Unfortunately for Fénelon (although he would have said "fortunately" as his cross to bear) these latter included not only Bossuet and his party but Madame de Maintenon and finally Louis XIV himself.

Reactions to the *Maxims* varied. Cartesian intellectuals, including the Jansenists, responded negatively to the seeming irrationalism of mystical experience as construed by Fénelon (thus tending to agree with Bossuet's criticism). The religious orders—Benedictine, Oratorian-Sulpician, Jesuit—knowledgeable about mysticism responded positively (partly, at least, because they tended to be anti-Jansenist). The heresy hunters of the Sorbonne, doctrinal policemen of the church, appreciated the subtlety and sophistication of Fénelon's accomplishment (partly because Fénelon had done his homework) but winced at some insufficiently cautious expressions. The most dramatic and damning response came, of course, from Bossuet himself, who saw the work as utterly hopeless *"galimatias"* (grandiloquent nonsense).

We are told by Voltaire (who despised Bossuet) that sometime during the period of February 20–23, 1697, Bossuet knelt before the king and repented of having consecrated Fénelon even while suspecting all the time that he was a heretic quietist.[374] Since that description comes from someone antipathetic to Bossuet, it may not be entirely trustworthy, although it is certainly consistent with the characters involved. Bossuet *must* have regretted what he had done, especially in view of the fact that

Fénelon's advocates now closed ranks. His supporters at court among the dévots were too powerful to be dismissed by one French bishop's opinion alone. As the publication of the *Maxims* quickly mushroomed into a cause célèbre and people took up opposing positions, Louis realized that he was in the middle of a hornet's nest. There was thus the possibility of a bloody fight within court circles—the last thing he wanted, given all of his other concerns. Bossuet and Louis in due course realized that appeal would have to be made to Rome for a judgment. The problem was that they preferred to avoid doing that. Getting the pope involved in French church politics raised Gallican hackles, in their reluctance to admit that Rome could exercise authority from afar *over* the French church. Fénelon had put them in a bind.

Any such appeal to the court of Rome would be politically complicated, involving not only issues of final arbitration and ultimate jurisdiction in strictly inner-churchly matters, but also the painful possibility that the pope might choose to plainly contradict both the opinion of the French episcopate and their king as well! So it was beginning to seem that Fénelon was making things complicated and awkward for Louis—and he hated that. It is one thing to be a nuisance but another to be a menace, and Fénelon was slipping into the latter category.

Sure enough, in May Fénelon would ask Louis's permission to make the trip to Rome in order to lay his *Maxims* at the feet of the pope. It was a decisive move on Fénelon's part and places him within the developing "ultramontanist" and therefore anti-Gallican tradition of papal authority. This was another strike against him from Louis's point of view because of its implication of *less* power for the French king and his bishops in final decisions about the church and *more* for Rome. And it became another piece of the whole process leading to the First Vatican Council where the nature and means of the church's "infallible" judgments in dogmatic matters would be officially defined. And so, this appeal to Rome by Fénelon, in addition to all that Rome already liked about the archbishop of Cambrai, certainly endeared him to Pope Innocent as well as to his secretary Cardinal Albani, soon to be Clement XI.

"The only proper course . . . is to suffer humiliation in peace. In peace, I say, since humiliation which is accepted angrily and reluctantly is in truth no humiliation at all."
—Letter to the Comtesse de Gramont,
November 17, 1694 (tr. McEwen)

"Any misfortune which touches us closely and is humiliating in its effect is of greater value than an angelic virtue which we complaisantly appropriate as our due. Fear not, therefore, to be weak. . . . The day will come when you will laugh."
—Undated letter, ed. Caron, 6:139 (tr. McEwen)

◆

SEVEN

Louis Thunders, the Pope Decides
FÉNELON HUMBLED

1699–1715

If Madame de Maintenon was a complex personality, Louis XIV was even more so. Raised by his mother, the devoutly Catholic Anne of Austria, to have an uncritical and unquestioning faith, he saw himself as one who was obedient to the spiritual authority of the church and thus intolerant of Jansenist deviations on the one hand and rebellious freethinking on the other. Protestants he abhorred as dangerous, discordant heretics.[375] National unity as represented by loyalty to the king, who embodied French "glory," was his supreme value.[376] Further, as he learned especially from Bossuet, his anointed royal sovereignty, absolute and requiring no accounting to any earthly authority, was legitimated by the church as "God's will."[377] Basing himself, thus, on the divine right of kings, he could expect and enforce total obedience from a subject people, who, for their part, expected him to operate with assertive and aggressive authority, with "the serenity and patience of those who participate in things eternal."[378] His subjects *wanted* him to be absolute, and he was more than willing to play the part to the hilt. Let those who would challenge him beware. As one historian, hostile to Fénelon, tells us, "Fénelon was to be the first man to teach humility to princes. We shall see what came of his lessons."[379] Indeed.

In becoming mistress, and finally wife, to Louis, Madame de Maintenon took on a monumental challenge—but one that she seems to have been (mostly) up to. Considering that Louis was someone whose very look caused people to freeze with fear, particularly if they sensed they had displeased him, whose "appetite for flattery was insatiable," and "who was continually preoccupied with the impression he created," he needed to be treated with care.[380] What Maintenon brought to the table, in addition to her native shrewdness and good sense, was a strong, even puritanical religiosity that Louis needed in order to steady himself. She became his strong anchor and trusted confidante in a sea of flattery, hypocrisy, fawning, and intrigue.

At this point, however, historians vary widely in their opinions, some seeing her influence as positive and essential to Louis's success, others seeing her as a cunning schemer, always using everything, including religion, to her advantage.[381] As we know, Fénelon saw her as a devout soul trying to grow and, although filled with pride and "high spirits" (*vivacité*), honestly trying through her special role as royal consort to have a good effect on Louis and, through him, on the French people as a whole.

— From the beginning of their relationship, Fénelon tried to give advice to Maintenon on how to deal with Louis in matters of faith.[382] The essence of the advice was: be a model for him of goodness, virtue, loving-kindness, mercy, patience, and so on, especially in the way you treat him when he mistreats you; do not push him to be more mature or more devout in faith than he is prepared to be, but wait for God's own time in such matters; never allow yourself to be manipulated by others in such a way that they can use you in order to gain access to him; never by your own lack of virtue in public bring discredit on him; be honest with him in private, but in a way that is always tempered by gentleness. Your job, Madame de Maintenon, is to play your role well as a follower of Jesus Christ, recognizing that all that comes is the cross of Christ beckoning to you. We have seen it all in Fénelon's general spiritual advice to her. In short, Madame (we might say), be a quietist saint with Louis and with everyone else as well!

The difficulty in all this advice, though, was pointed up by her own spiritual analysis of Louis: "he cannot understand the necessity of humbling himself and acquiring the true spirit of repentance," and, perhaps more damningly, "he is a saint at Versailles and an atheist in Paris."[383]

We have seen the tangle that Fénelon eventually got into with Guyon and Saint-Cyr and then the unhappiness that Maintenon began to feel with his spiritual teaching, all the time pouring this rumbling discontent into Louis's royal, but tin, ear on spiritual matters. There was also the rumor, never verified, that Fénelon had refused to approve of the proposed legitimating marriage between herself and Louis, and that this accounted for some of her animosity to Fénelon.[384] In any case, the last thing Louis needed or wanted, given his military, economic, and other political imbroglios as well as his aversion to religious "novelties," were clergy who fostered instability with strange ideas or by creating that worst monster of all—criticism and disobedience either with regard to Louis's public policy or his private life. He was getting enough of that already from various quarters.

It is in this context—namely, the tension created for Maintenon by Fénelon's criticisms of Louis, as well as the general uproar of developments at Saint-Cyr—that Maintenon's relations with Fénelon ruptured for good.[385] She, in fact, treasured for the rest of her life the direction that Fénelon gave her, but, put in a bind where she had to choose between what he was telling her and what loyalty to Louis required, the abbé was bound to come out on the short end.

— We can only imagine the chagrin and rage Louis might have felt at reading Fénelon's single most famous epistolary creation, the "anonymous letter to Louis XIV," composed probably around December 1693, and, more likely than not, never actually perused by the Sun King.[386] Jean Orcibal speculates that it may have been sent to Louis via Madame de Maintenon, who would have kept it to herself as an *aide-mémoire* (personal reminder) for gradually speaking some "hard truths" to Louis.[387] Surely Louis was averse to receiving one more stinging broadside about the political and economic grievances of French society. Discontent about Louis's war-making, especially in Flanders, with the accompanying ruinous taxation, combined with his disregard for the advice and authority of trustworthy advisors—relying rather on worthless sycophants—and coupled with food shortages and substantial suffering among the poor had caused public criticism to rise to an alarming level. After a series of military victories in the Low Countries from 1689 onward, things had turned sour by 1693, and Louis was in retreat and feeling besieged. It is probably not true that Fénelon took his life in his hands by daring to write an acerbic letter of reproach, since others were doing the same, but it seems likely that his forthrightness would have cost him dearly with the protective Madame de Maintenon, standing by Louis's side (as

Fénelon earlier had told her to do) and resenting his critics. But he wrote it anyway.

The letter is a powerful, unrelenting, eloquent scold from beginning to end, written with a devastating punch made all the more cutting by its artfulness. The central indictment is that Louis, by all of his war-making, has reduced France to the status of "a huge hospital, decimated and without means," and has at the same time, especially by his utterly unjust aggression against the Dutch alliance, created a situation in which "the Allies prefer making war unsuccessfully rather than concluding peace with you."[388] Louis has fostered misery at home and implacable enemies abroad, and the reason for this is the insatiety by which "you love only your own glory and your ease" in a court filled with "monstrous and irremediable luxury," along with his constant tendency to listen only to corrupt, or at best cowardly, political and ecclesiastical ministers."[389] Perhaps most damningly, "your religion consists only in superstitions, in petty superficial devotions." Fénelon warns that as things are going, the God of justice will humiliate Louis, unless he repents, unless "you . . . ask for peace and, by this act of shame, expiate all the glory that you have made your idol," since, he tells Louis, "you do not love God at all— you only fear him with the fear of a slave." The tragedy of the present situation is that a king who ought to have "a father's heart for his people," who ought "to find his glory in providing bread for them," who "has been put on earth for your people" has utterly failed.

What is striking in the letter, moreover, is that Fénelon, a monarchist to the core, has a touching faith in Louis himself as the anointed one. It is not too late, if only he will stop listening to false advice and will turn instead to the true Source of strength. We are reminded of precisely the same teaching that Fénelon was at the same time pouring into the young Duc de Bourgogne in the hope that the next ruler of France would be different. It is not the *system* that is corrupt (as Fénelon's later democratic readers tended to interpret him), it is the *people* who run it. Put good people in and it all changes. That is, interiority comes first and behavior second.

Perhaps the sharpest dig in the letter, and one that may have led to its never having been delivered, was the critique of two of Louis's most beloved councillors: "at least Madame de Maintenon and the Duc de Beauvilliers ought to have used your confidence in them to enlighten you. But their weakness and their timidity dishonor them and scandalize everyone. France is up against the wall . . . they do not love you, then, because we have to be prepared to anger those whom we love rather than flatter them and betray them with silence." *That* statement alone may have sealed Fénelon's fate with Maintenon, and we can only hope that Beauvillier, that utterly steadfast defender of Fénelon, never saw it. "You must humble yourself before God's hand if you do not want him to humble you," says Fénelon in a rather desperate, even pathetic, plea that he repeated later, almost word for word, to the young Duc de Bourgogne. The letter is not rude and mean-spirited, as its critics maintain, but is poignant and heartrending, as well as being a fine representation of Fénelon's capacity for the iron fist in the velvet glove.

In the meantime, though, in this period after the first publication of the *Maxims*, Louis's mounting exasperation with Fénelon would have been fed mostly by the growing, increasingly politicized and embittered theological controversy. Indeed, Louis gave Fénelon permission to appeal to the pope for guidance, in the hope that he would keep the debates as quiet and "in-house" as possible, while he himself plainly indicated to the pope that he disapproved of Fénelon's *Maxims*.[390]

But the controversy could not be contained. In due course both Fénelon and Bossuet, represented by partisans in Rome, steadily ratcheted up the intensity of exchanges, each side developing its own narrative of the events leading up to the *Maxims*. In Bossuet's version, the *Report on Quietism*, Guyon is represented as a pathological fanatic and Fénelon as a paragon of hypocrisy and betrayal with regard to Issy.[391] The latter made a spirited defense, and the character assassination intensified. Finally, the mudslinging having gone on long enough, a reluctant but beleaguered Innocent XII, weakened by age and illness but pressured by Louis's representatives to do *something*, rendered a verdict.[392]

During this period of 1697–99, while Fénelon was beginning his pastoral work in Cambrai, while various individuals and groups were still digesting the *Maxims*, while machinations on the part of the pro-Bossuet and pro-Fénelon factions slowly ground away at Rome and Fénelon's relations with Louis and Maintenon deteriorated, he carried on a running struggle. His opponents were the group of his principal theological and ecclesiastical critics from Issy days—Bossuet at Meaux, Godet des Marais at Chartres, and Noailles at Paris. Through letters, circulating pamphlets, and the official channel of "pastoral instructions" to their respective dioceses, the feud continued.[393]

— Almost immediately after the publication of the *Maxims*, in the latter part of February 1697, Fénelon requested and received from Madame de Maintenon an open hearing in her presence with Noailles, followed up by a written appeal.[394] There he began his defense by pointing to the "unresolved" issues from Issy: the nature of disinterested love, the trials or temptations facing the mystic who practices disinterested love, and the nature of passive prayer. He defended the circumstances involved in publishing the *Maxims* by arguing that he had given Noailles every opportunity to examine the work and to raise objections, he had secured approval from the Sorbonne ahead of time, he had tried in good faith to deliver copies to Madame de Maintenon and to Bossuet before publication, and so on. Informed by an apologetic and embarrassed Noailles that there would be a new examination of his work by commissioners approved by the king, Fénelon responded bluntly. Let such an examination be conducted in all rigor, he insisted, so that the examiners will carefully distinguish between matters essential to faith and morals and issues that remain debatable and variable among Catholic theologians. Let the final decision in no way be a superficial effort to accommodate the "finickiness" (*délicatesses*) of the bishop of Meaux or to be a whitewash of the genuine differences between himself and that prelate! And so the fight continued.

Fénelon and Bossuet Debate Again

The arguments advanced during the post-*Maxims* debate were intricate, subtle, and scholarly. The dispute often had the form of a logomachy, in which hairsplitting contentions about terms and definitions predominated. Fénelon composed explanations of what he intended to say in the *Maxims*, his critics formulated rebuttals, and there were rebuttals to the rebuttals. Gosselin summarized the substance in four points.[395]

1. The two men continued to disagree about the nature of love for God, Fénelon always insisting that the *motive* for loving God must at the highest level be completely disinterested love of God for the sake

of God's glory, even though the one who loves God *knows* that God always wishes to confer beatitude. It could be stated this way: in the moment that I love my spouse because she is lovable (pure, disinterested love), I do so with the knowledge that she fully loves me as well, but I do not do so *in order that she might love me as well* (somewhat interested love because hope is mixed in). Bossuet tried to squeeze around this in various ways, such as dismissing the language of the impossible supposition (I shall love God even if he sends me to hell) as a language of "amorous extravagance" on the part of some saints, but, as Gosselin shows, Fénelon had tradition solidly on his side.[396]

2. They continued to disagree about the nature of passive prayer. Does such prayer occur in a state of human powerlessness (Bossuet), or in an anxiety-free state of pure receptivity to God, peaceable but active in its own way (Fénelon)? Fénelon was careful here and had Bossuet on the ropes. When one listens, one is *doing* something, but in a "passive" kind of way. It was the old issue, again, of the so-called laziness attributed to those who practice passive prayer.

3. On the matter of what is called "passive prayer by state," they debated about the nature and place of "the mercenary spirit" in mature prayer. Recall here Fénelon's view that what makes prayer "passive" is its purely disinterested quality: if I am really listening to God, I *simply cannot* be self-concerned or agitated about my own welfare. He became increasingly sophisticated on this matter, so that in the later debate he argued against Bossuet that mature Christians desire a "supernatural end" for "supernatural reasons," that is, they desire salvation in accordance with *God's* goals and not because they want it for themselves, this latter being a natural desiring of a supernatural end. Natural loving is a good thing, says Fénelon (he is careful here), but supernatural loving is better, gathering up the natural human desire, already implicitly aimed at beatitude, in a more fulfilled and complete way.[397]

Put it this way: if, loving you, I do something good for you, and my pockets are in some way lined at the same time, then I have accomplished a supernatural end for a natural reason. Better, says Fénelon, to do something good for you in which I derive no profit (even the smug sense that I have done you a kindness). That is a supernatural goal for a supernatural reason—and this is what it means to love God purely. This last was the real issue between the two men, and, we might add, one that has troubled Christian ethics ever since Augustine.

For instance, there is the implication that for Fénelon the loving deeds of a pagan are genuinely good (as they were for Augustine) but imperfect, whereas for Bossuet, because these acts have no explicit reference to the Christian God as a warrant, they are "only natural" and worthless altogether (the more puritanical, almost Jansenist position). And, of course, these arguments by both men were backed up by massive reference to church councils, and decrees, and accepted writings by recognized authors, and similar resources.

4. The fourth issue involved experiences that may be peculiar to the passive state of prayer. Specifically, Fénelon had contended all along that some saints, in the passive state of prayer, "absolutely" renounce all hope of their salvation but continue to love God (on the "impossible supposition" that God has condemned them eternally). Bossuet considered this preposterous, but for Fénelon the issue was one of the extent to which "the mercenary spirit" is truly given up when we claim to love God.

In these areas of disagreement theologians have tended to come out on Fénelon's side, and over time Bossuet himself shifted in Fénelon's direction. Nonetheless, the church has never officially adjudicated such contentious points. Much of the official papal censure of the *Maxims*, as we shall see, centered on the way in which Fénelon *seems* to remove every element of fear and of hope from the dynamic of loving God in the highest states of prayer. For example, in the very moment that I seem to love, say, my spouse, or a friend, out of a sheer sense of what it is in them that makes them lovable and that draws my affection, have I *in that moment* ceased to fear the consequences of not loving the other person in such a (relatively) pure way, and have I ceased to hope for benefits to myself in so loving? Are the fear and hope swallowed up, as it were, in the loving?

Fénelon never hesitates to answer in the affirmative, having made a reference to friendship (and thus to Aristotle and St. Thomas Aquinas) explicitly. Surely in the *very moment* of pure loving, interested fear and hope have ceased to operate, but it is only a moment (however prolonged), and it might continue even while my conscious mind turns elsewhere. This idea remained ultimately incomprehensible to Bossuet and his supporters, and it was just too risky for church authority. This is why the condemnation of Fénelon would not be based on the claim that his maxims are wrong, but rather that they were "bad-sounding," "offensive to pious ears," "susceptible of a bad sense"—in other words, dangerous. Therefore, thought Fénelon, after the condemnation was enacted, no retractation was necessary (because he was not *wrong*), only silence (because he spoke *incautiously*).

In the meantime the wheels ground on. Madame de Maintenon remained very much at the center, eager now to make a complete break with any taint of quietism, alternately encouraging Bossuet, Noailles, and Godet des Marais in their attacks on Fénelon or criticizing them for their lack of energy in doing so. Melchior-Bonnet relates that she even attempted to recruit Malebranche into the onslaught, although that great thinker did not articulate his reservations about pure love, as we shall see, until a later time.[398] Louis, utterly exasperated with the situation, moved to have all of the nuns, including Madame de la Maisonfort, who had been influenced by Guyon and Fénelon removed from Saint-Cyr and packed off elsewhere. Concerted attempts at reconciliation among the combatants were attempted with the expedient of compromise formulations, but all to no avail. Bossuet and the others finally delivered on July 18, 1697, what Maintenon wanted—a formal condemnation by the French bishops of the *Maxims*.

Melchior-Bonnet's description of Fénelon's attitude at this point is, with a qualification, a good one: "there was in Fénelon's cry much pain and much pride. Pain because of the strong sense of injustice, since it clearly seemed to him that he was the victim of the fears, the deceptions, the vindictiveness, the petty and calculating righteousness of the first lady of the realm; pride also, because in his innermost conscience he opposed Bossuet's pompous [*trop grande*] theological simplicity and anger on the one hand to the elevated truths of the greatest saints and the wonders of the inner life on the other."[399] The qualification is that Melchior-Bonnet echoes a bit too much the verdict of Bremond here, namely, that well-intending clergy were trapped by an unscrupulous woman, Madame de Maintenon, who then is the villain in the drama. But that being said, it is unquestionable that Fénelon felt himself duty bound with regard to his theological principles, so that his position at this point, prior to any decision by higher authority (the pope), was "Here I stand; I can do no other."

When Fénelon finally asked Louis for permission to go to Rome to present his position,[400] the monarch refused, as Fénelon knew he would, insisting instead that the archbishop's cause would be represented by others—in due course, Fénelon's friend Gabriel de Chanterac, while the Bossuet faction would be led by that prelate's nephew, the abbé Bossuet.

In his formal request to Pope Innocent Louis appealed for a judgment on the *Maxims*, indicating at the same time, for the pope's edification, his personal disapproval of the work. On July 31, 1697, he ordered Fénelon to leave Versailles and to remain for the duration at Cambrai. "The enchanter," says Melchior-Bonnet, "was becoming a plague."[401] In a letter shortly thereafter to Madame de Maintenon, where Fénelon sought her forgiveness, he also wrote that "I return to Cambrai with a heart full of submission, of zeal, of gratitude, and of unlimited attachment to the king. My greatest sorrow is that I have fatigued and displeased him. . . . I will always pray for him . . . and my respectful attachment to you, Madame, will never diminish."[402]

The end result was that Louis finally did get what he wanted: a judgment against the *Maxims* and settlement of the conflict. But it all came only at the end of a process in which it was clear that Fénelon, having stood his ground and offered massive amounts of detailed explanations of "pure love," had won a major moral battle even if he lost the ecclesiastical war. Innocent XII was kindly disposed to Fénelon and hated being bullied by Louis, even though he knew that knuckling under would be inevitable. The pope was also disgusted by Bossuet. In his *Report on Quietism*, Bossuet had not only accused Fénelon of personal treachery, but he also compared him to Molinos.[403] With regard to Guyon, Bossuet described Fénelon, with an almost audible hiss, as "that woman's man."[404]

So the official commission met, and met, and met. The investigation gathered documents and testimony, correspondence and position papers flowed, influence was solicited in various quarters. The membership of the commission, deeply divided, was shuffled. But the end was a foregone conclusion. In the standard format of theological censure, a list of objectionable propositions extracted from, or implied by, the *Maxims* was produced. Innocent reviewed the text and passed it to his secretary, Cardinal Jean-François Albani, for final editing.[405]

Albani, the future Pope Clement XI, "deployed all of the resources of his subtlety in order to deceive Bossuet and his nephew,"[406] that is, to create the impression of a stronger condemnation than was actually the case. Indeed, the finished document, to Bossuet's ultimate disappointment and that of Louis as well, was not a solemn papal bull but a lesser communication known as a letter or "brief," further qualified by Innocent's *motu proprio*, which turns the brief into a personal pronouncement by the pope himself rather than by the whole papal curia. The result is that the objectionable propositions, twenty-three of them, were being censured by the pope as a disciplinary measure and not as an official and public condemnation of heresy. What could have been a judicial death sentence for Fénelon (so to speak) ended up as a stern pastoral action, a kind of fatherly cease-and-desist order.

As Ronald Knox put it, "Rome had pronounced on the doctrine without chastising the delinquent."[407] The condemnation, furthermore, was *global* in the sense that the real target was a tendency, a direction, an implication evoked by the *Maxims*. The danger was in what people *might* think, if they took the *Maxims* seriously. The menace, thought Knox, was "ultra-supernaturalism," that is, what I have called "angelism."[408] I don't think, however, that that was the pope's fear exactly, since, in fact, he thoroughly approved of all of Fénelon's ongoing explanations and clarifications. If we recall for a moment the condemnation of Molinos, we will remember that the great concern is not that people will somehow set the bar too high, but rather that *they will talk about setting the bar high and then use this as a cover* for license and the breaching of all boundaries. The pastoral problem is not the fear of asking too much of people, but rather of asking too much too soon, so that then they become cynical and devious. It's a fine dilemma.

Innocent wrote another brief a short time later full of praise and promotions for a number of church leaders, including some who had been strongly supportive of Fénelon during the official inquiry. As preceptor

and possible minister to a possible king of France, Fénelon had already
been designated for a cardinal's hat. There is strong evidence that the old
pope soon to die (Albani would become pope on November 23, 1700),
despite the censure, held Fénelon as a cardinal in petto, that is, one to
be officially named at some future opportune moment.[409] After all, said
Clement XI a little later with regard to Fénelon, "he was misguided only
by an excess of the love of God, for which he has paid with a great deal
of submission and humility. It is the case that the bishops of France have
been deeply lacking in charity toward their brother." Cooler and more
politic heads ultimately prevailed, mindful that such an honor would have
been a slap in the face to Louis. The promotion never happened.

The Condemnation

The opening paragraph of the papal brief *Cum alias,* dated March
13, 1699,[410] indicates that the "agitated uproar" in France following
the publication of the *Maxims of the Saints* requires a pastoral judgment
on the content of that book from the pope. Innocent indicates that the
outcome of a thorough process of examination by various authorities has
resulted in the judgment that the *Maxims* contains teaching "that could
lead the faithful into errors already condemned by the church," since it
contains propositions that, taken in their "plain sense" and in their logical
implications, are "scandalous and offensive to pious ears." The twenty-
three "bad-sounding" propositions are then listed.

For the most part, they sound very much like the complaints that
Bossuet had been aiming for some time at Fénelon but that Fénelon
insisted were true only of false mysticism. The twenty-third proposition
may be taken as typical:[411] condemned is the idea that pure love is the
only thing present in the interior life, where it becomes the only principle
and motivation for all deliberated (freely and consciously willed) and thus
meritorious acts. We know that Fénelon had not said quite that. What
he said was that at the *highest level* of interior life, where indifferent love
reigns, all other virtues are *incorporated as being of secondary importance, but
continue to operate in transformed fashion.*[412] But the nuances are lost here, especially if we recall that the real target of the condemnation is not specifics,

but a *tendency*. The first question for the papal examiners was that if you take the element of reward out of the practice of religion, will people still practice it? Even Thomas Aquinas admitted that sometimes there is material gain in our love for God. The great Lutheran theologian Philip Melancthon is often quoted as saying that "to know Christ is to know his benefits," but this ice is very thin: in the twinkling of an eye, religion becomes a market commodity.

The implication of the censured propositions was that Fénelon went too far by positing this idea of pure love as a "state," as something continuous and undifferentiated, a transtemporal experience of eternity absolutely perfected in a sustained and utterly self-forgetful, disinterested simplicity, where conscious and discrete acts of the human will are suspended. A modern way to say this might be that there is a spiritual condition in which the human soul is in a prolonged posture of "nonstop giving" to God without "expecting" anything. Fénelon had said that the expectation of receiving something good (ultimately, beatitude)—this being the virtue of hope—is "gathered up" into the loving, so that its operation is subordinated to love. It is a little like saying that the employees of a company should be loyal to the company's mission, even when you take away their incentives, *as long as they realize that the quality of their caring for the company is all that really matters in the end, because it is in that caring that a higher kind of benefit will accrue.* It raises also the difficult question of how to distinguish between the "benefits" of Christian faith (as in the Melancthon reference above) on the one hand, and the supposed "rewards" or "beneficial results" of Christian living, on the other. In the popular mind these become amalgamated, but Fénelon strove mightily to separate them, insisting that the former are quite real and the latter are products of interested self-love. In loving God I should expect transformation, not a bed of roses.

In any case, *Roma locuta est, causa est finita.* Rome has spoken, case closed. The papal brief was known in Versailles on March 22. Fénelon received it on March 25, and from the pulpit of his cathedral and in a follow-up letter immediately indicated his unconditional submission. Saint-Simon says Louis took the news with "evident satisfaction," and that when he twitted Beauvillier about it just as a meeting of the High Council was about to begin, the latter responded with great dignity; "Sir, I am M. de Cambrai's friend, and I shall always be so; but if he does not submit to the pope, I shall have no further intercourse with him."[413] Louis must have savored the moment, but not for long. What he didn't know was that another storm was about to break with the publication of Fénelon's *Adventures of Telemachus* in April. This was the final straw for Louis and what truly enraged him, while ensuring that Fénelon would live forever in the French political tradition.

The Telemachus

It is remarkable that during all of this gestation period of Fénelon's more and more subtly elaborated thinking on pure love, from the formation of the relationship with Guyon to the spiritual direction of Maintenon to the struggle with Bossuet, he had been tutoring the young dukes on the theory and practice, mostly practice, of wise leadership. The correlation was an easy one: "pure love" in action is what wise leaders actually do in practice, when their love for God is primary.[414] He then wrote a long didactic novel to drive the point home with his charges. The problem was that in order to describe with sufficient force how a good king rules well, he must also describe how a bad one rules poorly, and here he couldn't resist the temptation to paint the portraits vividly, too vividly. Louis and others thought they saw the point, and Fénelon was finished, as far as royal favor was concerned.

Composed over a substantial period for the Duc de Bourgogne and never intended by Fénelon for general publication, the *Telemachus* first appeared in partial form a few weeks after his papal censure, because an unfaithful copyist, unbeknownst to Fénelon, had delivered a copy to the printer.[415] Several thousand inaccurate copies of a work by the now notorious author of the *Maxims* were quickly disseminated. It sold robustly, and the general opinion was that Louis was the satirized target of the work. The print shop was shut down for having dared to circulate a work disrespectful to the state, and Louis moved quickly to strip Fénelon of his royal pension (he would still have his income as archbishop of Cambrai) and of the position as preceptor to the Duc de Bourgogne. Louis's sense of insult was quite palpable: "I knew quite well from the *Maxims* that the archbishop of Cambrai is a bad spirit, but I did not know that he was

a bad heart; I have just learned it from reading the *Telemachus*; ingratitude could not be pushed any further; his undertaking is one of eternally
crying down my reign."[416] Having already been banished to Cambrai in
1697, Fénelon "would never set foot in Versailles, or even Paris, again."[417]

The *Telemachus*, or *The Adventures of Telemachus, Son of Ulysses: Continuation
of the Fourth Book of Homer's Odyssey*, is a big work.[418] Displaying what Goré
called his "extreme virtuosity in the play of classical reminiscences,"[419]
Fénelon constructed in *Telemachus* an epic analogy to Homer's *Odyssey* that
functions either as a heroic adventure novel in its narrative format or in its
didactic material as a reflective exploration of political dynamics by means
of a fantasy voyage. The latter makes it akin to a work like Jonathan Swift's
slightly later *Gulliver's Travels*. It can be read as "picaresque romance" (the
hero gains wisdom in his travels)[420] or a utopian political manifesto (the
ideal society is a "'republican' monarchy")[421] simultaneously. It is a product
of an age in which political criticism was often expressed indirectly through
the creation of elaborate literary conceits.

The basic structure of the work is a travel narrative, in which Telemachus,
son of Ulysses (Odysseus), accompanied by a wise sage, Mentor (the god-
dess of wisdom, Athena, in disguise), goes in search of his father, absent
from home during the Trojan War. Mentor's task is to facilitate the process
"whose design is the formation of [Telemachus's] inner life."[422] Telemachus
represents humankind, weak, vain, ignorant, but seeking the good, while
Mentor is God's grace, turning the human need for transformation in
the direction of pure love. On the level of what is called a roman à clef,
Telemachus is the Duc de Bourgogne, more or less, and Mentor is his preceptor, Fénelon, more or less. The corrupt king Idomeneus is Louis XIV,
and other characters correspond to other of Fénelon's contemporaries.

The first aspect of the journey is purely moral: it is an opportunity for
Telemachus to suffer temptations, make bad choices, yield to seduction,
but also to learn by hard knocks that there is good practical common
sense in resisting all manner of deceitful and manipulative advisors, as
well as the grosser allurements of power, sensuality, and position. It is
the lesson of Fénelon's fables and dialogues all over again. Telemachus
must develop character, since virtue is much more than right actions. He
must grow out of his immature, impulsive, and shortsighted traits such as
impatience, combativeness, thoughtlessness. Indeed—and this is the real

point—before he can be a good leader, Telemachus must first be a good, even a sanctified, man.

The second element is more complexly ideological and reflective of Fénelon's political vision for a new society. It is formulated in classic Augustinian terms as a contrast between two cities or kingdoms, the first of which is heavenly and ideal and the second earthly and sinridden. The first "city" is La Bétique, which can only be described in a song performed for the entranced Telemachus. It is a peaceful, agricultural-pastoral, luxury-rejecting realm marked by brotherly love, the cultivation of simple crafts, the skill of conflict mediation, an abhorrence for conquest and domination, and domestic harmony. It is a place where the people, "so wise and so happy," live "by following nature and right reason."[423]

By contrast the "city" of Salente is a warlike, urbanized, luxury-enthralled domain led by a sensual, passionate, and aggressive ruler, Idomeneus. The first kingdom is successful because its policies are marked by "disinterest," thus giving us a picture of the ideal to be attained, while the second, where self-interest prevails, is a chaotic mess. In the course of a complex narrative of war, shifting military alliances, and political machination, Idomeneus has to learn from Mentor the folly of hostile aggression as an effective means for attaining worthwhile goals. "Idle ambition has brought you to the brink of ruin," says Mentor to Idomeneus, "by aiming at appearing great and powerful, you have almost destroyed your real power and greatness."[424] Idomenus allows Mentor to reorganize his kingdom on a rational, regulated basis, where immoderate greed and ambition can no longer create dysfunctional and unjust ways of living. All along the way Mentor provides Idomeneus, and thus Telemachus as well, with a stream of advice about social, economic, cultural, and political policies that will guarantee the harmony, peace, and just prosperity of a kingdom.

In fact, Mentor's advice is just the kind that Fénelon actually gave. In a letter of October 10, 1701, to the Marquis de Louville, now an advisor to the former Duc d'Anjou, lately become Philip V of Spain, Fénelon urges him to tell the new king that in a well-governed realm the leader sees to it that "the population grows; that all the people work, as their strength enables them, to cultivate the land; that everyone is cared for, provided that they work . . . that merit is rewarded . . . that royal authority is exercised in such a way that nothing is done from pride, violence, caprice, or out of weakness, contrary to the laws; that there is no graft or favoritism with the ministers. . . . The king must obey the laws and not himself. If he gives a command, it is not for his own benefit, but for the good of those whom he governs. He must be not only a man of law, but a man of God."

At the end of the narrative Telemachus, no longer an untutored and superficial boy, but now a man spiritually formed for leadership, falls in love with a virtuous woman, learns Mentor's real identity, and returns to Ithaca to join once again his beloved father in a new age of enlightened rule. As a work of fictional didacticism and moral allegory, *Telemachus* makes its points with literary elegance and cleverness. As pedagogy, it is "the culmination of Fénelon's theories of attractive education and indirect instruction."[425] As an optimistic vision of the future Fénelon hoped for in his beloved and purified France, it is wistful and poignant, while as satire it is a biting commentary on the impure present.

What complicates the vision contained in *Telemachus* is the fact that Fénelon was trying to make a lofty ideal, coherent at a theoretical level, meaningful at a practical level as well. For those who have loved the *Telemachus* it contains a vision of the godly prince who is himself Christlike, puts the needs of his people before everything else, administers justice impartially, works always for peace, and sets a standard of moderation in every respect for his kingdom. There is another side, though. For Fénelon's critics, the political vision contained in *Telemachus* has always seemed naïve, medieval-retrograde, aristocratic-elitist at heart, grounded in empty nostalgia, and, most damningly, reflective of a lack of realpolitik in Fénelon.[426] He contended that people practicing agriculture are more virtuous than people who work in shops and factories, that people living in small, rural communities are happier than those in dirty and crime-ridden urban complexes, that merchants who are "generous" and plan their commerce in cooperative concert with other commercial sectors are more successful than competitive sharks driven by the profit motive, that people who know their place in society and are content to stay there are better off than restless status seekers. In other words, a provincial aristocracy benignly solicitous for the welfare of local communities is more inclined to be virtuous than a bureaucracy gathered about an absolute monarch intent on aggrandizement and exploitation.

Furthermore, the ideal realm is conservative and reactionary in cultural style, eschewing the wastefulness and potential libertinism of innovative and experimental forms of expression. The pastoral spirit of La Bétique is anti-commercial and essentially anticapitalist, since a profit-seeking motive is nothing but greed. All of this is to say that Fénelon revealed his roots not only in the idealism of the philosopher-king of Plato's *Republic*, but also in the aristocratic elitism of the Old Regime (*ancien régime*), when regional nobles, focused on social harmony, presided benignly and paternalistically over populations of farmers, artisans, and tradesmen. One French critic (speaking in the dark and angry days right after World War II) calls his vision "state socialism, agrarian and Christian, a socialism imposed by a Christian aristocracy, presided over by a king," in which the people are treated as children.[427]

Although such a criticism has some truth in it—for Fénelon was aristocratic through and through—the negative spirit in which it is couched is not quite fair. Melchior-Bonnet, a modern French citizen, points to the fact that what is at work with Fénelon is the idea that commercial activity, rightly conceived and regulated within a society with a high ethic of public service, can, and should, produce a high level of welfare for the whole people, so that national militancy ceases to be the primary source of national vigor.[428] Such a vision is not only desirable for nations in the long run, it is also *necessary* for international survival. *That* is progressive, reality-based thinking, however difficult to implement in actual practice. Louis couldn't see it, but Fénelon could, and that fact puts him, paradoxically, on the side of the modern liberal social vision. It also puts him on the side of the internationalism and globalism of recent times.

But this is tricky. Where I think Louis (if he really read *Telemachus* through) would have blanched most of all, though, is when he read the description Mentor gives of the fragile nature of the ruler's fame and glory even under the best of circumstances. "Grandeur," says Mentor to Telemachus, "is like certain glasses that magnify every object. In high stations where the least things often have great effects, and where slight faults often produce the most fatal consequences, every defect appears more glaringly. The whole world has its eyes upon him who is highly elevated above others, watching his conduct and criticizing it with the utmost severity." But the people know nothing of the king's difficulties and struggles and pain, since they do not know that "a king, however wise and good he may be, is still only a man . . . scarcely has he repaired one fault when he falls into another."[429]

Thus passes the glory of the world, and uneasy lies the head that wears a crown! Fénelon's point is that the king, human as he is, and a kingdom, earthly as it is, can at best operate only with the less than ideal level of mixed love, where (as we recall from the *Maxims*) interestedness is always an element in what happens. Paradoxically Fénelon even makes room at this point for Adam Smith by recognizing (not as an exaltation, but as a concession!) that commercial life is not possible without self-interest. But such a standard of practice is *inferior* to the ideal, in which people would live simply and frugally in accord with their real needs—and not on the basis of ambition aimed at conquest and acquisition.

This is surely not what Louis wanted to hear, but it was what Fénelon hoped the Duc de Bourgogne *would* hear. The critics say that by this kind of teaching Fénelon unfitted the young duke to be a ruler in the hard school of reality, made him soft and overly spiritual, while his supporters say that he was nurturing the kind of monarch who, with suitable advisors at his elbow (Fénelon!), could have avoided the horrors of the Revolution of 1789. Alas, we will never know.

After April 1699, Fénelon and the young dukes were forbidden to have contact. The papal condemnation of propositions taken from the *Maxims* was ratified at a general assembly of the French clergy in 1700, and Fénelon's pastoral letters were not allowed to appear outside of his diocese. He was truly in exile. Nevertheless, his supporters and friends defiantly corresponded and often went to see him.

Madame Guyon remained in prison until 1703, after which she lived, much respected and influential, but not much in contact with Fénelon, for a good many years at Blois. Bossuet, permanently alienated from Fénelon and never ceasing to lambaste the errors of "pure love," died at Meaux in 1704, we are told, "after a long agony." "There is nothing more to settle between us," said Fénelon earlier. "I pray to God for him with all my heart."[430] We don't know if Bossuet's prayers contained similar sentiments for his erstwhile protégé.

"You truly know the truth insofar as you love it. When you love it, you know it well."
—LETTER TO THE DUC DE CHEVREUSE, ABOUT NOVEMBER 4, 1699

"Love is a great casuist for deciding doubtful matters . . . love makes us free, by simplifying without deregulating."
—LETTER TO THE COMTESSE DE MONTBERON, JULY 26, 1701

EIGHT

At Cambrai
"Pure Love" in Action

1695–1715

Opinions differed then, and probably always will, as to whether or not Fénelon truly "submitted" to the condemnation, especially since the condemnation of Jansenist ideas during this same era had made the whole concept of "submission" problematic. Outwardly speaking, there can be no question, since in all of his public statements and behaviors Fénelon conducted himself as a perfectly obedient son of the church. To the congregation in his cathedral on the day that he received official notice of the papal judgment he said: "May it please God that it would never be said to the contrary, and always remembered, that a pastor considered himself obligated to be more docile than the least sheep of his flock and that he put no limit to his obedience."[431] To Beauvillier he said, "For myself, I try to bear my cross in humility and patience. God has given me the grace to be at peace in the midst of bitterness and sorrow . . . it only remains for me to submit and to keep silent; which is what I have always wished to do."[432] "My submission," he said to the chevalier Ramsay with a sidelong look at the Jansenists, "was not a politic act, nor a respectful silence, but an interior act of obedience rendered to God alone."[433]

His assertion to Ramsay was that "the terms I used in explanation were not proper for a dogmatic work,"[434] and thus he would make no resort to the authority-dodging maneuvers of the Jansenists. They, when five heretical propositions were extracted from their work for condemnation, proceeded to create the famous distinction between *droit* (the church's "right" and power to judge infallibly the heretical nature of stated propositions) and *fait* (the church's fallibility in determining whether or not a particular text actually, in "fact," contains the condemned propositions). Since Jansen's *Augustinus* was being misunderstood, Jansenists argued, they would maintain "respectful silence" with regard to the pope's literary judgment. Nor did Fénelon assert in some ultimately rebellious way that he was right, and everyone else was wrong.

What he did claim, in a way that maintained his dignity and integrity, was that what he knew to be true in his heart never found its way into adequate verbal formulation, and therefore the *Maxims* were deficient and "susceptible of bad interpretations." "The pope understands my book better than I do, and on that I submit; but I understand my thought better than anyone else can."[435] The condemnation thus was just, but with the sad effect that the truth, the truth he was trying so hard to express, risked getting lost in the process. In time to come, he would defend his ideas in letters to the pope and to others in the form of clarifications, specifications, additional extrapolation, et cetera, but this was all private and informal.

The criticism that has been leveled against Fénelon, then and now, is a more subtle and inward one: that there was pride in his humility, a certain righteous superiority that manifested itself in an insufficient willingness to actually recant, to say that he had been dead wrong pure and simple. Some hold to the psychologizing view as well that ego simply reasserts itself in the "dramatic" character of his submission. There is the related tradition, disputed by some historians, that in 1714 Fénelon had a beautiful gold monstrance fabricated and then given as a thank-offering to his cathedral. Depicted on it, apparently, was a female allegorical figure representing "faith," trampling underfoot several books, including the works of Calvin and the *Maxims of the Saints*. The monstrance was believed to have been lost at the time of the Revolution of 1789. If true, the tradition suggests that Fénelon was, in a way, publicly "proud" of his total submission. Gosselin held that Fénelon was by means of this gift memorializing his agreement that the *Maxims* were inexact and thus condemnable, whereas Melchior-Bonnet suggests that he was perhaps engaging in a work of "reiterated repentance" in an implied contrast with Jansenist hypocrisy.[436] Alas, we can't be sure.

In any case, "silence" for Fénelon pertained only to the *Maxims*, since his actual voice would be stronger than ever now on a wide range of subjects (another mark of pride and even of spiteful vengeance, thought his critics). It would be preeminently a voice of *episcopal leadership* in his own diocese as well as in the continuing spiritual direction of a range of individuals. What emerges from this Cambrai period is the image of Fénelon, not so much as a writer and educator but more as a loving and beloved pastor, who faced the issues and needs of his community with a rugged, hands-on directness.

The goal of mystical prayer might be the "passive state," which could then be caricatured by its critics as idleness and immoral irresponsibility, but the lie was exposed when the time came for Fénelon to translate his prayer into concrete forms of pastoral care, service of human need, polemic against theological error, and criticism of those in secular or ecclesiastical authority. Then what seemed so "passive," so relentlessly inward and even solipsistic, could finally be viewed as a gathering of energies and a clarification of focus for what would be forcefully, even militantly, "active."

Deeply and Passionately Engaged

There was no dearth of activity in this busy, socially complex, and intermittently war-torn, recently annexed part of northern France.[437] The diocese itself was large, with four suffragan bishops for its major subdivisions centered at Arras, Saint-Omer, Tournai, and Namur. Long a part of the Holy Roman Empire and then under Spanish control, it had been ceded to France only in 1677, and Fénelon, thinking it more German than French, considered its people as "Low-Country Catholics" and "strangers to France."

There were complicated legal and financial issues regarding the endowments of the diocese, feudal responsibilities (such as collecting taxes) for the archbishop (since he was the duke of Cambrai as well), a number of religious communities needing episcopal oversight, as well as 764 towns for visitation![438] The regional nobility were difficult and adamant in their sense of local prerogatives, and thus Fénelon found himself in the role of counterbalancing the "rights" of his flock with the demands of the French king and royal officials. There was also a small seminary to supervise, this being a special love for Fénelon.[439] Good teaching was needed as well, because Jansenism was strong among many clergy and laity in the area, and the Calvinist Protestants were numerous. In short, he had his hands full but in time proved to be immensely effective and popular.

The chevalier Ramsay's idealized portrait of his beloved teacher deserves to be cited just for its eloquence. "The archbishop of Cambrai, excessively humbled, covered with shame, banished and confined to his diocese, enjoyed there that profound peace of mind, which never fails to accompany true virtue. He applied himself wholly to make men good and happy by discharging with great exactness all the functions of his Episcopal character." Ramsay adds that he was "far from turning spirituality into a dry and barren speculation," but that rigorously disciplined, he was cheerful and easy with others, famously generous with all that he had.[440] Even the cynical Saint-Simon joined the chorus of praise that streamed forth: "The life he led, after he retired to his diocese, was one of true piety and pastoral devotion. . . . His liberality, his accessibility, his sympathetic kindness to the poor, and politeness to persons of all classes; the mild wisdom of his government; above all, the natural charm of his manner, which enhanced the value of everything he said or did, endeared him to his people," though he could not resist adding: "yet there was something of the deliberate display of a man who has not yet renounced his worldly hopes, and wishes to stand well with everybody."[441] Saint-Simon definitely did not want to overstate matters even in the midst of praise!

Fénelon embraced an almost feverish busyness, a crushing load of work, in his pastoral role at this time. "There were," says Melchior-Bonnet, "two inseparable flipsides to his mission: to make a ponderous diocesan institution run in its temporal reality, its finances, its judicatory administration, its tangles with royal power and local oligarchies, under conditions that economic crisis and an almost permanent state of warfare made difficult; [and] to strengthen the faith of the people by organizing their religious practices with trained, virtuous and pious priests so as to shelter them both from the Jansenist sect and Protestant heresy." The question then arises: was he successful in all of this, as far as we know? "Pastoral visits, synods, seminary-work, episcopal instructions, preaching, distribution of the sacraments: the answer seems to be 'yes,' and even more, since he defends his people against adversaries of every kind, famine, soldiery, enemies, false prophets."[442]

What stands out in various records is the great generosity he manifested when a combination of famine and war swept through the area in 1708–10. He led in the distribution of emergency food and turned his episcopal palace into a hospital for the wounded of both sides, a "Noah's ark" in a flood of misery, says Goré. "Far from the dream of an ideal La Bétique and even from the reconstruction of a rational Salente [the good and bad kingdoms in *Telemachus*] . . . deprived fundamentally of everything, and without personal ambition, Fénelon was not attached to any political program in the measure that it was 'his own.'" Which is to say that "pure love" as he learned it from Guyon kept him from becoming "possessive" of his own efforts. He saw himself as free, in his own words to Chevreuse, "to die to himself . . . to act as if everything depended on how hard we try . . . while recognizing that, when all is done, we have not yet even made a beginning."[443]

The immediate context for much of his charitable activity in the Cambrai years was an environment of war and devastation, as rampaging armies moved through the area. The essence of it was that Louis, as part of the War of the Spanish Succession, was engaged from 1701 in an intermittent struggle against an alliance of Dutch, Austrian, and British forces for control of much of what constitutes modern Belgium, including the part of (now) northern France that contains Cambrai. After early successes, there was a series of defeats, followed by an intensifying whirlpool of financial and political crisis in France itself. Neither side in the military conflict in Flanders could decisively defeat the other, while the French armies, at a time when military organization was starting to become professional, generally suffered from incompetent amateur leadership. The period from 1708 to 1710 was particularly miserable with calamity on the battlefield and starvation and suffering all around. The chaos would not end until Louis agreed to the Peace of Utrecht in 1713. It is in this setting where Fénelon labored as peacemaker, negotiator, mentor to various figures, political advisor to Beauvillier and Chevreuse, and renewed spiritual guide and mentor to the Duc de Bourgogne that his social vision took on new and concrete form. Could *Telemachus* be made to work in the real world, he wondered?

This is also the time in which there developed a steady stream of foreign visitors to Cambrai, thus widening Fénelon's international status. There emerged a group of disciples, ready to start the machinery of the Fénelon legend. His popularity was high in liberal Holland, especially through the early dissemination of the *Treatise on the Education of Daughters*, and the condemnation of the *Maxims* immediately made him a persecuted hero. Visitors and students such as André-Michel Ramsay began to stream in. His influence in England began through contacts with the British officers in the anti-French coalition, but also as Quakers became interested in him, and, particularly, as the exiled James III, pretender to the British throne, came to pay a call.

The first collections of excerpts from his writings and addresses were put together during this time as well. These early gatherings formed the nucleus of later anthologies such as the *Instructions and Advice on Various Points of Morality and Christian Perfection* (a title assigned to the collection only by Gosselin in his critical edition) and began to make him known to a wide audience. The Fénelonian ideal of quietist pastoral work in peacemaking and universal charity, in which he will gradually emerge as a "man for all seasons," began to crystallize in this period. Woven into all of this was a renewed philosophical interest in restating the grounds for basic theistic belief and an apologetic interest in the authority and status of papal authority and of the claims of the Roman Church. There is also his assault on Jansenist teachings about the nature and working of grace in salvation. It would come back to questions of the credibility, as well as the desirability, of the concept of "pure love" again, as a final correspondence with Malebranche showed.[444]

If we were to ask ourselves what a human being who practices pure love looks like, there exists a remarkable document preserved by Bausset from a certain abbé Ledieu. This priest had been Bossuet's private secretary until that prelate's death, and he visited Cambrai shortly afterward in order to bring private letters to Fénelon. He had no particular reason to idealize Fénelon (quite the contrary), but he was touched by the "courteous" and "modest" treatment that he received from the archbishop, who promised him that he would respond "with the sincerity of a child" to any questions about quietism or the disputes with Bossuet that he might care to ask. The same writer also passed on a famous description of the household gathered at lively and lighthearted dinner in the episcopal palace, where Fénelon presided. At a table loaded with choice delicacies, "Fénelon ate very little, and only of mild food, and such as was not very succulent; in the evening, for example, he tasted only a few spoonfuls of milk and eggs, and drank but two or three glasses of a small white wine, weak in colour, and consequently in strength. It is impossible that anyone can be more temperate, and hence he is very thin: his countenance is clear and luminous, but without much colour; he carries himself very well, and on his return from a journey of three weeks, he did not exhibit any symptoms of fatigue or weariness."[445] Utterly without censoriousness toward the pleasures of others, and eminently hospitable, he was highly abstemious himself and instilled an atmosphere of generosity and grace to his surroundings.

❧ The work of spiritual direction moved in two directions—one that continued the earlier focus on the inward states of prayer, and one that was aimed more at individuals charged with the burdens of political responsibility and, potentially, the future of France. As an example of the first, we may take the series of letters addressed to the Comtesse de Montberon; for the second the letters both to the Duc de Chevreuse and then the renewed correspondence with the Duc de Bourgogne as the hope of the future are essential. The correspondence with the countess is especially abundant and lasted until Fénelon's death.

She was an interesting woman, and she brought out the best in Fénelon. Marie Gruyn, Comtesse de Montberon, married to an officer in the king's army, comes across as the personification of serious, well-intended, goodhearted religiosity—just the kind that is inclined to take itself *too* seriously. She suffered from that form of perfectionism usually called "scrupulosity," and Fénelon, having fought that battle with himself earlier, had a field day with her. As with all of his directees, he called her to a life of "humble simplicity" in which she would be "compassionate with the infirmities of others" and would manifest "true sensitivity without disdain or distaste for what seems small, weak, or unpolished."[446] In shaping a spiritual discipline, he advises her to listen to her heart, where she will discern her real needs, rhythms, and "attractions" (*attraits*), rather than her head, which is the ruthlessly exacting and ceaselessly self-critical source of "inquiétude" in her life.[447] He makes eloquent and repeated pleas to her, first, to maintain the normal disciplines expected of a devout Catholic, but then, second, to follow the impulse to break free from these when the energy of her prayer dictates. We must not hesitate, must not hold back, he says, when God's loving presence draws us in some fresh direction, as long as "it does not prevent us from feeling our fragility, our imperfection, our need for correction, and provided that it does not cause us to neglect any of our duties interior and exterior."[448]

It is precisely, Fénelon claims, when we yield to God's loving presence, give ourselves to it, that grace wraps the soul in peace, while at the same time empowering it for simple, quiet, and loving action with others. This "interior listening" to the divine Spouse results in exterior service. Human free will collaborates with divine energy and purpose for new possibilities of creative loving.[449] The personal challenge that Fénelon issued to Madame de Montberon in all of this was one of remaining mindful of her imperfections, while ceasing to be preoccupied with or tormented by them (the quietist "letting fall away").

But this kind of mental balance is remarkably difficult, because it requires a willingness to enter into the mystery of loving and being loved. In an extraordinary passage, Fénelon urges Madame de Montberon to remember that as she has the deep awareness of knowing that God loves her, she experiences "the whole thing inside herself as two infinitely opposed principles. She feels a weakness and an astonishing imperfection in what is her own, but [on the other hand] a transport of love so disproportionate to everything else, that she cannot attribute it to herself . . . it is like when a child whom one lifts up, far from believing itself taller, is afraid of falling, if it is not held with two hands at that elevation, so it is love which makes one truly humble . . . it occupies one in such a way as to make one forget oneself."[450] Such people, no longer obsessed with self, suffer quietly, so that about them "there is nothing dazzling, nothing remarkable, nothing distinct in the eyes of others, and still less in their own eyes. If you say to such a person that she suffers well, she doesn't understand. She doesn't know herself how she tolerates so much . . . and if she tried to puzzle out the reason, she would lose the simplicity of it . . . this is what we would call a 'good will'" (as opposed to normal "courage," a merely human virtue, Fénelon says).[451] Here we see Fénelon putting into practical terms his emphasis in the *Maxims* on the "state-quality" of mystical existence and the loss of self-awareness entailed.

For his part, M. de Chevreuse had worked earlier with Fénelon in tutoring the Duc de Bourgogne and had apparently flirted for a time with

Jansenist sympathies. He had become a strong advocate for Madame Guyon and stayed in touch with Fénelon after his departure for Cambrai. He was also a feudal overlord of the region in which Cambrai was located, as well as captain-lieutenant of Louis XIV's personal guard. He had been a longtime friend to Fénelon but also a problem, as indicated, for instance, in his precipitate publication of the *Maxims*. If it is fair to say that Madame de Montberon is the kind of overly diligent religious person who is inclined to make herself miserable, then Chevreuse is the kind who tends to bring misery on others, because everything will be done *his* methodical and exacting way. He is a man of affairs, accustomed to giving orders, and accustomed to being obeyed.[452]

In the spiritual direction he sought from Fénelon, which picked up speed in 1700, he reveals an intense, analytical, rational, somewhat obsessive, somewhat censorious, and anxious personality. Fénelon refers to Chevreuse's "restless spirit" a number of times,[453] and we already know from our review of Fénelon's psychological theory that anxiety is a sign of self-love. His advice, therefore, to Chevreuse constantly takes the form of urging him to take things slowly, moderately, one step at a time. On prayer he says, "begin with a small dose and increase it gradually," but also only "give as much time to prayer as would serve to attract, on every occasion, the inward peace and silence that is so essential." He urges Chevreuse to be gentle and forbearing in criticism generally, and in particular of a woman friend (the Duchesse de Beauvillier), remembering that as far as faults go, "the Apostles, after all, had plenty."

The problem for Chevreuse, as Fénelon makes clear, is that he is overdependent on meticulous and disciplined religious practice and the assurance that it brings, so that when the well seems to run dry he is in despair (a point that will also be important for Fénelon in his anti-Jansenist polemic). Thus, Fénelon contends that "in truth one never prays so sincerely as when one is tempted to believe that one has ceased to pray at all."[454] "Impatience for visible and sentient truth" is the great enemy, because, in its anxious need for proof, it is the antithesis of the dark night of faith, of that "Jesus Christ who was abandoned on the Cross by His Father." There is an echo here of some of his earliest advice to the duke: "Do not trust in your own intelligence . . . be simple, and be strong in your simplicity."

In one particularly hard-hitting letter that must have been difficult for Chevreuse to read, Fénelon comes down hard on his pettifogging, nitpicking, "exhausting to himself and everyone else" style of leadership. He points out to the duke that there is a "subtle temptation, namely, that the multitude of affairs entrains you rapidly" and that being pressed by a steady flood of demanding business, he follows too much "his spirit of anatomy and of exactitude in each thing." The result is that everything takes too long, delays become longer, and inefficiency follows. He tells Chevreuse that "if you cut things short, each thing would be placed in a larger perspective, and would find its level of priority without difficulty . . . by trimming away all that is not essential, and by avoiding a blinding exactitude that destroys what is necessary by superfluity."[455] Again, greater interior silence and a consequently less agitated approach to matters would help greatly. We have no trouble recognizing in the duke a classic example of the leader who dreads failure and then micromanages everything, thus setting himself up for what he fears most.

Political Hopes and Disappointments

Now, as it happened, with a royal force operating in Flanders from 1699 onward, Chevreuse and Beauvillier were often out in the field with the army, keeping a preceptorial eye on the maturing Duc de Bourgogne, encouraged by Louis to get his military "spurs." His former charge's love for Fénelon never having flagged, on September 6, 1702, young Louis was allowed to post a letter to his old mentor and to have a brief public meeting. Bourgogne's words brought deep joy to Fénelon: "I pray you be assured of my warmest friendship at all times as in the past," and Fénelon in turn judged Bourgogne "stouter" with "better color."[456] It soon became clear that in their renewed relationship, his old hopes for the young duke were stimulated again: that he might one day be king of France in a time of freshly anointed, spiritually enlightened leadership! The old tone of instruction revived. Writing to Beauvillier, he urges him to remind Bourgogne that if he is "thrown upon his own resources to the exclusion of God and of the grace that derives from Him, his whole being would wither away and that very world that made him forget God would serve as a divine instrument of destruction for the punishment of his ingratitude . . . and in failing God he would presently be found to have failed the world as well which would then turn from him in disgust."[457] So, perhaps the best was yet to come, and perhaps he, Fénelon could yet make a significant contribution to a politically and socially redeemed nation.

As the war drums started to beat in the summer of 1701 Fénelon began sending to Chevreuse a remarkable series of "memorials," or political letters of counsel, that he hoped would influence official policy decisions by the king and his council.[458] It is through these documents that his reputation as a "pacifist" started to grow, although the term is not strictly accurate. What we quickly discover in reading the memorials is the pragmatic argument that the making of war as an instrument of national policy is usually self-defeating, because however effective it may be in the short run, it creates worse problems for everyone, including the victor, in the long run. An inclination toward peace is not so much a matter of absolute principle as it is a matter of rational wisdom learned from experience.

In the first of these communications on the matter with Chevreuse, dated August 8, 1701, Fénelon lays down a list of credible and specific, highly informed reasons why Louis XIV, however just his cause, will be doing much more harm than good by resorting to warfare in Flanders. Determined to defend the rights of the king of Spain, a member of his own Bourbon family, over the Lowlands, Louis put himself in opposition to the rest of Europe. Fénelon acknowledged the justness of the cause but insisted with carefully wrought argument, backed up with many specifics, that a war with the Allies would be prolonged, fruitless, and ultimately counterproductive for France. However, once the war began, in a communication in 1702, he urged vigorous prosecution with the argument that "the cause which he [the king] now sustains is clearly quite just . . . he could, by wanting to avoid the war, actually make it happen." Don't make war, but if you do, get it over with quickly. As things developed, the war dragged on indecisively and fruitlessly for years, Louis suffered a major defeat at Malplaquet in 1709, and by 1710 Fénelon was describing vividly the damage that had been done and the need (Louis's cause and that of France having been vindicated) to make an honorable peace.

His central point with Chevreuse is that the making and sustaining of a war, however just the cause, generates at the same time corruption on every level: greedy and vicious people are rewarded; resources are squandered and the nation reduced to poverty; human life is wasted under incompetent military leadership that cannot care for the wounded or even properly feed the troops; a precipitating cause, however worthy initially, becomes an idolatry; and cynicism replaces faith.

In fact, Chevreuse, Beauvillier, and others heard Fénelon's voice, and he became a presence in the mechanics of a complicated, on-again, off-again set of peace negotiations, earning respect from representatives of both sets of the opposing forces. Perhaps, then, it is better to describe him as a "peacemaker," rather than a "pacifist" in the strict sense. Melchior-Bonnet says it very well: "You get the sense that Fénelon saw 'winning the war' as hardly credible, with things coming down in the end to the real question of finding money and provisioning the army [that is, the question of how to pay for all of this]. But for the preparation of peace, this diplomat born with a sense for modalities, advantages, nuances, as the only instrument for escaping humiliation and the only true glory for the king of France, was called to serve as mediator."[459]

Opinions will always differ as to whether the peacemaking advice Fénelon gave to the French negotiators was wise or not. Writers in the nationalist and royalist traditions argue that Fénelon was a defeatist and betrayed Louis, urging him to give the Allies what they wanted—to stop supporting the territorial claims of the king of Spain in the Low Countries, to recognize the Protestant William as legitimate king of England rather than the Catholic pretender, James III, and so on— while writers in the liberal and republican traditions argue that Fénelon prophetically recognized that the age of absolute monarchs and their imperialistic ambitions was over. Melchior-Bonnet calls Fénelon in his approach to the possibilities of international justice and his vision of royal leadership an "anti-Machiavelli."[460] I would call him a "pure-love actualist," that is, someone who thought that leaders really can make pure love work in the political arena, if they are sufficiently virtuous and sufficiently willing to pay the cost. They must also realize that the implementation of pure love will always be a progressive undertaking, a matter of moving closer to the goal, without ever reaching it, and thus never an all-or-nothing proposition.

These years have a gray quality. The war in the Cambrai area ground on for years, routine pastoral work had to be done, and spiritual direction continued mostly through letters. The sources that we have indicate that Fénelon attended to masses of legal and financial detail in a complex jurisdiction weighted with archaic ecclesiastical structures and requirements. He also stayed in touch with family members, primarily sisters, nieces, and nephews who sometimes came to Cambrai to visit. Debates over Jansenism filled the whole period, but it was the crisis over the royal succession that provided the next major focus of energy for the aging archbishop.

It is in the period of 1710–11 that Fénelon, aware that King Louis was aging, stressed, and struggling with illness, produced two works intended to assist the Duc de Bourgogne in the event that divine Providence were suddenly to bring that young man to the throne of France. At the time of writing, the grand dauphin Louis, weak and sickly, was the heir apparent. But not for long, for this Louis died on April 14, 1711, leaving Bourgogne as next in line. The hopes of the devout circle at court soared in an almost messianic frenzy, as of course did those of Fénelon. There was the sudden and likely prospect that France would have a new and enlightened, deeply spiritual king. And his first minister would be none other than his old tutor! That was the hope on the part of many. Given the possibility that Louis XIV might not live much longer, Fénelon moved quickly to provide some resources for the heir apparent.

The first work was entrusted to Beauvillier, who would make it available for inspection by the young duke if his moment of glory in fact were to materialize. It has the form of a penitential aid for the monarch who is preparing for sacramental confession. Entitled *A Form for Examining Conscience with Regard to the Duties of a King*, it consists of a series of questions, which the royal penitent is to consider by way of assessing his spiritual state before God.[461] In effect, the questions articulate the Fénelonian understanding of what is required for a king to be truly godly. Most important is the emphasis on justice in everything the king does. The list of questions is long. Does the king operate within the law at all times?

Does he choose upright and uncorrupt judges for the realm? Does he mind the welfare of all the people in the administration of economic and commercial matters? Does he put a stop to a range of corrupt administrative practices, such as the selling of offices to incompetent persons or the appointment of persons to office, who, not being adequately paid, then fleece those whom they should serve? Does he avoid the injustice done to other nations by making wars of conquest or by breaking treaties? Does he consult the wisest and most suitable advisors before deciding to make war? Is he fair and merciful to defeated enemies? In a *Supplement* the king is reminded that "All the nations of the earth are only different families of the same community of which God is the common Father," says Fénelon, for "the natural and universal law by which God wishes the nations to be governed is that we are to prefer the public good over against individual interest." In other words, the king, as he prepares to confess, must examine his conscience with respect to the ideal of disinterested love on a wide range of very practical matters! "The love of the people," avers Fénelon, "the public good, the general interest of society, these are the immutable and universal law for sovereigns."

The second document is the *Plans of Government Intended for Presentation to the Duc de Bourgogne*, worked out with Chevreuse in November 1711, also known as the *Tables of Chaulnes* because of the name of the town where they were presented and the list form that was used.[462] It lays out two agendas for Bourgogne in the event of his coronation. The first is to bring the War of the Spanish Succession to an end as rapidly as possible, while at the same time reorganizing the high command of the army to operate in a more functional, competent, and rational way than it had done under Louis XIV. The second is a more ambitious and more detailed scheme for restructuring the essential institutions of the French state— the military, court at Versailles, interior administration of the kingdom, church, aristocracy, and justice system—by a variety of measures that would promote productivity, weed out abuses, clarify lines of authority, and restore high ideals for those persons obligated to the service of the country. Two proposals that must have been dear to Fénelon's heart were the doing away with the system of pensions that allowed an idle aristocracy to live at Versailles and the restoration to the bishops of full power to uproot Jansenism in their dioceses and to enforce papal decrees.

The sweep of the *Tables* is ambitious and breathtaking. There would be a structural redistribution of power and privilege in the governing of France. Its weakness to its critics has always been its hierarchical emphasis on the roles of nobility, episcopate, and judiciary operating in the manner of an informed and enlightened elite, an upper-class establishment, who have finally been given a free hand to run the country the way it *should be run* (Saint-Simon called it a kind of idealizing throwback to the time of Louis XIII, before the nobility had been reined in and neutered by Louis XIV). Its Achilles's heel is its Old Regime monarchist failure to recognize the growing role of the new mercantile middle class for France's future, as well as the rise of the class conflict inevitably being generated by the irreversible process of industrialization.

Then all of this hope came crashing to the ground. First Bourgogne's wife suddenly died with an infectious fever, and then, very shortly thereafter, the young duke himself died on February 18, 1712.[463] Everyone was thunderstruck, and Louis's last years were immediately cast under a shadow as the succession moved to a great-grandson, now only four years old. The extraordinary thing was that Fénelon, greatly saddened and even dismayed, was not crushed or despondent. He immediately sent condolences to Louis and Maintenon, despite all that had happened. No pettiness here.

In fact, shortly thereafter Madame de Maintenon discovered in a folder of Bourgogne's a number of tender letters that Fénelon had written to the young man. She read them to Louis, who was so touched that he ordered them to be burned. Later she confided to Beauvillier that never had anything quite so beautiful or so good ever been said to, or about, their grandson.[464] One suspects a twinge of justified guilt on the part of the royal couple.

And Fénelon took the blow more philosophically, one might say, than would have been expected. One view is that his initial reaction can best be understood from within the context of a growing pessimism about human nature and the fate of all things earthly.[465] "I am seized with horror, seized with illness where there is no malady," he said with seeming despair to Chevreuse, and with even more pathos. "God formed this young prince, adorned him, prepared him for very great good. He let the world see

him, and before long destroyed him." But there is no real despair. Quite
the contrary. Fénelon took it all in the spirit of Job's praise: "The Lord has
given, and the Lord has taken away: blessed be the name of the Lord." His
whole spirituality, after all, is one of embracing the calamitous development precisely as a "cross," as something from God that causes suffering,
but that is also grace-laden for those who would practice "pure love." It
is no wonder, then, that he rebounded quickly, despite his own fragile
health and disgust at times with ineptitude and corruption.[466]

We have notes gathered by Chevreuse of suggestions made by Fénelon
right after Bourgogne's death.[467] The savvy old archbishop saw it coming.
There would be a regency after Louis XIV's death and thus a fight for
control among the leading nobility. Civil war must be avoided at all
costs, he thought. A wise governing council must be created. The child-
heir, who will become Louis XV, will be immature for years to come and
therefore must have the most mature guidance. Beauvillier is just the man,
says Fénelon, and he looks forward to that nobleman's central role in the
new council, where he may also be the primary educational supervisor of
France's next king. And so on. Fénelon never gave up; there is no pessimism,
but rather endless hope of the kind that is "swallowed up" in love!

The Anti-Jansenist

And so, returning to the theory of pure love, we come to Fénelon's
last great theological struggle, running all through the Cambrai years.
It was with the Jansenists. And it was, to a degree, part of a lingering
doctrinal aftermath of the condemnation of the *Maxims of the Saints* and
Fénelon's defense there of quietist-mystical spirituality. If we recall that
the Jansenists were anti-mystical and anti-quietist, as in Pierre Nicole's
1695 attack when Fénelon was on the ropes, then we can see that he had
(although he denied it) a score to settle. The time had come, and he got
to make some points once more. Indeed, becoming a kind of "hammer of
the Jansenists," he made them squirm.

But, as he viewed it, the context was pastoral and not personal. It was a
question of protecting the flock. His archdiocese needed to be defended,
he thought, from the heretical and duplicitous Jansenists, while the nation

of France needed to be freed from the kind of politically disloyal ferment that the Jansenists tended to create. The bishops of the church needed the power to discipline these disobedient sectarians, who, professing to be loyal Catholics and submissive subjects, were, as Fénelon thought, neither.

There were in the diocese of Cambrai plenty of clergy and laity sympathetic with Jansenism, and we know that Fénelon complained early on in a memoir—sent to Chevreuse in 1702 in hopes that he would show it to Louis—that his diocese was full of clergy trained at Louvain in Flanders, where Jansenist influence was strong. His hope was that Louis, made aware of this pervasive Jansenism and hating sectarianism, would take steps to block these clergy from ecclesiastical preferment. A particular lament at first was that he did not have a seminary in his own diocese, except the inadequate one at Douai, where he could train clergy properly.

He began to remedy this last deficiency shortly after arriving at Cambrai, so that by 1704 he had, with the help of Saint-Sulpice, a seminary up and operating at the cathedral. It was a special love, and he took a personal interest in the training of the seminarians, conducting frequent examinations, but always with a certain gentleness. "In addition to the instructions he gave," says Ramsay, "on feast-days and at retreats, he conducted weekly conferences on the principles of religion. He wanted each student to articulate his difficulties. He would listen with infinite patience and respond with paternal kindness." Respecting every objection, however clumsily stated, he had a way of structuring a discourse that solved every difficulty without embarrassing the student.[468] He also conducted conferences with the clergy of his diocese, aimed at averting the Jansenist danger.

What was at stake with the Jansenists? Right up until his death in 1715, Fénelon would write polemics and critiques aimed at this Catholic deviation, as he saw it.[469] In essence, two basic issues rankled for him. The first involved his perception that churchmen of Jansenist sympathies denied the authority of the church in doctrinal matters in a particularly odious way: they conformed outwardly, but dissented inwardly. Rome had denounced their doctrines, but they refused to yield, so that for Fénelon, who had, in Melchior-Bonnet's happy phrase, embraced a "true mystique" in which "consented submission is the highest degree of love," their lack of submission was unforgivable.[470]

But the second and more substantive concern theologically was the issue that contorted this whole period, namely, the question of how grace works in the human soul. How does God's grace touch and transform our created, but also our sinful, human nature? How do we know it when it happens? Is grace, when it comes, an irresistible, overwhelming, *necessitating* force, driving us to our knees and then lifting us to the skies, as the Jansenists tended to think? Or is it a beckoning, attracting, intensely inviting and compelling, though quite resistible, *draw*, often slow and gradual in its working, as Fénelon tended to think? This issue runs like a faultline through the whole modern history of Christianity.

Let us consider both of Fénelon's anti-Jansenist concerns, while acknowledging that the second is of greater interest.

We recall that the Jansenists, condemned in the five propositions of the 1653 papal bull *Cum occasione*, and required to sign an oath of assent (called the Formulary of Alexander VII), took the position that although the church is infallible in judging (has the "right") the orthodoxy or heresy of isolated propositions, it is not so in determining whether, "in fact," a particular extended text really expresses those propositions. Thus, they contended that the *Augustinus* of Jansen did not contain the condemned propositions, and that, therefore, their position would be one of "respectful silence" with regard to the pope's decision that Jansen was a heretic. Matters thus rested for a time in this qualified submission, until a little pamphlet, the *Case of Conscience* in 1702, raised the *droit* vs. *fait* issue again in such a crafty way as to win fresh approval for the concept of "respectful silence" from a number of theologians at the Sorbonne. An explosion ensued, in which the pope finally moved to rebuke the Sorbonne authorities, who then quickly backpedaled.

Now, as things heated up, everybody had something to say on the issue, including Fénelon. In a series of pastoral instructions to his diocese in 1704–5 and in a correspondence that continued until his death, he argued the case for the infallible ability of the church to judge the orthodoxy of dogmatic statements *and of dogmatic texts*. In other words, the church can say authoritatively not only that Jansen's doctrine is heretical (the *droit*), but also that this doctrine is actually contained in the book (the *fait*) authored by him. "Respectful silence" by the Jansenists with regard to the church's decision regarding what the *Augustinus* says, its "plain sense," is thus hypocrisy and culpable disobedience, a failure on their part to give true "inward assent."

⚫ François Lamy, a Benedictine priest and "disquieted soul" with whom Fénelon corresponded for years about theological matters, in a letter of June 2, 1704, to Fénelon summarized the logic of the argument very concisely in a simple syllogism: since the church is infallible in its decisions for preserving Catholic faith (later Fénelon would say that Christ promised this power and thus it is supernatural), and since this power must include the ability to judge the status of dogmatic pronouncements of any kind, therefore the church's infallibility includes the ability to discern with absolute certainty the plain sense of any dogmatic text. And that settles it!

When Clement XI, at Louis's insistence, finally came out with a decree on the "respectful silence" issue, *Vineam Domini*, on July 15, 1705, and said essentially what Fénelon had already said, the latter energetically defended the pope's pronouncement. However, it is also true that *Vineam Domini* does not use the term *infallible* to describe the church's teaching authority and that, thus, Fénelon was ahead of the curve in so employing it. But he was careful to insist that this attribute adheres to the *office* of the pope, not to his *person*. Gosselin, a nineteenth-century pre-Vatican I churchman, makes a similar case by saying that it is the *church's* infallibility, not the *pope's*, that Fénelon emphasized. One irony is that Fénelon, having worked hard to assert papal authority, incurred the wrath of some ultramontane extremists who thought that he waffled.

The second issue, namely, that of the nature of the working of grace, is more complex and includes, in addition to some explicit critiques of the Jansenists, a particular correspondence with François Lamy in 1708–9 on predestination and a pastoral instruction written in 1714. The last work is an imitation of the form of Pascal's famous *Provincial Letters*, in which that writer attacked the moral casuistry of the Jesuits. In Fénelon's usage the fictional letters contain imagined dialogues between an orthodox Catholic (himself, of course) and a Jansenist and are intended to expose doctrinal error and its undesirable moral consequences. What we quickly see in all of this material is that his objections to the Jansenist view of efficacious grace link up very clearly with his support for mystical prayer and the spirituality of pure love.

The context is complex and is best framed as an expression of the incessant battle that went on about the interpretation of Augustine. Everybody in the seventeenth century—Protestant or Catholic— appealed to that church father as a major authority on doctrine, and particularly the doctrine of *grace.* And since grace is the God-given means, through Christ, of human salvation, the doctrine of grace involved the whole understanding of how salvation, the salvific process, actually works in the souls of human beings.

All Catholic theologians, Fénelon and the Jansenists included, were anxious in their interpretation to avoid the heresies of Pelagianism and semi-Pelagianism on the one hand, and Calvinist Protestantism on the other. To that end, three questions emerged in their efforts to forge a correct understanding of Augustine. It is in the answers worked out to these questions that interpreters differed from one another, sometimes bitterly.

First, *how and by what means* does grace work its saving effect in our souls? Second, why does this grace seem to work effectively only in *some souls, but not in others?* Third, what is the *actual experience* of this grace, the sign of authenticity by which we may know that we are experiencing the real thing? In practice, when a theologian worked out answers to these questions, the result was a package deal, a formulation that answered all three at the same time. Our disengaging of the three questions is, therefore, a bit artificial, but it allows us to get some clarity. Here it is that we can see more of Fénelon the theological wrestler in the ring, intensely intellectual to the last. The difference between his views and those of the Jansenists are carefully and finely wrought.

With regard to the first question, the *how,* all parties shared the same idea, straight from Augustine, that God's grace works in the lives of Christians by means of what is called the "efficacious call." The idea is that grace "happens" in our lives when we hear ourselves being addressed, through Scripture or inwardly or both, by the word of the Gospel. Precisely because that word comes from God, it must be *effective* since God's purposes cannot fail; that is, in the language of the time, God's grace is always "efficacious in itself," requiring no human input to achieve its goal. But this was where the first crunch came. It is the first point of difference between Fénelon and his opponents: the Jansenists say that God's word will be *invincibly, necessarily, irresistibly* successful, whatever the dispositions and inclinations of the human recipient, since God has willed that person's salvation.

Not so, says Fénelon. In fact, when God issues the efficacious call, it is done in such a way as to be *congruent* with the personality, circumstances, and spiritual readiness of the individual. That is, when the call comes and we hear it for the first time, it has been customized, as it were, to the needs of the soul of the individual. And this customizing happens because a free human consent is always required and thus must be *elicited and not forced*. God does not bully us, even in offering the gift of salvation. Instead God makes the Gospel attractive and alluring, so that our desiring is activated. For this reason, Fénelon is classed by historians as a "congruentist" in his understanding of the working of grace.

It is still the case, however, that by issuing the congruent call God cannot fail. Salvation is still a pure gift of grace. "The act of the [human] will," says one modern interpreter of Augustine, "is evoked by the persuasive quality of the call, and this is something that does not lie within man's power. . . . The human mind and the affections are open, to be sure, to realities and values beyond itself, and it is not always in a posture of indifference towards them; but [also], however strongly the mind is drawn toward something, or however hesitant it may be, still the resulting act comes from within the mind itself."[471] *Grace, for Fénelon, is not invincible, but is infallible.*[472] But this is where the second question comes up: why call grace infallible, when clearly it falls flat with some people? Why do some turn away, unattracted and even indifferent to God's gracious offer? This is the issue of predestination.

Indeed, another place where all followers of Augustine agreed was that God wishes to save everyone but has determined that, in fact, some will be lost. It's not that efficacious grace fails with some people; it never had a chance in the first place. But the challenge was to understand how God's eternal choice of the saved (their *election*) still respected their free will, still took seriously the real human capacity for turning away from God. The Jansenists responded that there is mystery here, that God saves those who are chosen, and that those who are saved are the chosen ones. God's will in this is inscrutable. End of discussion.

Not so, says Fénelon. And he availed himself of a theory called "Molinism," associated with the Jesuit Luis de Molina and considered one of the characteristic doctrines of the Jesuit order. In fact, Fénelon averred, God *knows* from all eternity those persons who will in fact respond to the offer of grace, and *those* are the chosen ones. God operates with a special kind of knowledge (called "knowledge of hypothetical future contingents" or "middle knowledge," in technical language) by which it can be known in advance how a given individual will freely respond under a given set of circumstances. Imagine, says Fénelon, in a masterful illustration, "a prophet who would have the ability to read his friend's heart, to know with infallible prescience what that friend would decide to do under such-and-such set of circumstances, and who could thus see the perfect means for persuading the friend to act in a good way. He will know with certainty [infallibly] the perfect means for dissolving all resistance and all opposition on the part of his friend's will to a well-advised course. In just such a way does God act interiorly to work in us a good will that we cannot generate for ourselves."[473] God's saving will is infallible, but in being crafted to attract some and not others, it is also loving and fair, not harshly irrational and arbitrary. The two traps that Fénelon wanted to avoid in expounding Augustine have thus been skirted: the individual who is saved is saved not *because* she will respond with faith (Pelagianism) or because grace is *irresistible* for someone predestined for salvation (Calvinism), but because God already knows in *a special, timeless way* that she will freely respond in a positive manner to the gracious offer.[474]

And then the difference of opinion between Fénelon and the Jansenists on the third question followed logically. The authentic experience of saving grace had the character of a "victorious delectation," they agreed. But what is that? What does it mean to "delight," and to do so "victoriously," in God? The Jansenists contended that the recipient of irresistible grace finds that his natural ability to enjoy earthly goals has now shifted to an ability to enjoy heavenly goals. Such is the depth of our sin, said Jansen, that God must use our love of pleasure as the means of our salvation. So it is that the redeemed sinner took pleasure in sin before, but now he takes pleasure in the doing of God's will, and, as a result, finds the strength to live a more Christlike life. All the passion of which persons are capable turns around one hundred and eighty degrees, but it is the *same* passion.

It's not hard to see the problem with this Jansenist view, which has a very long history and often reemerges in popular religiosity. But unless conversion changes something about how the human psyche reckons rewards and satisfactions, it will remain a sham ("skin deep," we might say). Fénelon, thus, will have absolutely none of it. For him this is where the bankruptcy of the Jansenist way of looking at the working of grace is revealed. The fundamental problem, he claims, with this whole Jansenist way of looking at grace as irresistible, and at predestination as irrational and arbitrary, is that it turns God into a purveyor of pleasure for the benefit of a chosen elite. This, however, (he might say) is not God *loving* us; it is God *catering* to us. *That way* of looking at God is blasphemous, since it falls into the trap, once again, of picturing God as a force at *our* disposal. It is, in short, a form of self-love. The central thrust of his quietist-mysticism, and the emphasis on pure love, had been to try to stop that way of operating in prayer, and everywhere else as well.

To Lamy Fénelon made the case here with special clarity.[175] Given the fact, he argues, that the essence of sin is self-love, the "me" in everything, God's grace must come to me in a way that humbles the "me." And it will do this precisely by breaking me of dependence on props, so to speak, for my ego. The problem with the Jansenist idea that saving grace is irresistible and comes as an overwhelming delight in God's will is that it plays to the tendency that all pious people have to become "hooked" on consciously felt "delights" and "fervors" and "consolations," on ecstatic and visionary experiences that thrill a person's sensibility, and that have, thinks Fénelon, very little to do really with God.

The technical way he frames his objection is to say that for the Jansenists God's grace seizes the "unreflecting [*indélibérée*] will" of a person. Much later, in the 1714 pastoral instruction modeled as a dialogue with a Jansenist, he makes the same point by claiming, in Melchior-Bonnet's words, that "Jansenism encourages Epicureanism under an appearence of austerity."[476] The Jansenists, by arguing that God uses spiritual pleasure to draw us away from earthly pleasure, fail to show that it is the "good, the beautiful, and true" that brings us delight: it is only the *delighting*, the "rush" of the experience itself, that brings delight. In the twinkling of an eye, we are addicted to the pleasure.[477] What then tends to happen, Fénelon says to Lamy, is that when the pleasures wane, when God ceases to send spiritual sweets, the life of prayer collapses. It is the temptation to think that I am not one of God's chosen ones when the lights go out, the going is difficult, and there is not much satisfaction at the end of the day. That is the problem with religion based on the pleasure principle: it works only in fair weather and as long as God keeps catering to our lower urges.[478]

Saving grace, says Fénelon, actually comes to the "reflecting [*délibérée*] will"; it appeals to the highest *moral* sense, which always entails an agonized sense of our need to be, in Fénelon's term of choice, the "child" once again. "True prayer," he writes, "is in the spirit and the will," where the "delectation is the prayer itself." The delight is "pure will, the will or love completely nude, very dry." In other words, the true work of grace is to enable the activity of pure love to make possible for the will to experience, *for the first time*, simple pleasure in doing what is loving *because it is loving, and for no other reason.*[479]

The alternative, he says, is a prayer life that derives its pleasure from satisfaction in "an augmentation of the virtues," that is, a spiritual self-righteousness rooted in the "signs" of irresistible grace, which then becomes "enthusiasm" and "fanaticism," a privileged and delusional access to God—precisely what the Jansenists would be accused of. Grace, rightly discerned and rightly received by the individual, is "hidden" from view, profoundly interior, unclear even to the individual herself, difficult and cruciform in sacrifices, yet issuing in quiet perseverance, gradual transformation, service to the neighbor. This is too low-key for the Jansenists, and it lacks, we might say, crowd appeal.

In the end, Fénelon advised Lamy to stop worrying about these abstruse matters so much, to invest his energies in devoting himself to God and neighbor with pure love, to believe that grace had been given to him in abundance, and not to fret about whether he was one of the "predestined"—better to leave that matter "hidden" in the heart of God, as well as in his own. "Peace," he says, "does not come with a clarity that is impossible in this life, but rather with a loving acceptance of darkness and uncertainty."[480]

So it is that Fénelon's dispute with the Jansenists became another chapter in his crusade for pure love. Jansenism has a long history, and people, especially French writers, still take sides, sometimes with great energy. In the complicated politics of Jansenism, Port-Royal would be destroyed in 1712 and Clement XI would issue in 1713 the papal bull *Unigenitus*, a root-and-branch condemnation of the Jansenists and their institutions, insisting that the French bishops drive them out of the church. A nightmare then ensued that went well beyond Fénelon's time.

Last Efforts and Faithful to the Last

Fénelon's constant reading of Augustine during this period, his dissatisfaction with the Maurist-Benedictine edition of Augustine's collected works, and his interest in producing his own edition of the writings of this church father are strong reminders of the intensity of his continuing and fundamental loyalty to the literature of the classical world. The struggle with the Jansenists further stimulated this loyalty in some interesting, even ironic, ways. One of these was the crystallizing of his interest in what theologians call "natural theology," that is, the effort to see what can be said about the existence and attributes of God without appealing to the special revelations of the great religions. We saw that Fénelon made a highly philosophical stab at this kind of theology in the early Cartesian-influenced work, where the reality of God is, he claims, inferrable from the activity of the thinking intellect. Now he did something strikingly inconsistent, it seems.

Or was it inconsistent? He had nieces and nephews coming to visit him at Cambrai, and he was more immersed in the affairs of the seminary than ever. Further, his unflagging faithfulness in the daily pastoral round, sometimes with unsophisticated, unlettered folk, continued at a steady pace. He was also conscious, more than ever, of the rhythms of his aging body and refers more and more to various ailments, aches, and pains. We must not think that because he was hard on the Jansenists regarding their pleasure-driven spirituality that he was insensitive to ordinary human satisfactions. Even more, he would not have been in any way ungrateful for such. He was no Epicurean, but neither was he a puritan! There is a better way: to be thankful for what comes in the course of nature, neither exaggerating it artificially nor discounting it contemptuously, but respecting it as a manifestation of the loving energy of God. Call it a touch of Franciscan asceticism in Fénelon, because it may have provided a basis for his next work.

Given his distaste for any spirituality based on felt, sensual "delights," even of a cerebral kind, one is surprised to discover that during this time of pastoral care at Cambrai, he seemingly struck an opposite tack. In a work of 1712 entitled *Demonstration of the Existence of God Drawn from the Spectacle of Nature and of Human Knowledge,* he set out an apologetic for the reality of God based on commonsense observation.[481] In this composition Fénelon gives us a more "exterior" and "physical" case for God, one that moves from outer observation to inner life, rather than the earlier "interior" and "metaphysical" view that disregards sensory perceptions. The title of the work suggests a kind of concession to everyday experience rather than an appeal to esoteric sophistication.

The argument is intended to be straightforward and relies heavily on the philosophical work of the Roman Cicero's summaries of ancient Greek philosophy, especially *On the Nature of the Gods.* The basic idea is that the observable universe has all of the properties of a work of art, from which one can infer the existence and nature of the creating Artist. If one approaches the natural world with an open mind and heart, says Fénelon, its harmonies reveal the laws that are the manifestation of an infinite Will. This orderly structure even manifests itself, as Augustine teaches, in the working of human memory and consciousness, despite all of our limitations and weaknesses. We are reminded again that Fénelon holds very much to the Platonist-Augustinian view that our mental life is not derivable from potentialities of the physical world, and that recognition of this fact immediately points one to an origin for the mind in the realm of spirit, that is, God.

Unlike the earlier argument, influenced by Descartes, where it is the existence of "ideas" in and of themselves that points to God, the contention here is grounded more in the everyday experience of contingency. While my experience of free will shows me that I can turn in various directions, I am also brought face-to-face with my creaturely dependency on the world around me. And that world itself points to the incorporeal God on whom corporeal nature is dependent. He contends against the ancient Epicureans and modern materialists that what is incorporeal is not reducible to what is corporeal, that materialism cannot explain the fact of conscious freedom, and that the only *rational* choice is to bow before the God who is infinite, ordering, creating Reason.

How sad it is, says Fénelon, when people see only the painting and not the Painter. Thus, we are left with a paradox. In his prayer at the conclusion of the work he says, "O God, while a great many do not discover you in the beautiful spectacle that you provide in the fullness of nature, it is not because you are far from each of us. Each of us touches you with our hands, and yet sensations and feelings deflect our perception . . . [for many] you are a reality too deeply within themselves, where they never go, and you are for them a hidden God. Because this intimate part of themselves is a place far distant from their view, they live in a state of alienation. The order and beauty which you spread on the face of your creatures are like a veil that hides you from their sick eyes." Such persons, he says from his classical sources, are "blinded by the light of the Sun."[482]

This is the humanistic side of Fénelon, the part of him that remained resolutely anti-Jansenist, so that for all of his use of the language of human "nothingness" before God, there is no denial that we can take steps *in the direction of God, and that we must take these steps,* since God "necessitates" no one; but there is also the associated insistence that we cannot complete the act without divine assistance. And one part of that assistance is the experience of the given goodness of the ordinary world as we find it. And then, acknowledging that we cannot save ourselves, we can recognize what we need in order to be saved and can reach for it. For Henri Gouhier, it is this robust faith in what human reason can do that decisively separates Fénelon from the Jansenist Pascal.

This fascination of Fénelon's in the revelatory power of what is orderly and artful in nature carried through, of course, into the crafted elegance of his discourse, the famous "Fénelonian style." The eloquent letters never ceased to flow. Having been a member of the Académie Française, the French Academy (created by Louis XIV to be an elite group of recognized writers authorized to pass "critical" judgment on works of literary art), since 1693, when the honor accrued to him as preceptor for the Duc de Bourgogne,[483] he was asked by the Academy in 1713 to prepare a report regarding the content of a dictionary and other possible handbooks contemplated for official publication. The purpose was to produce resources that would stabilize the "proper" literary usage for the rapidly evolving French language. Central to the discussion was a much-vaunted debate between the "Ancients," those who thought that classical models should always predominate, and the "Moderns," those who exalted new forms and experimentation.

The essence of Fénelon's response was contained in a metaphor.[484] The classical forms in rhetoric, music, poetry, tragedy, comedy, and historiography are complete, effective, plain, and direct, he says, and yet we have the example of the Gothic architects who thought they could make improvements with a style that is fussy, ornate gingerbread-in-the-sky. Older is not better, although it tends to be more solid. By all means let us have both, he says, with a dictionary to stabilize French usage, but with the aggressive importation of new terms that enrich the language. Let the academy manage the process. In other words: regulated innovation. A nice and conciliatory compromise!

The *Letter* was enormously successful, absolving Fénelon of any doctrinaire classicism by offering a deep veneration of tradition balanced by the refusal to idolize the past.

The Finale of "Pure Love"

Theological reflection in the midst of Jansenist sectarianism, Protestant heresy, and increasing secular-materialist indifference to religion finally brought Fénelon to the last substantive intellectual effort of his life— conversations on the "truth of religion" with André-Michel Ramsay and on the superiority of the Catholic Church with the Protestant pastor Pierre Poiret.

Ramsay was a migrant young Scotsman and spiritual seeker who had spent time in Holland at Rijnsburg, near Leiden, where Poiret had gathered a special sort of spiritual community of the kind called "pietist" by historians. Deeply dedicated to the ideal of pure love as the Holy Spirit-driven essence of Christianity, Poiret, though a Calvinist Protestant, was enamored of the Catholic mystics. Antoinette Bourignon was the exemplar, but Madame Guyon, he believed, articulated the ideal as well. And, of course, he was well aware that the papal church had condemned these mystics. Ramsay imbibed deeply at Poiret's well. Then in due course he moved on to Fénelon in Cambrai, where he became a disciple, taking the place of the faithful Langeron as Fénelon's secretary, when that priest died in 1710.

In conversations, and seemingly in letters,[485] Fénelon evangelized Ramsay, showing him that the ideal of pure love must have concrete embodiment in a specific revelation, Christianity, and a specific institution, the Catholic Church, if it is to be spiritually viable. Without those embodiments pure love could become chaotic and pathological fanaticism, unrestrained, undisciplined, manipulated by charlatans, and subject thus to the self-love that is its opposite. Ramsay accepted these arguments—although, as we will note later, only for a time—and then put Fénelon in touch with Poiret.

In a famous exchange of letters in 1712–13,[486] the two had a dialogue about the nature of the church, Fénelon congratulating Poiret on his embrace of Catholic mysticism but puzzled at his insistence on remaining Protestant. Poiret's response was basically, first, to point to the corruptions of Catholicism, an example in point being Fénelon's own condemnation, and then to make the case, in a way that would become typical of modern times, that all outward forms are "variable" and "relative" anyway as long as the spirit of love within is right. Love cannot be "forced" by anyone, said Poiret, and Fénelon in response insisted that true love will require submission to constituted authority with its authorized symbols as "the necessary means." It is extraordinary that Fénelon, so agonizingly mindful of the spiritual snares of outward observance, could, in the final analysis, affirm such observance as a necessary safeguard. Poiret was not convinced, and there the matter rested, and, many would say, still rests.

And so, Fénelon finished out his time in lively dialogue with a range of partners, the rounds of pastoral care with a cathedral staff and congregation, visits from family members, and, of course, a regimen of prayer. Productivity remained unabated. But his health always having been, as Bausset put it, "delicate," it was, of course, just a matter of time in an area of violent tumult and harsh climate.

What seems to have been the final blow took the form of a carriage accident. Out on a pastoral call, he tumbled from the vehicle when it overturned during the crossing of a stream sometime during September 1714. Badly bruised, chilled, and shaken up, he barely survived. But this time he could not bounce back. His decline was inexorable during that last hard winter. "Privations are the bread of the strong," he would have said, not excepting himself from that stern reminder.

"A traveler who is marching across a vast plain sees nothing ahead of him but a slight rise which ends the distant horizon. When he tops this rise, he finds a new stretch of country as vast as the first. . . . In the daily round, God constantly shows us new countries."

—INSTRUCTIONS AND ADVICE, 33

"I was once as wise as any. Thinking I saw everything, I saw nothing."

—INSTRUCTIONS AND ADVICE, 22 (TR. EDMONSON)

Fénelon for Us

In the Introduction I cited Melchior-Bonnet's statement that "every age has its own Fénelon." So, the first question that emerges from this biography is: Who is Fénelon for *our* age? The second question is: Why Fénelon now?

My answer to the first throughout has been that he is the Christian thinker and writer who forces us to reassess the nature and the potential of love—first love of God or the Absolute, and then love of neighbor or the Other—as the ultimate issue for understanding human wholeness, or the lack thereof, both for individuals and for the world community. He forces us to ponder the issue of what it is that makes love "pure," and then how it is that this "pure love" might show itself in the concrete circumstances of actual human lives. It is by means of asking, and suggesting answers to, these questions that Fénelon imparts a particular wisdom, which, he claimed in Christian terms, is the "wisdom of the Cross."

The background, as I have indicated everywhere, is St. Augustine's adaptation of Plato's vision. In his commentary on the First Epistle of John, the great love-epistle of the New Testament, Augustine expounded the meaning of one of the Beatitudes, Matthew 5:8, "blessed are the pure in heart, for they shall see God," with the help of 1 John 3:2, "we shall be like him [God], for we shall see him as he is." "The whole life of a good Christian," Augustine says, "is a holy desire. You don't yet see what you desire, but desiring makes you capable of being filled when what you desire to see comes. If you have a pocket or a sack you want to fill, and you know the immense amount of what you are to be given, you stretch whatever it is that you have to fill. . . . In the same way God stretches our desire by making us wait; he stretches our soul by making us desire; and by stretching our soul he enlarges its capacity. So let us desire, dear friends, because we are to be filled."[487]

In essence, all of Fénelon is commentary on this passage, further elaborated by the interlocking chain of concepts.

Desire is the activity of the will, and the supreme and final expression of the will is love, the "enlarged" heart (in Guyon's phrase), which by nature always seeks its ultimate destination in God while always being encumbered by desires for things that are less than God. That encumbrance is a product first of our own mortal and finite nature, so that we can never know the world as clearly as God knows it, and, second, of our wills, which are perverted from birth by the human history of bad choices. The net result is what Fénelon calls "self-love," the ever-present *moi* in all that we say or do.

A major component in the moral discourse of Fénelon's time, as we saw, was the analysis of the vicissitudes of this self-love and the calamities to which it leads. It was also clear that by "self-love" Fénelon did not mean what we mean by "self-care" or good "self-esteem." Rather, his understanding, typified in Louis XIV's love of "glory," comes closer to what we mean by the immature, infantile, narcissistic, impoverished, minimal, psychologically stunted, false "self" (depending on which paradigm you prefer). The soul "annihilated" and reborn in the presence of God, therefore, is the recovered "self," now freed from self-absorption and its associated self-inflation. But freed for what? Henri Bremond thought it was for pure creativity, for release from all that is "neurasthenic" in the personality (we would say "neurotic"). The virtue of Fénelon's "mysticizing" of this hunger to be freed from the self, said Bremond, is that it makes the interior life "dazzlingly sublime," an adventurous search for the springs of energy deep within.[488]

In more recent French interpretation, which emphasizes Fénelon's use of the negative, *neantic* language of the French school and of the Spanish mystics such as John of the Cross, he is seen as one who helps us to accept a cognitive paradox: we are utterly mortal and limited "nothings" who, by miraculous grace manifested in the liberating power of reason, can know "something." Or differently stated: precisely by knowing that I am nothing I "know" everything, and I am thus prepared to enter the human community intelligently and compassionately. One implication would be

the paradoxical statement that God is present in our lives as an absence—
as one for whom we hunger but do not "have"—the human correlate of
which is the state of not-knowing. This is Fénelon the postmodernist.[489]

But my emphasis here has been more ethically oriented, because I
am interested in how the one who thinks and prays profoundly is also a
person of action. I wanted to trace his development from the lively intel-
lectualism of his youth, through the intense relationship with Guyon and
the "pure love" controversy, to the concreteness of his pastoral work. The
very vibrancy of his practical ministry should have shown all of his critics
that "pure love" is not an empty abstraction or just a nice idea. Further,
by highlighting Fénelon's constant rejection of the "mercenary spirit" as
the basis of true loving (with all of the intellectual difficulties thereby
entailed), I have chosen to give central place to the motivational, morally
oriented element of *indifference* as the basis for his understanding of "pure
love." To be freed from the "me" is equivalent to being freed from the
enervating "what's in it for me?" It was, and is, also a way of being freed, as
I have suggested, from the stifling egocentrism and complacent materialism of class-conscious vanity.[490]

It is one thing to say, as in the contemporary analysis of human
behavior on the basis of sociobiology and evolutionary psychology,
that all human behavior is driven by fundamental needs for the survival
of the self or of one's own group. It is another thing to settle for that
analysis as an adequate characterization either of the ideal standard or of
the motivational dynamic that ultimately serves the human community
at an optimal level. One of my favorite contemporary neuroscientists,
V. S. Ramachandran, himself no robust theist but fighting back against
scientific reductionism, puts it this way: "Science tells us we are merely
beasts, but we don't feel like that. We feel like angels trapped inside the
bodies of beasts, forever craving transcendence."[491] In fact, Fénelon spoke
to the "angel" in us, trying to get out. But that is not "angelism." His way
of putting the matter is that freedom from self-absorption is freedom for
service, which in turn is freedom to love and glorify God alone.

It is important to see also that the contribution of Guyon and French
school mysticism to Fénelon lies hidden in Augustine's use of the word
stretch in the quotation above from the tractates on 1 John. Augustine

himself had some deep roots here, some of them going back to Greek predecessors such as Origen of Alexandria, slightly later contemporary of that Clement of whom Fénelon made use in his comments to Bossuet at the time of the Conferences of Issy. In this perspective from the early Egyptian Church, God "uses" the conditions of our mortality, and our own mistakes, as a school in our world of "soul-making" for teaching hard, morally transformative truth. We saw that Guyon with her ideas about the holy "child" and the virtues of suffering brought Fénelon to new awareness of the ways in which the dryness, emptiness, and sense of forsakenness in his spiritual life can be seen as "signs" of grace, that God is in fact drawing the soul closer to himself, that is, is "stretching it" for further filling. Augustine's "stretching" surely captures some of Fénelon's use of "passivity." Bremond had it right here. Passivity is, in Bremond's aesthetic formulation at the end of his master work, "active receiving," the analogy being to a harp played by a harpist: the instrument is passive only in that it does not initiate but is active once it is plucked.[492] So it is that we are stretched and endure and grow.

But the buyer should be cautious here, since everything can be flattened. The contemporary emphasis on passivity in the practice of meditation, for instance, is a valuable *technology* of mental emptying, often for therapeutic purposes, but not a loss of self in the paradoxical sense desired by Fénelon. For the latter, there must be a genuine desire to love God by diminishing the self before one can approach God "in spirit and in truth." If that desire is present in the form of the "desiring not to desire" so as to "desire with the will of God," that is, for reengagement in the world on behalf of all that God desires, then the "passivity" of the higher prayer *may* come as pure gift, accompanied by the "dry peace" of a tranquility in which concern for self has disappeared.

One might ask the question: is Fénelon's "pure love" identical with Buddhist "compassion"? André-Michel Ramsey, too restless to stay forever in any particular religious form, answered in the affirmative. As we saw, though, Fénelon resisted a universalizing impulse, and we ought to take him seriously. Bossuet feared that "pure love" led to a kind of final abandonment of Christianity, although Fénelon tried (unsuccessfully) to quell his fears.

Furthermore, if we ask the question about the dispute between Fénelon and Bossuet, we see, as many have suggested, that it was not so much a matter of who was right or wrong. It appears that they operated on different levels. Bossuet was, we might say, a *realist*, convinced that in the world as experienced, grace can do only so much—and so compromises are called for, if greater evil is *not* to be done and some measure of good *is* to be done. Fénelon is the *idealist*, convinced that grace can change everything, *including, and especially including*, himself (and hence the element of submission in his makeup), and then there will be a new world. A great deal of day-to-day operation will always go on in Bossuet's mode, but without Fénelon's larger view—and people who embody it—we are lost in the grand sweep of things.[493]

I think that Fénelon's spiritual writings will always appeal to people who have his high idealism about love and loving deeds, but also his elegiac sense of the sadness of the world as it normally is. And there really *is* great sadness in him, a sense of the loss of innocence and the need to create it anew, if only the wayward will can be turned toward God. The pain of all this is immense. Thus, Melchior-Bonnet can describe Fénelon in the final analysis as one who proposes "a mystique of the will," so that, as he says, "we should not wish to free ourselves from what we suffer, since it belongs only to God to distribute crosses and consolations."[494] And to Madame de Montberon he says, "Walk your walk well. All the fiddling that you try to do with it just puts a cloud between you and God."[495] Jeanne-Lydie Goré sums it up thus: "at the dawn of the century of Enlightened thinkers, he recalled that our clearest certitude is the knowledge that we can have of our limit, and that our greatest wisdom is the acceptance of this limit as a cross."[496]

In a recent essay on "God as Infinite Love" in the Catholic Christian tradition, David Tracy recalls a passage from Dostoevsky used by Dorothy Day, great leader of the Catholic Worker Movement: "Love in action is a harsh and dreadful thing compared with love in dreams. Love in dreams is greedy for immediate action, rapidly performed and in the sight of all. Men will even give their lives if only the ordeal does not last long but is soon over, with all looking on and applauding as though on the stage. But active love is labour and fortitude. . . . Just when you see with horror that in spite of all your efforts you are getting further from your goal instead of nearer to it—at that very moment . . . you will reach it and behold clearly the miraculous power of the Lord who has been all the time loving and mysteriously guiding you."[497] If we inserted the words "and in spite of all you endure" after "in spite of all your efforts," and if we realize that what Fénelon meant by "self-love" is close to "love in dreams," we have a fair approximation to his spirituality.

To my second question—Why Fénelon now?—I would suggest that his spirituality of pure love speaks to the disillusionment that so many people feel with regard to conventional religiosity. Religion often seems like a consumer product—something packaged and marketed for quick gratification at the cheapest possible price to the buyer. We place an order in a restaurant and God the restaurateur responds—more or less. The result is that "God" becomes a target for all of our projected needs, and, sure enough, religion becomes contemptible. Self-love corrupts everything, as idealistic people always come to realize.

On the other hand, his call to pure love puts Fénelon on the heights. He sets a high standard by challenging us to take God seriously, and by making spirituality a matter not of blissful contentment or contrived ecstasy, but of patient, steady, grueling discipleship. He empowers us for real action, because we are being stripped clean inside. He makes it clear that much of faithful living is a matter of "taking the hit" (crosses!), whatever it is, learning from it, and getting up again. Good spirituality is a matter of being "cracked open" again and again. If love really is love, it looks like the Cross.

Certainly his whole life testified to this perspective. He worked it out intellectually. Then his defense of Guyon made him mature as a human being, and his submission after the condemnation of the *Maxims* made him tough and resilient in the spirituality that he espoused but had yet to live fully. Pure love is a spirituality for people who are determined to keep their heads in the clouds, and their feet on the ground, he might have said at Cambrai. I cannot imagine a spirituality that is more needed for our own times, when it is likely that persons will claim one of those extremes without the other!

That last debate with the Jansenists makes the point. As we saw, it was part of a long, complicated struggle in the spirituality of the period with the "psychology of grace." How does God "speak" inside us? In the tradition of both Pascal the Jansenist and Fénelon the anti-Jansenist we talk about the religion of the heart as opposed to the mind. The difference was that Pascal had experienced what we have come to think of as the prototypical conversion-experience—deeply emotional, shattering, pinpointed in time, bringing the convicted and helpless sinner to his knees. Pascal saw his experience as implying an utter rupture between the God of the philosophers and the God of Abraham, Isaac, and Jacob. But Fénelon is different. His God is not one of the raw passion of encounter; his God is the one of "dry peace," approached through prolonged and serious cerebral labor. The process was energized and deepened by Guyon's interiority, and then advanced through privations and defeats to a life marked by deep humility and unrelenting service. For him the "heart" is our freed capacity for loving God and being loved by God wherever we are, and with whomever we are. For Fénelon the God of Abraham, Isaac, and Jacob *is precisely* the God whom the philosophers are seeking and of whom they catch glimpses, but *only* glimpses. I contend that it is Fénelon's spirituality that we need, not Pascal's, in a time when the claims of reason are intensely compelling, but not necessarily empowering.

Fénelon's spirituality is austere, to be sure. But it carries the promise of human potentialities unleashed for solid, reality-based discipleship, rather than a pleasure trip marked by ceaseless self-serving calculation. If he was right in saying that privations are the bread of the strong, and if he was right in thinking that these privations, rightly embraced, are the journey deeper into the love of God, then the Gospel journey really is the royal way of the Cross! And it is the true God that both walks with us and waits for us at the End.

ACKNOWLEDGMENTS

In a book about the apostle of pure love, my first debt has to be to my wife, Virginia, the one with whom I have experienced, in human terms, the purest love. She has been, and continues to be, for me (in the words of the Book of Common Prayer) "a strength in need, a counselor in perplexity, a comfort in sorrow, and a companion in joy." My son, John, enters the picture as well. He loves very purely and thus is an inspiration, but he would probably challenge the concept on philosophical grounds.

My first intellectual debt is to Frederick Wheelock, formerly of the Darrow School, and John Zarker, formerly of Dartmouth College, both of whom taught me to cherish the classical literature of Greece and Rome.

My second intellectual debt is to Eugene TeSelle, my doctoral dissertation supervisor at Vanderbilt University, who taught me to value and understand the patristic age of the church's life, and especially St. Augustine. Gene has been over the years a model of kindness, patience, and sophisticated criticism.

I owe a large professional debt to Calvin Kropp, my pastoral counseling supervisor in Atlanta. He helped me a great deal with the theology/psychology interface. I do not think that Fénelon's inner experience would ever have interested me quite so much, had it not been for Cal.

I owe much to several congregations of the Episcopal Church, who have heard me out on several of the themes in this book. But most of all, I am indebted to the late Sara Craig of the Cathedral of St. Philip in Atlanta, and latterly, to Lewis Doggett of the Church of the Incarnation in Highlands, North Carolina.

My principal literary sources should be acknowledged as well: Jean Gosselin for his critical edition of Fénelon's collected works, Jean Orcibal for the magnificent modern edition of Fénelon's correspondence, Sabine

Melchior-Bonnet for the latest and quite comprehensive biography of Fénelon in French, Chad Helms for his edition, with a fine introduction, of selections (particularly the *Maxims*) from Fénelon's work, and finally Henri Gouhier for the best of books on Fénelon as a philosopher. My debt to Henri Bremond is evident throughout.

I have gathered scholarly resources from a variety of sources: the libraries of Emory University and Georgia State University in Atlanta primarily, but also the library of the University of Texas in Austin, and the library of Vanderbilt University. The online resources of archive.org were invaluable. Last of all, my thanks to Jon Sweeney, Robert Edmonson, and the editorial staff of Paraclete Press. They have the competent Fénelonian eye for style, reinforced by M. de Cambrai's "iron fist in a velvet glove."

Where I have used existing translations of French texts I so note, but otherwise translations are my own. In the case of the titles of nobility I have kept the French form—since the translation of such titles seems awkward at best—but I have capitalized the title in accordance with English usage. Thus, the Duc de Bourgogne and Marquise de Maintenon, and so on. The individual may then be referred to in shorthand fashion as "Bourgogne," or either "Maintenon" or "Madame de Maintenon," and so on.

NOTES

❖

INTRODUCTION: MAN, QUIETIST, MYSTIC

1 Gosselin, *Oeuvres complètes*, 8:541. From a letter of 1714 to an unnamed female recipient. He also describes his care, at age sixty-three, of his "vast diocese" as "a crushing burden." References to the volumes of Gosselin's Paris edition (also known as the Edition of Saint-Sulpice) of Fénelon's writings and correspondence will be by volume and page number.

2 Ramsay, *Histoire*, 197: "a chest-inflammation with continuing fever."

3 Ibid., 200.

4 Fénelon, "Testament" of May 5, 1705, Bausset, *Histoire*, 4:393–97.

5 For a synthesis of all of the details of the circumstances of Fénelon's death, see Tison, "Monseigneur," 170–72, and Melchior-Bonnet, *Fénelon*, 408–10. For Fénelon's deathbed appeal to Louis XIV, the full text is in Bausset, *Histoire*, 4:386–87.

6 *Maxims of the Saints*, preface. All references to the *Maxims* will be to Chad Helms's fine translation in *Fénelon*.

7 Knox, *Enthusiasm*, ch. 11, "Quietism: The Background."

8 Bremond, *Histoire littéraire*, vol. 11, pt. 2, ch. 1. References to Henri Bremond's multivolume work, the *Histoire littéraire*, published between 1916 and 1933 (the last volume being a posthumous editing by others), are to the volume, part, chapter, and (sometimes) page numbers.

9 Knox, *Enthusiasm*, 249.

10 The most masterful and complete survey known to me of the history of the study of mysticism is Bernard McGinn, *Foundations*, appendix, but see also Schmidt, "Making." I accept McGinn's argument that it makes more sense to define the goal of mystical experience as the "experienced presence of God," rather than "union with God."

11 Bremond, *Histoire littéraire*, vol. 1, pt. 3, 18, 400.

12 An example would be Jerome Neufelder and Mary Coelho, eds., *Writings on Spiritual Direction by Great Christian Masters* (New York: Seabury, 1982).

13 *Instructions and Advice*, 24.

14 D'Aguesseau, *Oeuvres*, 13:167, cited by Orcibal, *Correspondance*, 1: 9. References to Jean Orcibal's eighteen-volume critical edition of Fénelon's complete correspondence will be by volume and page numbers.

15 Bausset, *Histoire*, 1:142.

16 Saint-Simon, *Mémoires*, tr. Arkwright, 1:141–43. Most references to Saint-Simon's memoirs will be to this six-volume English translation. A few references are to the more recent three-volume translation of selections by Lucy Norton.

17 Melchior-Bonnet, *Fénelon*, 8: "To encounter Fénelon is to undergo being seduced by him."

18 Ibid., 12.

19 Far and away the definitive study of the use and interpretation of Fénelon in France in the eighteenth century is Chérel, *Fénelon*. For the Anglo-Saxon countries, see Orcibal, *L'influence spirituelle*. There is a specialized set of studies on Ramsay. The best place to start is with Neveu, "La 'science divine.'"

20 The interested reader would enjoy a poignant essay based on a popular radio program, by French journalist Pierre Sipriot, 1951, entitled "L'admirable Monsieur du Télémaque." On the role of the *Telemachus* during the nineteenth century as part of a literature "of the people," see Gesse, *Fénelon*.

21 Bausset, *Histoire*, 3:498, says of the Marquis de Fénelon, as he was preparing for publication the first authorized collection of Fénelon's spiritual works: "He [that is, the Marquis] had equally the most religious veneration for the memory of Madame Guyon: he had had relations with her since his youth; and he did not believe himself to be under less obligation to her than to his uncle for the principles of religion, and the sentiments of tender and affectionate piety that she held and developed in the depth of her heart."

22 Jean-Pierre de Caussade, *Spiritual Instructions.* The first edition appeared in 1711. It is a defense of Bossuet's views on prayer, but with supportive citations from Fénelon. Thus Caussade is often described as "Fénelonizing" Bossuet.

23 Ward, *Experimental Theology in America,* is now the comprehensive treatment of the Guyon-Fénelon influence in nineteenth-century America.

24 McManners, *Church and Society,* 350.

25 Ibid., 351.

26 From Maxime LeRoy's introduction to Sainte-Beauve, *Port-Royal,* 1: 69.

27 A synthesis of Sainte-Beuve's writing on Fénelon is in Sainte-Beuve, *Portraits,* vol. 2.

28 Ibid., 349.

29 Ibid., 353.

30 Ibid., 362.

31 Ibid., 382.

32 McManners, *Church and Society,* 361.

33 Ibid., 178.

34 Ibid., 361.

35 This is the central argument of Bremond, *Histoire littéraire,* vol. 4.

36 Thomas Merton, in McEwen, *Fénelon,* 11.

37 Called by Melchior-Bonnet, *Fénelon,* 20, "the inexhaustible and multiform theme of the secret Fénelonian garden."

CHAPTER ONE: CLASSICAL EDUCATION AND PRIESTLY FORMATION.
   (1651–1677)

38 The latter is the preferred dating by Orcibal, *Correspondance,* 3:480, for technical reasons.

39 Cognet, "Fénelon" (1964), 151; Helms, *Fénelon,* 3; Orcibal, *Correspondance,* 1:31; and Bausset, Histoire, 1:3, respectively.

40 Helms, *Fénelon,* 3.

41 Secret, "Avec Fénelon en Périgord," 145, is a lyrical evocation. "Between the countryside and the soul of Fénelon, between the

slopes and sweet hills and the work of Fénelon, between the music of the wind in the somber yews of Périgord Noir and the incantation of Fénelon's style, there is a mysterious consonance, a secret harmony."

42 Bausset, *Histoire*, 1:381–85; Helms, *Fénelon*, introduction; and Orcibal, *Correspondance*, 1, pt. 1, have detailed information on family background and connections.

43 Bausset, *Histoire*, 1:5.

44 Goré, *L'Itinéraire de Fénelon*, 37.

45 Ibid., 38, citing a remark from Bremond.

46 Maland, *Culture and Society*, is a superior overview of the literary-artistic-educational culture of this era.

47 Goré, *L'Itinéraire de Fénelon*, 45.

48 Cited by Helms, *Fénelon*, 306, n. 11.

49 Bausset, *Histoire*, 1:8.

50 Gobinet seems also to have been an early source for the influence of Francis de Sales on Fénelon. See also Helms, *Fénelon*, 10.

51 Bremond, *Histoire littéraire*, vol. 3, pt. 2, ch. 5, "The Excellence of M. Olier," is remarkable here. An interesting aside is that in the early 1920s Bremond was forced to rewrite this chapter of the *Histoire*, because contemporary Sulpicians objected to what they considered a defamatory portrait of Olier in the original draft. Olier was under consideration at Rome at that time for canonization, but his personal history was complex, and he remains one of the few founders of French seventeenth-century religious orders who have not in fact been canonized.

52 Ibid., vol. 1, pt. 1, 1. The first edition was in 1668, the eighth in 1694. With constant revision, the work remained enormously popular.

53 This is a central thesis of Gouhier, *Fénelon philosophe*.

54 Bremond, *Histoire littéraire*, vol. 1, pt. 1, 1, 14.

55 Goré, *La Notion*, ch. 1.

56 Chadwick, "Indifference and Morality," 208–9.

57 Chad Helms, *Fénelon*, 5, 11, and passim, especially emphasizes the power of the Fénelon-Tronson connection. Helms's excellent pages, 11–19, on the influence of Saint-Sulpice and the French school on Fénelon's early development should be read as well. In the tradition

of modern Catholic authors, Helms applauds Tronson's influence on
Fénelon, e g , 11, 67, while lamenting that of Guyon.

58 This is the thesis of Henri Bremond in the *Histoire littéraire*, namely,
that the devout humanism of the French school was theocentric
by emphasizing God-centered prayer rather than anthropocentric
by emphasizing a moral and ascetical discipline deriving from
human capacities. This last is the whole complex of techniques and
methods that promise to deliver God over to us, if only we do them
correctly. Bremond (polemically and controversially) considered the
latter typical of post-Ignatian Jesuit spirituality. McGinn's comment
(*Making*, 280) is astute: "Bremond's positions were controversial,
especially his support of Fénelon over Bossuet in the dispute
over pure love and total abandonment, and his delineation of the
opposition between two great parties, the group dedicated to the
ideal of pure love and that which favored the practice of asceticism."

59 Kleinman, *Revolution*, for general treatment.

60 Bremond, *Histoire littéraire*, vol. 1, pt. 1, 3, 57, and 91.

61 Letter to Madame de Montberon, January 29, 1700.

62 For references to Francis de Sales's two famous books, I am using the
translations of the *Introduction to the Devout Life* and the *Treatise on the
Love of God* by John K. Ryan.

63 M. Buckley, "Seventeenth-Century French Spirituality," 34–35.

64 Ryan, *Introduction*, 1:3; 1:1; 1:5; 1:20–21.

65 Ibid., summary at 5:2–16; 5:14; 2:17.

66 Ibid., 3:37; 4:3; 4:8–9; 4:13; 3:10.

67 Ryan, *Treatise*, 1:15; 2:17.

68 Ibid., 2:22; 5:1–2; 6:8; 6:9; 6:10.

69 Ibid., 9:2 (twice); 9:3 (twice); 10:13; 9:4.

70 Ibid., 9:4; 9:5; 12:13.

71 Bremond, *Histoire littéraire*, vol. 3, pt. 1, 1, 22.

72 As noted by Helms, *Fénelon*, 307, n. 19; and see Bremond, *Histoire
littéraire*, vol. 3, pt. 1, 1 and following.

73 The best introduction to the writings of the French school, along
with extensive selections, is Thompson, *Bérulle*.

74 See, for instance, ibid., 174, which contains a portion of Bérulle's
description of the repentance of Mary Magdalene as she encountered

the Lord: "This is the moment when you [O Lord] ignite its flames [of love] in her heart. The sacred fire of this love is born in the waters that flow from the eyes of this humble sinner."

75 Ibid., 146.

76 Bausset, *Histoire*, 1:28.

77 Ibid., 1:30.

78 Thompson, *Bérulle*, 232.

79 Ibid., 237.

80 Ibid., 262–66.

81 Ibid., 270.

82 Bremond, *Histoire littéraire*, vol. 3, pt. 2, 5, 408, n.1.

83 Ibid., ch. 8.

84 Bausset, *Histoire*, 1:51.

CHAPTER TWO: RISING INTELLECTUAL STAR (1675–1689)

85 Bausset, *Histoire*, 1:141, 143.

86 Gosselin, *Oeuvres complètes*, 1:101–6, gives reasons for the early dating. The text is in ibid., 6:567–605.

87 La Bruyère, *Les caractères*, 15, 1.

88 Bausset's summary of this material (*Histoire*, 3:479) is notable: Fénelon "does not wish to be an orator, but wants only to be a pastor . . . who gives to village and country people instructions conformed to their simplicity and adapted to their intelligence . . . who gives up that eloquence . . . that mixes in a vain desire for glory."

89 Melchior-Bonnet, *Fénelon*, 68: "an enormous success."

90 Helms, *Fénelon*, 22–24, 115–32.

91 Ibid., 118.

92 Ibid., 123.

93 Ibid., 131.

94 Ibid.

95 Bausset, *Histoire*, 1:33.

96 Goré, *L'Itinéraire de Fénelon*, 90.

97 The comprehensive discussion of Nouvelles Catholiques and of Fénelon's role as director is Orcibal, *Correspondance*, 1, pt. 2, ch. 4: "Fénelon Superior of the Nouvelles Catholiques."

98 At the surprisingly young age of twenty-seven, says Bausset, *Histoire*, 1:48.

99 Barnard, *Fénelon on Education*, xiv.

100 Orcibal, *Correspondance*, 1:159.

101 Ibid., 3:143–44, for background on Charlotte. Fénelon's letters to her would be among his most profound and carefully wrought.

102 Ibid., 1, pt. 2, ch. 6.

103 Ibid., 171.

104 Ramsay, *Histoire*, 10.

105 We are in a quite tangled, and obscure, area of Fénelon's life here. On the whole subject of Fénelon's use of "accommodationist" methods in the Poitou mission, see Orcibal, *Correspondance*, 1:176–77; on the charge of Jansenism, ibid., pt. 2, ch. 6; on his early loss of bishoprics, Bausset, *Histoire*, 1:50, and Cognet, "Fénelon" (1954), 154. The latter suggests that Fénelon's beginning acquaintance with Guyon in 1688 also began to sour him with Harlay, who, as archbishop of Paris, was charged with her prosecution.

106 Orcibal, *Correspondance*, 1:181, notes that ironically Fénelon and the Protestant Jurieu were in agreement here: forced conversion is a travesty and simply induces hypocrisy.

107 Cited, for instance, by Barnard, *Fénelon on Education*, xvii–xviii. The reference is to the "Supplément" to the *Examen*, Gosselin, *Oeuvres complètes*, 7:102.

108 Texts in Gosselin, *Oeuvres complètes*, 5:563–603 and 1:147–202, respectively.

109 Melchior-Bonnet, *Fénelon*, 57.

110 Goré, *L'Itinéraire de Fénelon*, 100–30, has a particularly vivid sketch of the profound literary and artistic classicism of this Germigny milieu. Melchior-Bonnet, *Fénelon*, 53–57, lays greater emphasis on Bossuet's imposing presence at the center of conversation.

111 Goré, *L'Itinéraire de Fénelon*, 109: Fénelon owed to him "logical solidity" as well as clear thinking about principles of virtue.

112 Barnard, *Fénelon on Education*, 143, n. 88.

113 Louis Cognet, "Fénelon" (1967), 962 considered both works to be immature and mediocre compositions. But Cognet, usually very wise about Fénelon, was wrong here, as I try to argue in the text.

114 The text is found in Gosselin, *Oeuvres complètes*, 1:1–88, but also in a more modern critical edition edited by Dumas, *Traité de l'existence de Dieu*, 91–173.

115 See Gouhier, *Fénelon philosophe*, 127–31, for hypotheses regarding the origins and dating of this work.

116 Ibid., 33–40, for circumstances and dating. Text is in Gosselin, *Oeuvres complètes*, 2:70–157.

117 This is Gouhier's phrase, ibid., 19–25, in a section entitled "Augustinianism Cartesianized and Cartesianism Augustinianized."

118 *Demonstration*, chs. 7, 8, and 17.

119 The whole section, Gouhier, *Fénelon philosophe*, ch. 3, pt. 3, is crucial.

120 Ibid., 141.

121 Ibid., 146.

122 *Demonstration*, chs. 29, 50, and 54.

123 Gouhier, *Fénelon philosophe*, 163.

124 Dreyfus, *Malebranche*, introduction, sec. 4, "The Joint Opposition of Bossuet and Fénelon," 136.

125 *Refutation*, ch. 22.

126 Riley, "Malebranche's Moral Philosophy," 248.

127 Gouhier, *Fénelon philosophe*, 41, 50.

128 Gouhier's discussion here, ibid., 43–52, is masterful.

129 Dreyfus, *Malebranche*, introduction, sec. 4, "Concluding Remarks."

130 *Refutation*, chs. 33–34.

131 Gouhier, *Fénelon philosophe*, 71.

CHAPTER THREE: PEDAGOGUE TO ROYALTY (1689–1697)

132 Maland, *Culture and Society*, 234, describes Colbert as "a ruthless and ambitious bureaucrat who drilled himself to stand quietly in the shadow of Louis' greatness."

133 For brief sketches of the early popularity of this work, see Orcibal, *Correspondance*, 1:184ff., and Gosselin, *Oeuvres complètes*, 1:84–85. See also Ward, *Experimental Theology in America*, 86–88, for its reception in liberal Europe and in America.

134 La Bruyère, *Les caractères*, 3, 49.

135 Fénelon, *Education*, 7 (tr. Barnard).

136 Ibid., 6.

137 Ibid., 10.

138 Ibid., 12.

139 Melchior-Bonnet, *Fénelon*, 115.

140 Translated in Barnard, *Fénelon on Education*, 97–107.

141 See also Fénelon's letter to Madame de Montberon of April 15, 1700, for the same idea.

142 As suggested by Orcibal, *Correspondance*, 1:192ff.

143 See Barnard, *Fénelon on Education*, xviii; but Saint-Simon also says that Beauvillier applied to Saint-Sulpice for advice and that Fénelon was highly recommended, *Memoirs*, tr. Arkwright, 1:141.

144 Letter from Tronson to Fénelon of August 1689.

145 Bausset, *Histoire*, 1:130.

146 Cited in Melchior-Bonnet, *Fénelon*, 85.

147 Barnard, *Fénelon on Education*, xviii–xix.

148 Bausset, *Histoire*, 1:145.

149 Saint-Simon, *Memoirs*, for the year 1711, tr. Norton, 2:145.

150 Sainte-Beuve, *Portraits*, 1:419.

151 Ibid., 432.

152 English translation, Barnard, *Fénelon on Education*, 117–21.

153 Ibid., 111–16.

154 Ibid., 113.

155 Ibid., 114.

156 Ibid.

157 Ibid., 115–16.

158 Saint-Simon, *Memoirs*, for the year 1710, tr. Norton, 2:53–54.

159 Text in Gosselin, *Oeuvres complètes*, 6:335f.

160 Melchior-Bonnet, *Fénelon*, 123–25, for the chorus of praise.

161 Ramsay, *Histoire*, 16.

162 Melchior-Bonnet, *Fénelon*, 120.

163 Bausset, *Histoire*, 1:228.

164 Sainte-Beuve, *Portraits*, 2:350.

165 For what follows the best general introduction is Helms, *Fénelon*, 24–65.

166 Fumaroli, *Le Poète*, 426–35.

167 For overview and introduction to La Fontaine, see his *Selected Fables*, tr. Applebaum.

168 Ibid., X, 14 (167).

169 Fénelon's Latin text is reproduced by Bausset, *Histoire*, 1:378.

170 Texts in Gosselin, *Oeuvres complètes*, 6:344–83.

171 Ibid., 6:195–233.

172 Helms, *Fénelon*, 27.

173 Number 15 in the Gosselin collection, *Oeuvres complètes*, vol. 6.

174 Ibid., #20.

175 Helms, *Fénelon*, 31–32.

176 Gosselin, *Oeuvres complètes*, 6, #29.

177 Text in Gosselin, *Oeuvres complètes*, 6:233–334.

178 For all of the examples from Fénelon's *Dialogues*, one may consult ibid., numbers 36; 55; 25, 27; 6; 8, 64; 35, 56, 61; 1.

179 Sainte-Beuve, *Portraits*, 2:370.

180 Letters of March 21 and November 14, 1690. Bausset, *Histoire*, 3:541, notes the "admirable frankness" of Fénelon's "reproach of Madame de Gramont for her faults." The collection of Fénelon's letters to the Comtesse de Gramont long enjoyed its own separate history of transmission and use by aristocratic readers.

181 As in the letter of February 23, 1690.

182 Letters of November 17, 1688, and October 2, 1689.

183 Letter of March 21, 1692.

184 Letter of July 22, 1690.

185 Letter of November 17, 1690.

186 Goré, *L'Itinéraire de Fénelon*, 340.

187 Letter of June 1, 1689.

188 Letter of June 6, 1689.

189 Letter dated sometime in 1689.

190 Letter of August 7, 1689.

191 Ibid.

192 Identification of the recipient is difficult; see Orcibal's discussion, *Correspondance*, 3:151–52.

193 Letter dated sometime in 1688, tr. Helms, *Fénelon*. 194.

194 Letter of June 1690.

195 Letter of June 23, 1690.

196 Letter at the end of July 1690.

197 Orcibal, *Correspondance*, 1:219–21.

198 Gosselin, *Oeuvres complètes*, 1:86.

199 Text in ibid., 5:673–85.

200 Orcibal, *Correspondance*, 1:221, and n. 112.

201 Gosselin, *Oeuvres complètes*, 5:673, 680, 684.

CHAPTER FOUR: MADAME GUYON: THE CATALYST (1688–1695)

202 For a brief, general treatment of La Rochefoucauld on self-love, see Blackmore and Giguère, *Collected Maxims*, xxiv–xxvi.

203 *Instructions and Advice*, 25.

204 Rehearsals of her life and career before the collaboration with Fénelon are based mainly on the *Autobiography*. Her writings are gathered in *The Unabridged Collected Works of Jeanne Guyon*, ed. Kahley.

205 Melchior-Bonnet, *Fénelon*, 97, referring to Saint-Simon's comment. The slur is Saint-Simon's takeoff on the title of Madame Guyon's book.

206 Now it is possible to greatly romanticize this meeting and the whole ambience. Michael de la Bedoyère, *The Archbishop and the Lady*, is a highly imaginative, novelistic recreation. Since the meeting occurred in the fall season, the author begins, "The half-light of the autumnal afternoon would be in keeping with the dark and ample clothes of the ladies, relieved, in the case of the Duchess [Béthune-Charost], perhaps, by a soft-colored lace shawl and a muslin *fichu* at her neck" (p. 11). And so on. Bedoyère's chapter on the beginning of the Fénelon-Guyon relationship is entitled "Fénelon Entranced." Hollywood would have a field day, but I am trying here to reframe the connection between these two mystics on a more cerebral basis!

207 Letters to Guyon of July 26, 1689, and to Maintenon of January 1690.

208 Cognet, "Fénelon" (1964), 164. In "Fénelon" (1967), 965, Cognet adds the descriptors "introverted, analytical, deductive and cold"!

209 Merton, in McEwen, *Fénelon*, 18: she was this "dangerous woman" to whom he fled from his "cool security."

210 Cognet, *Crépuscule des mystiques*, 123–24.

211 Goré, *L'Itinéraire de Fénelon*, 338.

212 With regard to their first meeting, Guyon said: "We had some conversations on the subject of the inner life, in which he offered many objections to me. . . . The difficulties he offered only served to make clear to him the root of my sentiments," *Autobiography*, 3:11.

213 Goré, *L'Itinéraire de Fénelon*, 374ff.; see also Bremond, *Apologie*, 132–33, and Melchior-Bonnet, *Fénelon*, 88–89.

214 Bossuet, *Remarks on the Response of the M. the archbishop of Cambrai to the Report on Quietism*, art. 3.2. *Oeuvres complètes*, 10:353. In the second century in Asia Minor, Priscilla, a prophetess, claimed to be directly inspired to speak by the Holy Spirit, and Montanus was the interpreter of her prophecies. This is what Fénelon's age called "illuminism."

215 Orcibal, *Correspondance*, 1, pt. 2, ch. 10, has done a careful analysis of the whole range of Guyon's statements about her relations with Fénelon. It is abundantly clear, to say the least, that she never limited the independence of his thinking, however much he felt free to appropriate her ideas.

216 Letter to Tronson of November 6, 1694.

217 Melchior-Bonnet, *Fénelon*, 96.

218 Letter of October, 16, 1689.

219 Bremond, *Apologie*, 36.

220 Ibid., ch. 1, where Bremond describes how, during the seventeenth century, the term *quietism* became freighted, so to speak, with a host of negative connotations.

221 For the text of Molinos's *Spiritual Guide* I am using the 2010 edition and translation by Robert Baird. References to the *Guide* are to its book, chapter, and paragraph numbers respectively.

222 Taylor, *Sources of the Self*, 188, refers, in a striking phrase, to "a new, strong localization" of the soul.

223 Baird, *Spiritual Guide*, I, 1, 1, and I, 1, 3.

224 Ibid., I, 6, 40.

225 Ibid., I, 9, 52; I, 14, heading; I, 14, 106; I, 17.

226 Ibid., II, 3, 18; I, 4, 22; II, 17, 128.

227 Ibid., III, 1, 8; II, 1, 2; III, 3; III, 10, 95.

228 Ibid., III, 13, 120; III, 16, 147; III, 20, 193–194; III, 21, 203.

229 Baird, *Spiritual Guide*, B. McGinn, introduction, 21–39.

230 Guyon, "The Swallow" (Kahley, *Unabridged Collected Works*, 369).

231 Guyon, "A Child of God Longing to See Him Beloved" (Kahley, ibid., 372).

232 References in the paragraph are to Guyon, *Method*, preface (Kahley, ibid., 234f.), and *Autobiography*, ibid. 1:5 (Kahley, ibid., 20).

233 Marquet, "L'expérience religieuse," 156.

234 Cognet, "La spiritualité," 275.

235 Guyon, *Method*, 2 (Kahley, *Unabridged Collected Works*, 238).

236 Guyon, *Method*, 4 (Kahley, ibid., 241–42).

237 Guyon, *Method*, 3 (Kahley, ibid., 239–41), and *Autobiography*, 1:11 (Kahley, ibid., 47–50).

238 Guyon, *Method*, 11 (Kahley, ibid., 249).

239 Guyon, *Autobiography*, 1:11 (Allen, *The Autobiography of Jeanne Guyon*, 67–70).

240 Guyon, *Method*, 12 (Kahley, ibid., 251), and *Autobiography*, 2:4 (Allen, ibid., 231).

241 Guyon, *Method*, 18, 19, and 20 (Kahley, ibid., 257, 258, 262).

242 Bremond, *Apologie*, 71, calls Saint-Cyr "half convent, half pedagogical beehive."

243 Melchior-Bonnet, *Fénelon*, 142.

244 Orcibal, *Correspondance*, 1, pt. 2, ch. 9, is a comprehensive discussion of Fénelon's involvement at Saint-Cyr.

245 Cognet, *Crépuscule des mystiques*, 75ff.

246 Marquet, "L'expérience religieuse," 161.

247 Guyon, *Autobiography*, 1:19 (Allen, 124–25).

248 Cognet, *Crépuscule des mystiques*, 63–64.

249 The most famous example is the sketch of the faux dévot by La Bruyère in 13, "de la mode," of *Les caractères*.

250 In the sketch and synthesis that follows, I am drawing on the letters written to Guyon by Fénelon in the years 1689–90. Sometimes I refer to Guyon's letters to Fénelon as well, as these are cited in the notes and commentary of Orcibal's edition of Fénelon's *Correspondance*.

251 Bremond, *Histoire littéraire*, vol. 3, pt. 3, 1.

252 Ibid., 448.

253 Chad Helms evokes this theme nicely in *Fénelon*, 33–36.

254 La Bruyère, *Les caractères*, 8, 2.

255 Orcibal, *Correspondance*, 1:197–98, n. 6, gives details.

256 Letter to Guyon of December 2, 1688.

257 Guyon, *Autobiography*, 2:18 (Allen, ibid., 323).

258 Letter to Guyon of March 3, 1689.

259 Melchior-Bonnet, *Fénelon*, 315.

260 Letter to Guyon of May 11, 1689.

261 Letter to Guyon, dated by Orcibal, *Correspondance*, in January–February 1689.

262 Guyon is clear in the *Autobiography*, e.g., 3:8, that the states of "Jesus Christ Crucified and the Child" move in tandem.

263 Letters to Guyon of March 28, 1689; April 8, 1689; April 30, 1689; and May 11, 1689.

264 Bremond, *Apologie*, 33–34, paraphrased.

265 Cognet, *Crépuscule des mystiques*, 77.

CHAPTER FIVE: MADAME DE MAINTENON, SAINT-CYR, AND THE QUESTION OF "PURE LOVE" (1689–1697)

266 Texts are to be found in Gosselin, *Oeuvres complètes*, 6:5–71 and 6:72–160, respectively. For English translations, generous selections from the *Instructions and Advice* are to be found in Edmonson, *Complete Fénelon*; much of the *Manuel de Piété* is in the same volume. For an almost complete text of the *Instructions and Advice* in English, one still has to search out a copy of the 1947 Stillman translation, entitled *Christian Perfection*. Citations from the *Instructions and Advice* throughout this biography are from this Stillman translation, unless otherwise noted.

267 Orcibal, *Correspondance*, 1, pt. 2, ch. 9, traces out the connections of their acquaintance.

268 V. Buckley, *Françoise d'Aubigné*, is the latest, somewhat inaccurate, treatment. She keeps referring to Fénelon as a Jesuit.

269 Cognet, "Fénelon" (1954), 156.

270 In a letter (though probably a compilation) to her, dated by Orcibal, *Correspondance*, in January 1690, Fénelon lays out a catalog of her

"faults" (at her own request) in scathing terms. Complete English translation by Helms, *Fénelon*, 169–76.

271 Orcibal, *Correspondance*, 2:212.

272 Gosselin, *Oeuvres complètes*, 6:48, 55. The collection known as the *Manual of Piety* was compiled from earlier and smaller gatherings. The prayers cited here were originally part of the *Meditations on Various Subjects drawn from Holy Scripture* and the *Personal Conversations* [with God] *for the Principal Annual Feasts*. Helpful introductory comments and translations by Robert Edmonson, CJ, are found in *The Complete Fénelon* (159–60, 225–31, for comments; 210, 235–36, for prayers cited).

273 Letters to Maintenon of Christmas Day 1689; January 1690; April 2–5, 1690; September 3, 1690; and January 18–24, 1691.

274 *Instructions and Advice*, 5 and 24.

275 Letter to Maintenon of January 1690.

276 Ibid.

277 Melchior-Bonnet, *Fénelon*, 99ff.

278 Letter to Maintenon of January 1691.

279 Ibid.

280 *Instructions and Advice*, 1 (tr. Edmonson). This advice is found everywhere in Fénelon's writing to his female directees in particular.

281 Ibid., 2.

282 Ibid., 27.

283 Letter to Madame de Gramont of June 1691.

284 Letter to Madame de Gramont of May 25, 1691.

285 Letter to Madame de Gramont of October 2, 1689.

286 *Instructions and Advice*, 34.

287 A major theme of the letter of January 1690, and the one that will eventually get him into trouble with her!

288 Letter to Madame de Maintenon of October 1690.

289 There is probably some truth in Bremond's accusation (*Apologie*, 72–73) that she was an insecure parvenue who yearned to live up to Fénelon's standards and could not do it, collapsing into a mass of scruples instead. We can make the same point more compassionately by saying that she had been put in a very difficult position and simply expected too much of herself.

290 For much of what follows, up to and including the publication of the *Maxims*, far and away the best modern treatment has been Cognet, *Crépuscule des mystiques*, which superseded Bremond, *Apologie*.

291 Bremond, *Apologie*, 71: she was "young, affectionate, capricious, infinitely seductive."

292 Orcibal's comment, *Correspondance*, 2:341, that Maisonfort manifested *répugnances si évidentes* at the taking of vows is wonderfully revealing.

293 Particular examples would be the letters to Madame de la Maisonfort of December 17, 1690; February 29, 1692; and April 5, 1693.

294 References in Cognet, "Fénelon" (1964), 133ff.

295 Text in Orcibal, *Correspondance*, 2:285–87.

296 Orcibal, *Correspondance*, 3:248.

297 Cited in Cognet, *Crépuscule des mystiques*, 206.

298 Text in Orcibal, *Correspondance*, 1:302–12.

299 Cognet, *Crépuscule des mystiques*, 167, with sources for the supposition.

300 Ibid., 172.

301 Ibid., 179.

302 Letter to Bossuet of July 28, 1694.

303 Cognet, *Crépuscule des mystiques*, 97, calls Bossuet's rationalism an "a priorism," meaning that he operated with unexamined assumptions about how religious experience should be understood. Bremond, *Apologie*, everywhere argues that Bossuet developed an idée fixe about Guyon, i.e., a perception that no amount of reality would alter!

304 Cognet, *Crépuscule des mystiques*, 195.

305 Ibid., 198.

306 Melchior-Bonnet, *Fénelon*, 159: Bossuet considers her "more of a disordered visionary than a dangerous quietist."

307 The statement is actually attributed to Pope Pius IX in the nineteenth century in connection with the First Vatican Council and the dogma of papal infallibility.

CHAPTER SIX: FROM ISSY TO THE *MAXIMS* AND BEYOND: FÉNELON AT HIGH NOON (1694–1699)

308 These texts are not found in Gosselin, *Oeuvres complètes*. Jeanne-Lydie Goré, *La Notion*, 195–292, has reproduced them with commentary.

309 September October 1694, suggests Cognet, *Crépuscule des mystiques*, 240.

310 Also not found in Gosselin, *Oeuvres complètes*. Paul Dudon, ed., *Le Gnostique*, is a critical edition.

311 Letter to Bossuet of July 14, 1694.

312 I thus avoid the whole question raised by the postmodern theologian Michel Certeau in *Mystic Fable*, 108–112, of whether Fénelon's effort to show that Guyon's ideas were not new, but actually were old, was well advised. Certeau argues that Bossuet has been unfairly trashed for pointing out that Guyon's ideas were in fact quite new, or "different," by comparison with the past. He was right, says Certeau, while defenders like Fénelon always try to make of Christian tradition a smooth "homogeneity."

313 This is the central thesis of Goré, *La Notion*.

314 The classic texts are John Cassian, *Conferences*, 9 and 10. For instance, Cassian exhorts his monks to "an unceasing prayerfulness," which is a "continual serenity of prayerfulness," ibid., 9.2 (tr. Chadwick).

315 Passages cited by Cognet, *Crépuscule des mystiques*, 242.

316 *On the Authority of Cassian*, 14 (in Goré, *La Notion*, 266–67).

317 Ibid., 267, n. 14.

318 Ibid., 145: "The state of indifference is none other than the passive state . . . indifference then poses the problem of [the nature of] contemplation for Fénelon."

319 *Memoir on the Passive State*, 1–3 (ibid., 194–95).

320 Ibid., chs. 4 and 8.

321 Ibid., 232: "the ensemble witnesses to the profound spiritual culture acquired by Fénelon during these years."

322 *Memoir on the Passive State*, 17ff., and 38 (ibid., 207ff., 219).

323 Ibid., 246: "with a neatness and freedom" not so evident in later writings.

324 Text in Bossuet, *Oeuvres complètes*, 9:620–80.

325 Cognet, *Crépuscule des mystiques*, 263.

326 Ibid., 241–46.

327 Letter to Madame de la Maisonfort of February 17, 1695.

328 Details and citations are all found in Orcibal, *Correspondance*, 1, pt. 2, ch. 11.

329 Helms, *Fénelon*, 95.

330 From Issy, article 19, cited by Cognet, *Crépuscule des mystiques*, 288.

331 Ibid., 290, 301.

332 Letter to Madame de Maintenon of September 1696.

333 Gosselin, *Oeuvres complètes*, 1:33.

334 Text in ibid., 2:226–29.

335 Articles of Issy, 24, 1, 21, 2, 3, 7, 6, 8, 18, 10, 15.

336 Ibid., 11 and 25, 22, 23, 16 and 26, 17, 10, 9, 19, 28, 21.

337 Ibid., 31, 32, 34.

338 Letter to Maintenon of March 7, 1696. The Articles are "my rule of faith," he says.

339 Melchior-Bonnet, *Fénelon*, 195: "with much finesse."

340 Not included in Gosselin, *Oeuvres complètes*, but first edited and published by Chérel, *Explication des articles*.

341 Letter to Tronson of February 26, 1696, cited by Cognet, *Crépuscule des mystiques*, 365.

342 Chérel, *Explication des articles*, 7.

343 Text in Bossuet, *Oeuvres complètes*, 9:461–67.

344 Cognet, *Crépuscule des mystiques*, 379: a work of "great virulence."

345 Melchior-Bonnet, *Fénelon*, 199.

346 Letter to Maintenon of September 1696.

347 Letter of Tronson to Chevreuse, February 2, 1697.

348 Cognet, *Crépuscule des mystiques*, 395.

349 Text in Bossuet, *Oeuvres complètes*, 9:474–605.

350 Ibid., 477.

351 Ibid., 596.

352 From a 1701 address of Bossuet to the clergy of Meaux, cited by Fénelon in an unsent letter to Clement XI of March 8, 1701. Bossuet's defenders here contend that he had Thomas Aquinas solidly on his side. Paul Dudon ("Bossuet," 1880–1881), for example, claimed that Thomas takes the position that our love for God, our friendship with God, must be based on a perception that such loving is good and beneficial for us. But Thomas is more subtle than that. His theory of love is rooted in the concept of "connaturality," that is, the idea that there is an essential affinity between the lover's desire for what is good and the goodness contained in the beloved object. In the

case of God, who is pure goodness, our love for him will be *primarily* a matter of loving him for his own sake, although *secondarily* we may love him for the sake of favors received. Cf. *Summa Theologica*, IIa IIae, q. 27, art. 3 (Dom. Ed., 3:1301).

353 His term in the letter to Madame de Maintenon of September 1696.

354 Ibid., where Fénelon admits that the language of the mystics and even of the "principal Fathers" has "exaggerations."

355 In the unsent letter to Clement XI of March 8, 1701.

356 Helms, *Fénelon*, 216–20. The text of the *Maxims*, a condemned document, does not appear in official editions of Fénelon's work, such as that of Gosselin, *Oeuvres complètes*. This text was first republished separately only in the nineteenth century, and then in a critical edition by Chérel in 1911. Specific references to the *Maxims* are to the page number in the Helms translation, *Fénelon*.

357 Bossuet, *Oeuvres complètes*, 9:586.

358 *Maxims*, preface, *Fénelon*, 212.

359 *Maxims*, exposition, ibid., 220.

360 *Maxims*, art. 4, ibid., 228.

361 *Maxims*, art. 44, ibid., 294.

362 *Maxims*, art. 14, ibid., 250.

363 *Maxims*, art. 5, ibid., 233, where Fénelon says that the idea that "holy indifference is an absolute suspension of the will [is a] monstrous extravagance."

364 *Maxims*, arts. 8 and 9, ibid., 236–240.

365 *Maxims*, art. 16, ibid., 254–55.

366 *Maxims*, art. 10, ibid., 241.

367 Cognet remarks: "For [Fénelon], in effect, the graces and mystical states were the flowering of sanctifying grace, the normal crowning of the interior Christian life, culminating in absolute abandonment to God and holy indifference, and he considered as completely secondary and accessory the extraordinary phenomena on which, by contrast, Bossuet set so much store." "Fénelon" (1967), 971.

368 *Maxims*, art. 11, *Fénelon*, 244.

369 Chadwick, "Indifference and Morality," 222ff.

370 *Maxims*, arts. 19, 21, 23, 29, and 30.

371 *Maxims*, arts. 31, 32, 33, 35, and 36. For instance, art. 36: "Christian souls that have been transformed no longer ordinarily have need of certain arrangements either with respect to places or times, or even of specific formulas or of meticulously researched [perhaps "strained"] practices for their interior spiritual exercises." *Fénelon*, 285.

372 *Maxims*, arts., 41, 44, and 45.

373 Gouhier, *Fénelon philosophe*, 105.

374 Voltaire, *The Age of Louis XIV*, 38, in *Oeuvres complètes*, 21:387.

CHAPTER SEVEN: LOUIS THUNDERS, THE POPE DECIDES: FÉNELON HUMBLED (1699–1715)

375 Erlanger, *Louis XIV*, 29.

376 Ibid., 104. See Boulenger, *National History of France*, ch. 10, for a good treatment of Louis XIV with regard to religion.

377 Bossuet, *Politics Drawn from the Very Words of Scripture*, *Oeuvres complètes*, 7:595–776. In this elaborate and classical treatment Bossuet derives the authority of the hereditary French monarchy directly from the fatherhood of God. Such royal rule is to be godly, compassionate, and just, but it is also to be absolute, so that the "judgments of the sovereign are to be as if from God himself," ibid., 4.1 (O. c., 629).

378 Erlanger, *Louis XIV*, 110.

379 Ibid., 68.

380 Ibid., 118, 176.

381 Buckley, *Françoise d'Aubigné*, for instance, is pro-Maintenon, and Erlanger, *Louis XIV*, is anti-Maintenon. Bremond, *Apologie*, hated her, probably unfairly.

382 As, for instance, in the letters to Madame de Maintenon of January 1690; April 2–5, 1690; and September 26, 1692.

383 Citations from Boulenger, *National History of France*, 239, 260. It should be noted that Louis actually had his own spiritual advisor, the Jesuit Father de la Chaise. This man was highly critical of the hyper-piety of the courts dévots circle, and was frequently at odds with Maintenon. She thought that he was much too quick to endorse Louis's lukewarm piety and to oppose her in her calling to convert Louis to true religion. Cf. Guitton, "Un conflict."

384 Bausset argued that this rumor was spread by Fénelon's enemies after his death in order to make him more odious to Maintenon, and that it was "imprudently" spread by his supporters in order to create the impression at Rome that he was being sacrificed by a vengeful woman. But there has never been any proof for the rumor. *Histoire*, 2: 357–360.

385 Helms, *Fénelon*, 76–77, mentions other possibilities, but they are essentially variations on Bremond's parvenue theory, namely, that Maintenon was an insecure social climber who took advantage of people, including Fénelon, only as long as they proved to be useful.

386 Text, Orcibal, *Correspondance*, 1:274–80; Helms, *Fénelon*, 198–205, with introduction, 81–84.

387 Orcibal, *Correspondance*, 2:418–49, also noted by Helms, *Fénelon*, 82.

388 Citations are from the Helms translation, *Fénelon*.

389 Orcibal, *Correspondance*, 2:404, notes that Bossuet had even spoken to the king of "his right of conquest as attested in Scripture." In fact, that concept is omnipresent in the work mentioned in n. 377 above, composed actually for the instruction of the Dauphin as the next king of France.

390 Letter from Louis XIV to Innocent XII of July 26, 1697.

391 Text in Bossuet, *Oeuvres complètes*, 10:300–338. In the *Report*, 11 (*O. c.*, 337) he calls Guyon "an ignorant and visionary woman."

392 Orcibal, "Fénelon et le quiétisme. II," gives all the details.

393 The best overview of this period, and the points of debate, is still the "Analyse raisonnée" of Gosselin, *Oeuvres complètes*, 1:177–254.

394 Called a *Mémoire*. Text in ibid., 2:252–55.

395 Ibid., 1:211ff.

396 As an interesting aside, it appears to have been about this time that Fénelon prepared a long memo (never sent) for Bossuet with regard to a passage in a recently published biography of the Ursuline nun Marie Guyart, known as Marie of the Incarnation and often considered the French Teresa. In the passage, Marie describes her dark night of the soul, in which she has a vision of being cast into hell, so that God's justice would be satisfied. She says that "in a moment his goodness and mercy, through a secret outpouring of his spirit, aroused in the higher part of my soul a desire to be cast

into hell. . . . I saw that I deserved hell and that the justice of God would never be wrong in casting me into the abyss. I had a strong desire for this, although I would never want to be deprived of the friendship of God." In other words: Send me to hell, O Lord, if your love requires it.

Gosselin knew about the memo, but chose not to include it in the collected works, because it was never sent. Apparently, Fénelon considered it an example of the "impossible supposition" among the saints. Paul Dudon, "Lettre autographe," speculates on why it was never sent. The passage from Marie may be found in *Marie of the Incarnation*, ed. Mahoney, 141–42.

397　While Thomas Aquinas was not yet the official authority for Catholic theology that he would become at the end of the nineteenth century, it is clear that both Fénelon and Bossuet are struggling with him. On the question of whether charity precedes hope, Aquinas asserts that there is perfect, and there is imperfect, love. "Perfect love is that whereby a man is loved in himelf, as when someone wishes a person some good for his own sake; thus a man loves his friend. Imperfect love is that whereby a man loves something, not for its own sake, but that he may obtain that good for himself; thus a man loves what he desires," *Summa Theologica*, IIa IIae, q. 17, art. 8 (Dom. Ed., 3:1241).

397　Melchior-Bonnet, *Fénelon*, 218.

399　Ibid., 221.

400　Letters to Louis of May 12, 1697, and to Madame de Maintenon in late July 1697.

401　Melchior-Bonnet, *Fénelon*, 223, with an ironic twist on Saint-Simon's favorite term for Fénelon.

402　Letter to Madame de Maintenon of August 1, 1697. It is easy to see from a letter like this why Fénelon can be accused of "feline" (McManners) craftiness. And yet the letter comes across as sincere, despite its fulsomeness.

403　What Bossuet actually wrote was that while he had called Fénelon a second Molinos, he had no intention of casting aspersions on M. de Cambrai's personal conduct or the direct implications of his teaching. Nonetheless, he insisted, the underlying principles of

Molinism were present in Fénelon's doctrine. *Report on Quietism,* 2 (Bossuet, *Oeuvres complètes,* 10:300).

404 Bossuet's favorite dismissive phrase for Guyon is "that woman and her books." Cf. ibid., 11 (*O. c.,* 10:336).

405 Orcibal, "Fénelon et le quiétisme. 2," refers colorfully to the whole process in Rome as "a hard combat"!

406 Cognet, "Fénelon" (1964), 162.

407 Cited by Helms, *Fénelon,* 111.

408 Knox, *Enthusiasm,* 347ff.

409 Orcibal, "Fénelon et le quiétisme. III," 242ff.

410 Text in Gosselin, *Oeuvres complètes,* 3:405–11.

411 Also instanced and discussed by Helms, *Fénelon,* 108.

412 *Maxims,* art. 33, Helms, *Fénelon,* 281, begins: "In the passive state there is a union of all love's virtues that never excludes the distinct exercise of each virtue."

413 Saint-Simon, *Memoirs,* tr. Arkwright, 1:343–44.

414 I thus follow the views of Patrick Riley, *Telemachus,* xxi, who contends that in this composition we have "a political version of Fénelon's 'disinterested love of God.'"

415 Tison, "Monseigneur," 162. The detail comes from Voltaire, *The Age,* 32, who called the *Telemachus* "one of the finest monuments of a flourishing age" (tr. Brumfitt, 177).

416 Melchior-Bonnet, *Fénelon,* 256.

417 Riley, *Telemachus,* xv. All citations from the *Telemachus* will be from this excellent edition and translation.

418 Critical introductions are in Helms, *Fénelon,* and Riley, ibid. Helms's introduction excels as literary analysis, Riley's as political-scientific analysis.

419 Goré, *L'Itinéraire de Fénelon,* 549.

420 Ibid., 550.

421 Riley, *Telemachus,* xvii.

422 Melchior-Bonnet, *Fénelon,* 126.

423 *Telemachus,* bk. 7 (Riley ed., 114).

424 *Telemachus,* bk. 10 (Riley ed., 152).

425 Melchior-Bonnet, *Fénelon,* 60.

426 According to Voltaire, when Louis engaged Fénelon in conversation about the ideas in *Telemachus*, the king came away convinced that his grandson's preceptor was "the finest spirit, but also the greatest fantasist, in his kingdom." *The Age*, 38 (*Oeuvres complètes* 21:390).

427 Mousnier, "Les idées politiques," 202–3. As pointed out to me by Eugene TeSelle, this is part of the dark side of the theme of childhood in French political discourse, where the long-standing custom was for the leader to address the people as "my children."

428 Melchior-Bonnet, *Fénelon*, 129–30: "Whereas war divides people, commerce unites them."

429 *Telemachus*, bk. 10 (Riley ed., 158).

430 Letter to Beauvillier of August 1, 1697.

CHAPTER EIGHT: AT CAMBRAI: "PURE LOVE" IN ACTION (1695–1715)

431 Tison, "Monseigneur," 161–62.

432 Letter to Beauvillier of March 29, 1699 (tr. McEwen).

433 Ramsay, *Histoire*, 74.

434 Ibid., 74–75.

435 Cited in Bremond, *Apologie*, 184.

436 Melchior-Bonnet, *Fénelon*, 368.

437 The best short treatment of the Cambrai ambience is Tison, "Monseigneur." For much more detailed treatment see Deregnaucourt and Guignet, *Fénelon*.

438 For this detail, see Melchior-Bonnet, *Fénelon*, 263.

439 Orcibal, *Correspondance*, 27:391–95, has the history here. It was a fragile operation, eventually folded into Saint-Sulpice in Paris in 1713, so that Fénelon on his deathbed could ask the king to look after it.

440 Ramsay, *Histoire*, 156, 162, 165–66.

441 Saint-Simon, *Memoir*, tr. Arkwright, 5:77–84.

442 Melchior-Bonnet, *Fénelon*, 268, 295.

443 Goré, "Fénelon ou du pur amour," 71–72.

444 Briefly, there were two "rubs" with Malebranche in Fénelon's later years. The later event, in 1713, involved a convoluted affair in

which Malebranche came to believe that Fénelon had accused him in one of his works of "Spinozism." Because, as we recall, Malebranche identified the general providence of God with the laws of nature, it was easy for critics to argue that he, Malebranche, was in league with the Spinozist view that God and nature are one and the same. In a correspondence Fénelon assured a ruffled Malebranche that he had done no such thing, whatever his other criticisms. Source documents are in Nicolas Malebranche, *Oeuvres complètes*, 19:835ff.

The second issue concerns Malebranche's critique of Fénelon's anti-Jansenist understanding of God's sanctifying grace as an experience devoid of ordinary human pleasure. Malebranche found this view "unnatural," and since God works through nature and our natural processes of loving, while still respecting our freedom, as un-Christian as well. In an effort to distance himself from quietism Malebranche had published his *Treatise on the Love of God* in 1697, thus setting himself in opposition to Fénelon.

445 Bausset, *Histoire*, 2:394 (tr. Mudford, 2:427).

446 Letter to Madame de Montberon of January 29, 1700.

447 Letter to Madame de Montberon of April 15, 1700.

448 Letter to Madame de Montberon of June 13, 1700.

449 Letter to Madame de Montberon of June 17, 1700.

450 Letter to Madame de Montberon of December 26, 1700.

451 Letter to Madame de Montberon of January 5, 1701.

452 For citations from the letters to Chevreuse and Bourgogne, I am using McEwen, *Fénelon: Letters of Love*.

453 For instance, the letter to Chevreuse of January 27, 1700.

454 Undated letter to Chevreuse (McEwen, 151).

455 Letter to Chevreuse of December 30, 1699.

456 Letter to Beauvillier of September 1702.

457 Letter to Beauvillier of January 27, 1703.

458 Text in Gosselin, *Oeuvres complètes*, 7:149–81.

459 Melchior-Bonnet, *Fénelon*, 336.

460 Ibid., 338.

461 Text in Gosselin, *Oeuvres complètes*, 7:85–102.

462 Text in ibid., 182–88.

463 The couple's first son had already died, and the second would die shortly thereafter.

464 Ramsay, *Histoire*, 195–96.

465 Melchior-Bonnet, *Fénelon*, 393.

466 Saint-Simon took Fénelon's quick reimmersion in the political flow as just another evidence of his "ambition" (*Memoirs*, tr. Arkwright, 5:82).

467 Text in Gosselin, *Oeuvres complètes*, 7:189–84.

468 Ramsay, *Histoire*, 92. On the history of the seminary, see Orcibal, *Correspondence*, 27, appendix.

469 The amount of text material is massive, comprising part of Gosselin, *Oeuvres complètes*, 3, and all of 4 and 5.

470 Melchior-Bonnet, *Fénelon*, 357.

471 TeSelle, *Augustine*, 275.

472 Actual formulation from Eugene TeSelle, personal communication.

473 Letter to Lamy of May 3, 1708, slightly paraphrased.

474 Gouhier, *Fénelon philosophe*, 52–54, is especially good here.

475 Letter to Lamy of October 26, 1704.

476 Melchior-Bonnet, *Fénelon*, 383. The reference is to *Pastoral Instruction in the Form of Dialogues on the System of Jansenius*, letter-dialogue 23. Gosselin, *Oeuvres complètes*, 5:436–43.

477 An interesting parallel is in the modern view of addictionology that "once an addict, always an addict," since it is only the element that one is addicted to that changes in the process of recovery. There is wisdom here, of course, despite Fénelon's objection.

478 The question is a difficult one. It should be noted that Thomas Aquinas is cautious. He argues that there is pleasure in loving God, but that the goodness of this pleasure "is due not to the mere fact that it is pleasure, but to the fact that it is perfect repose in the perfect good," *Summa Theologica*, 1a IIae, q. 34, art. 3 (Dom. Ed., 2:738). In other words, the pleasure that comes from loving God is unique in nature. That seems to have been Fénelon's point.

479 Gouhier, *Fénelon philosophe*, 77, also contends that we have here a definition of true freedom: "the pleasure that the will takes in wishing to wish well what it wishes." One is reminded of Søren Kierkegaard's later dictum that "purity of heart is to will one thing."

480 Cited in Melchior-Bonnet, *Fénelon*, 373.

481 Text in Dumas, *Traité de l'existence de Dieu*, 11–90.

482 *Demonstration*, 92. Ibid., 89–90 (slightly paraphrased).

483 Bausset, *Histoire*, 1:231.

484 *Letter to the Academy*, 10. Text in Caldarini, *Lettre à l'Académie*.

485 Text in Gosselin, *Oeuvres complètes*, 1:201–26.

486 The text of Fénelon's letters to Poiret is in Orcibal, "Une controverse"; the text of Poiret's letters to Fénelon is in Chevallier, "La réponse de Poiret."

EPILOGUE: FÉNELON FOR US

487 Augustine, *Homilies on the First Letter of John*, 4.5, in *Love One Another*, tr. Leinenweber.

488 Bremond, *Apologie*, 455. It is no accident that French adaptations of Freudian psychoanalysis have specialized in exploring the nature of narcissistic neurosis and narcissistic personality dynamics.

489 Thus, Gouhier, *Fénelon philosophe*, 163, for instance, can compare Fénelon's insights about human experience to those of André Gide.

490 This is a central thesis of Robert Spaemann, *Reflexion und Spontaneität*.

491 Ramachandran, *The Tell-Tale Brain*, 291.

492 Bremond, *Histoire littéraire*, vol. 11, pt. 2, 2, 364ff.

493 It may also be the case that Bossuet was simply a man of the past, of the seventeenth century, with his realism and rationality and dogmatism, while Fénelon was the voice of the future, with his flowing style and reforming ardor and humane sensibility. This was the shrewdly wrought view of M.-H. Guervin, "Bossuet and Fénelon," 567–68, in a detailed comparing and contrasting of the two men.

494 Melchior-Bonnet, *Fénelon*, 433.

495 Letter to Madame de Montberon of June 23, 1703.

496 Goré, *L'Itinéraire de Fénelon*, 726.

497 From *The Brothers Karamazov*, in Tracy, "God as Infinite Love."

SELECTED BIBLIOGRAPHY

I. WORKS AND CORRESPONDENCE OF FÉNELON

Fénelon, François. *Oeuvres*. Edited by Jacques Le Brun. 2 vols. Paris: Gallimard, 1983–97.

——. *Oeuvres complètes, précédées de son histoire littéraire*. Edited by Jean Gosselin. 10 vols. Paris: Gaume, 1848–52.

——. *Correspondance de Fénelon*. Edited by J. Orcibal, J. Le Brun, and I. Noye. 18 vols. Paris and Geneva: Droz, 1972–2007.

——. *Explication des articles d'Issy*. Edited by A. Chérel. Paris: Hachette, 1915.

——. *Explication des maximes des saints*. Edited by A. Chérel. Paris: Bloud, 1911.

——. *Le Gnostique de saint Clément d'Alexandrie, opuscule inédit*. Edited by Paul Dudon. Paris: Beauchesne, 1930.

——. *Mémoire sur l'état passif, L'autorité de Cassien, Annihilation*. Edited by Paul Dudon and printed in Goré, *La Notion*. See General bibliography below.

——. *Traité de l'existence de Dieu*. Edited by Jean-Louis Dumas. Paris: Éditions Universitaires, 1990.

——. *Lettre à l'Académie*. Edited by E. Caldarini. Geneva: Droz, 1970.

II. MODERN TRANSLATIONS WITH CRITICAL INTRODUCTION AND COMMENTARY

Barnard, H. C., trans. *Fénelon on Education: A Translation of the "Traité de l'Éducation des Filles" and Other Documents Illustrating Fénelon's Educational Theories and Practice*. Cambridge: Cambridge University Press, 1966.

Edmonson, Robert J., CJ, and Hal M. Helms, ed. and trans. *The Complete Fénelon*. Brewster, MA: Paraclete Press, 2008.

Helms, Chad, ed. and trans. *Fénelon: Selected Writings*. Classics of Western Spirituality. New York and Mahwah, NJ: Paulist Press, 2006.

McEwen, John, ed. and trans. *Fénelon: Letters of Love and Counsel*. New York: Harcourt, Brace, 1964.

Riley, Patrick, ed. and trans. *François de Fénelon: Telemachus, Son of Ulysses*. Cambridge: Cambridge University Press, 1994.

Stillman, Mildred Whitney, trans., and Charles F. Whiston, ed. *Christian Perfection, by François de Salignac de la Mothe Fénelon*. New York: Harper & Row, 1947.

III. MODERN COLLOQUIA AND COLLECTIONS ON FÉNELON

Cuche, F.-X., and J. Le Brun, eds. *Fénelon: Mystique et Politique (1699–1999)*. Actes du colloque international de Strasbourg pour le troisième centenaire de la publication du *Télémaque* et de la condemnation des *Maximes des Saints*. Paris: Honoré Champion, 2004.

Derégnaucourt, Gilles, and Philippe Guignet, eds. *Fénelon: évêque et pasteur en son temps, 1695–1715*. Actes du colloque Cambrai, 15–16 septembre, 1995. Lille: Centre d'Histoire de la Région du Nord et de l'Europe du Nord-Ouest, 1996.

Guervin, M.-H., ed. *Dix-septième siècle* (1951), nos. 12–14, for the *Société d'Étude du XVIIe Siècle*. Tricentenaire de Naissance de Fénelon, special issue. Leduc-Fayette, Denise, ed. *Fénelon: Philosophie et spiritualité*. Actes du colloque organisé par le Centre d'Étude des Philosophes Français, Sorbonne, 27–28 mai 1994. À la mémoire de Henri Gouhier (1898–1994). Geneva: Droz, 1996.

III. GENERAL

Aquinas, Thomas. *Summa Theologica*. English Dominican edition, Christian Classics reprint. 5 volumes, Westminster, MD: 1981 (originally published by Benziger, 1948).

Augustine. *Love One Another, My Friends: St. Augustine's Homilies on the First Letter of John*. Translated by John Leinenweber. San Francisco: Harper & Row, 1989.

Bausset, Cardinal de. *Histoire de Fénelon, archevêque de Cambrai, composée sur les manuscrits originaux*. 3rd ed. 4 vols. Versailles: Lebel, 1817.

———. *The Life of Fénelon, Archbishop of Cambrai*. Tr. William Mudford. 2 vol. London: 1810.

Bedoyère, Michael de la. *The Archbishop and the Lady: The Story of Fénelon and Madame Guyon*. London: Collins, 1956.

Bossuet, Jacques-Bénigne. *Oeuvres complètes, précédées de son histoire par le cardinal de Bausset*. 12 vols. Nancy, 1863.

Boulenger, Jacques. *The National History of France: The Seventeenth Century*. London: William Heinemann, 1920.

Bremond, Henri. *Apologie pour Fénelon*. Paris: Perrin et cie, 1910.

———. *Histoire littéraire du sentiment religieux en France depuis la fin des guerres de religion jusqu'à nos jours*. 11 vols. Paris: Bloud et Gay, 1916–33.

———. *A Literary History of Religious Thought in France from the Wars of Religion Down to Our Own Times*. Edited and translated by K. L. Montgomery. Vols. 1–3. New York: SPCK, 1928–36.

Buckley, Michael J. "Seventeenth-Century French Spirituality: Three Figures." In *Christian Spirituality 3: Post-Reformation and Modern*, edited by Louis Dupré and Don E. Saliers, 28–68. New York: Crossroad, 1989.

Buckley, Veronica. *Françoise d'Aubigné, Madame de Maintenon: The Secret Wife of Louis XIV.* New York: Farrar, Straus and Giroux, 2008.

Cassian, John. *Conferences.* Edited by Owen Chadwick. The Library of Christian Classics. Philadelphia: Westminster, 1958.

Caussade, Jean-Pierre de. *Spiritual Instructions on the Various States of Prayer according to the Doctrine of Bossuet, Bishop of Meaux.* Edited by Algar Thorold, first published 1931. Springfield, IL: Templegate, 1964.

Certeau, Michel de. *The Mystic Fable.* Volume 1: *The Sixteenth and Seventeenth Centuries.* Edited by Michael B. Smith. Chicago: University of Chicago Press, 1992.

Chadwick, Owen. "Indifference and Morality." In *Christian Spirituality: Essays in Honor of Gordon Rupp*, edited by Peter Brooks, 205–30. London: SCM Press, 1975.

Chérel, Albert. *Fénelon au XVIIIe siècle en France (1715–1820): son prestige-son influence.* Paris: Hachette, 1917.

Chevallier, Marjolaine. "Deux reactions protestantes à la condemnation de Fénelon: Pierre Jurieu et Pierre Poiret." In the Cuche and Le Brun collection, 147–61.

———. "La réponse de Poiret à Fénelon." *Revue d'histoire de la spiritualité* 52 (1976):19–47.

Cognet, Louis. *Les origines de la spiritualité française au XVIIe siècle.* Paris: La Colombe, 1949.

———. "La spiritualité de Madame Guyon." In the Guervin collection, 269–75.

―――. *Crépuscule des mystiques. Bossuet Fénelon* Tournai. Desclée & Co., 1958.

―――. "Fénelon." *Dictionnaire de spiritualité*, 5:151–70. Edited by M. Viller et al. Paris: Beauchesne, 1964.

―――. *Le Jansénisme*. Paris: Presses Universitaires de France, 1964.

―――. "Fénelon." *Dictionnaire d'histoire et de géographie ecclésiastiques*, 16: 958–87. Edited by R. Aubert. Paris: Letouzey et Ané, 1967.

Daniélou, Madeleine. "Fénelon Éducateur." In the Guervin collection, 181–89.

Dudon, Paul. "Bossuet." *Dictionnaire de spiritualité*, 1:1874–83. Edited by M. Viller et al. Paris: Beauchesne, 1937.

―――. "Lettre autographe et inédite de Fénelon à Bossuet sur le sacrifice absolu du salut." *Révue d'ascétique et de mystique* 18 (Jan. 1937):65–88.

Erlanger, Philippe. *Louis XIV*. Edited and translated by Stephen Cox. New York: Praeger, 1970.

Fontenelle, Bernard Le Bovier de. *Dialogues of the Dead, in three parts*. Translated by John Hughes. London: Tonson, 1730. Gale editions reprint.

Fumaroli, Marc. *Le Poète et le roi: Jean de La Fontaine en son siècle*. Paris: Éditions de Fallois, 1997.

Gesse, Frédéric. "Fénelon au XIXe siècle: De J. Joubert à G. Bruno." In the Cuche and Le Brun collection, 549–66.

Goré, Jeanne-Lydie. "Un aspect de l'éthique fénelonienne: l'anéantissement du moi." In the Guervin collection, 254–68.

―――. *La notion d'indifférence chez Fénelon et ses sources*. Paris: Presses Universitaires de France, 1956. Contained also are *Le mémoire sur l'état passif, De l'autorité de Cassien*, and *Sur l'anéantissement*.

————. *L'Itinéraire de Fénelon: humanisme et spiritualité.* Paris: Presses Universitaires de France, 1957.

————. "Fénelon ou du pur amour: à la politique de la charité." *Dix-septième siècle* 90, no. 1 (1971): 57–73.

Gouhier, Henri. *Fénelon philosophe.* Paris: Vrin, 1977.

Guervin, M.-H. "Bossuet and Fénelon." *Dix-septième siècle* 16 (1952):545–68.

Guibert, J. de. "Bremond (Henri)." *Dictionnaire de spiritualité,* 1:1928–38. Edited by M. Villar et al. Paris: Beauchesne, 1964.

Guitton, Georges. "Un conflit de direction spirituelle: Madame de Maintenon et le Père de la Chaize." *Dix-septième siècle* 29 (1955):378–95.

Guyon, Madame Jeanne. *The Autobiography of Jeanne Guyon.* SeedSowers, n.d. ** (This is a reprint of the Thomas Taylor Allen translation of 1897. In some passages it is more dependable than the Kahley edition.)

————. *Unabridged Collected Works.* Edited by Glenn Kahley. Breinigsville, PA: n.p., 2006.

Hogarth, Henry. *Henri Bremond: The Life and Work of a Devout Humanist.* London: SPCK, 1950.

Joppin, Gabriel, SJ. "Fénelon et le quiétisme. 1. Le problème théologique." In the Guervin collection, 215–26.

Kleinman, Ruth. *A Revolution in Charity.* Hyattsville, MD: Institute of Salesian Studies, 1968.

Knox, Ronald. *Enthusiasm: A Chapter in the History of Religion, with Special Reference to the XVII and XVIII Centuries.* Oxford: Oxford University Press, 1950.

La Bruyère, Jean de. *Les caractères* [*Characters*]. Translated by Jean Stewart. New York: Penguin, 1970.

La Fontaine, Jean de. *Fables choisies* [*Selected Fables*]. Edited and translated by Stanley Appelbaum. Mineola, NY: Dover, 1997.

La Rochefoucauld, François de. *Collected Maxims and Other Reflections.* Translated by E. H. and A. M. Blackmore and Francine Giguère. Oxford: Oxford University Press, 2007.

Lorson, Pierre. "Guerre et paix chez Fénelon." In the Guervin collection, 207–14.

Magnard, Pierre. "La querelle des augustinismes." In the Leduc-Fayette collection, 135–54.

Maland, David. *Culture and Society in Seventeenth-Century France.* New York: Scribner's, 1970.

Malebranche, Nicolas. *Malebranche: Traité de la nature et de la grâce.* Edited by Ginette Dreyfus. Paris: Vrin, 1958.

————. *Oeuvres complètes.* Edited by A. Robinet. Bibliothèques des Textes Philosophiques. 20 vol. and index. Paris: Vrin, 1958–70.

Marie of the Incarnation. *Selected Writings.* Edited by Irene Mahony, OSU. Classics of Western Spirituality. Mahwah, NJ: Paulist, 1989.

Marquet, J.-F. "L'expérience religieuse de Jeanne Guyon." In the Leduc-Fayette collection, 155–76.

McGinn, Bernard. *The Foundations of Mysticism.* New York: Crossroad, 1991.

McManners, John. *Church and Society in Eighteenth-Century France.* Vol. 2, *The Religion of the People and the Politics of Religion.* Oxford: Oxford University Press, 1998.

Melchior-Bonnet, Sabine. *Fénelon.* Paris: Éditions Perrin, 2008.

Merton, Thomas. "Reflections on the Character and Genius of Fénelon." In the McEwen anthology, 9–30.

Molinos, Miguel de. *Miguel de Molinos: The Spiritual Guide.* Edited by and translated by Robert P. Baird. Introduction by Bernard McGinn. Classics of Western Spirituality. New York and Mahwah, NJ: Paulist Press, 2010.

Mousnier, Roland. "Les idées politiques de Fénelon." In the Guervin collection, 190–206.

Neveu, Bruno. "La 'science divine' du chevalier Ramsay." In the Leduc-Fayette collection, 177–96.

Orcibal, Jean. "Fénelon et le quiétisme. 2. Le procès de *Maximes des Saints* à Rome." In the Guervin collection, 226–42.

————. "Fénelon et le quiétisme. 3. La soumission de Fénelon et son cardinalat manqué." In the Guervin collection, 242–53.

————. "L'influence spirituelle de Fénelon dans les pays anglo-saxons au XVIIIe siècle." In the Guervin collection, 276–87.

————. "Une controverse sur l'Église d'après une correspondence inédite entre Fénelon et Pierre Poiret." *Dix-septième siècle* 4 (1955):396–422.

Pryce, Elaine. "'Upon the Quakers and the Quietists: Quietism, Power and Authority in Late Seventeenth-Century France, and Its relation to Quaker History and Theology." *Quaker Studies* 14, no. 2 (2010): 212–23.

Ramachandran, V. S. *The Tell-Tale Brain: A Neuroscientist's Quest for What Makes Us Human.* New York: Norton, 2011.

Ramsay, André-Michel de. *Histoire de la vie de Messr. François de Salignac de la Motte-Fénelon, Archevêque Duc de Cambray.* With *Discours philosophique sur l'amour de Dieu.* La Haye: Vaillant, 1723.

Riley, Patrick. "Malebranche's Moral Philosophy: Divine and Human Justice." In *The Cambridge Companion to Malebranche,* edited by Steven Nadler, 220–61. Cambridge: Cambridge University Press, 2000.

Sainte-Beuve, Charles Augustin. *Port-Royal.* 5 vols. Paris: Gallimard, 1953.

————. *Portraits of the Seventeeenth Century: Historic and Literary.* 2 vols. Translated by Katherine P. Wormeley. New York: Frederick Ungar, 1964.

Saint-Simon, Duc de. *Mémoires.* Edited by A. de Boislisle. 43 vols. Paris: Hachette, 1879–1928.

————. *Mémoires.* Abridged ed. Translated by Francis Arkwright. 6 vols. London: Stanley, Paul & Co., 1915.

————. *Mémoires.* Abridged ed. Translated by Lucy Norton. 3 vols. New York: McGraw-Hill, 1967–2007.

Sales, Francis de. *Introduction to the Devout Life.* Translated by John K. Ryan. New York: Image Books/Doubleday, 1972.

————. *Treatise on the Love of God.* Translated by John K. Ryan. Rockford, IL: Tan Books, 1975.

Schmidt, Leigh Eric. "The Making of Modern Mysticism." *Journal of the American Academy of Religion* 71, no. 2 (June 2003):273–302.

Secret, Jean. "Avec Fénelon en Périgord et en Quercy." In the Guervin collection, 141–45.

Spaemann, Robert. *Reflexion und Spontaneität: Studien über Fénelon.* Stuttgart: Klett Verlag, 1990.

Taylor, Charles. *Sources of the Self: The Making of the Modern Identity.* Cambridge, MA: Harvard University Press, 1989.

TeSelle, Eugene. *Augustine the Theologian.* New York: Herder & Herder, 1970.

Thompson, William M., ed. *Bérulle and the French School: Selected Writings.* Translated by Lowell M. Glendon, ss. New York and Mahwah, NJ: Paulist Press, 1989.

Tison, Pierre. "Monseigneur François de Salignac de la Mothe-Fénelon, Archevêque-Duc de Cambrai: Quelques Notes." In the Guervin collection, 146–72.

Tracy, David. "God as Infinite Love: A Roman Catholic Perspective." In *Divine Love: Perspectives from the World's Religious Traditions*, edited by Jeff Levin and Stephen G. Post, 131–62. West Conshohocken, PA: Templeton Press, 2010.

Voltaire (François Marie Arouet). *The Age of Louis XIV and Other Selected Writings*. Translated by J. H. Brumfitt. New York: Twayne, 1963.

———. *Oeuvres complètes*. Paris: Imp. de la Societé littéraire-typographique, 1784.

Ward, Patricia A. *Experimental Theology in America: Madame Guyon, Fénelon, and Their Readers*. Waco, TX: Baylor University Press, 2009.

INDEX OF PROPER NAMES

ABOUT PARACLETE PRESS

WHO WE ARE

Paraclete Press is a publisher of books, recordings, and DVDs on Christian spirituality. Our publishing represents a full expression of Christian belief and practice—from Catholic to Evangelical, from Protestant to Orthodox.

We are the publishing arm of the Community of Jesus, an ecumenical monastic community in the Benedictine tradition. As such, we are uniquely positioned in the marketplace without connection to a large corporation and with informal relationships to many branches and denominations of faith.

WHAT WE ARE DOING

Books

Paraclete publishes books that show the richness and depth of what it means to be Christian. Although Benedictine spirituality is at the heart of all that we do, we publish books that reflect the Christian experience across many cultures, time periods, and houses of worship. We publish books that nourish the vibrant life of the church and its people—books about spiritual practice, formation, history, ideas, and customs.

We have several different series, including the best-selling Paraclete Essentials and Paraclete Giants series of classic texts in contemporary English; A Voice from the Monastery—men and women monastics writing about living a spiritual life today; award-winning poetry; best-selling gift books for children on the occasions of baptism and first communion; and the Active Prayer Series that brings creativity and liveliness to any life of prayer.

Recordings

From Gregorian chant to contemporary American choral works, our music recordings celebrate sacred choral music through the centuries. Paraclete distributes the recordings of the internationally acclaimed choir Gloriæ Dei Cantores, praised for their "rapt and fathomless spiritual intensity" by *American Record Guide*, and the Gloriæ Dei Cantores Schola, which specializes in the study and performance of Gregorian chant. Paraclete is also the exclusive North American distributor of the recordings of the Monastic Choir of St. Peter's Abbey in Solesmes, France, long considered to be a leading authority on Gregorian chant.

DVDs

Our DVDs offer spiritual help, healing, and biblical guidance for life issues: grief and loss, marriage, forgiveness, anger management, facing death, and spiritual formation.

Learn more about us at our website:
www.paracletepress.com, or call us toll-free at 1-800-451-5006.

Discover Paraclete Giants

The Complete Madame Guyon

ISBN: 978-1-55725-923-3
304 pages, $24.99

Guyon's theology and spiritual writing opened new doors to people from all walks of life who yearned for spiritual joy and wisdom. These new translations include her popular *A Short and Easy Method of Prayer*, her biblical commentary on the Song of Songs, and examples of her passionate poetry, some of which has never before been translated into English. The historical introduction explains the events in Guyon's life, first as an aristocratic wife and mother of five, and later as a widow traveling around Europe as an author, who ended up incarcerated in the Bastille by the direct order of Louis XIV. Guyon suffered ten years of incarceration and accusations of heresy. Cleared of all charges at the end of her life, in her writings Madame Guyon testified to the goodness and holiness of God.

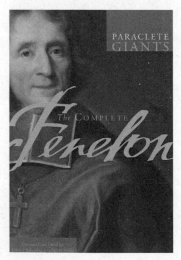

The Complete Fénelon

ISBN: 978-1-55725-607-2
338 pages, $24.95

Christians are now rediscovering the wisdom of François Fénelon, a controversial theologian and spiritual thinker who showed how it was possible to have devotion and faith in the original Age of Reason. His writings have never been as accessible as they are now in *The Complete Fénelon*, which includes more than one hundred of his letters and meditations. Also translated here into English for the first time are Fénelon's reflections on the seasons and holidays of the Christian year.

Available from most booksellers or through Paraclete Press:
www.paracletepress.com; 1-800-451-5006.
Try your local bookstore first.